Pascal
for
Engineers

Pascal for Engineers

William H. Jermann
Memphis State University

PRENTICE HALL, Englewood Cliffs, New Jersey 07632

Library of Congress Cataloging-in-Publication Data

Jermann, William H.
    Pascal for engineers / William H. Jermann.
        p. cm.
    ISBN 0–13–652892–9
    1. Pascal (Computer program language)   I. Title.
QA76.73.P2J47   1989
005.13′3—dc20

Editorial/production supervision: George Calmenson
Cover design: Lundgren Graphics, Ltd.
Manufacturing buyer: Donna Douglass

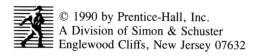
LIMITS OF LIABILITY AND DISCLAIMER OF WARRANTY:
The author and publisher of this book have used their best efforts
in preparing this book. These efforts include the development,
research, and testing of the theories and programs to determine their
effectiveness. The author and publisher make no warranty of any kind,
expressed or implied, with regard to these programs or the documentation
contained in this book. The author and publisher shall not be liable in any
event for incidental or consequential damages in connection with, or arising
out of, the furnishing, performance, or use of these programs.

Printed in the United States of America
10 9 8 7 6 5 4 3 2 1

ISBN   0-13-652892-9

Prentice-Hall International (UK) Limited, *London*
Prentice-Hall of Australia Pty. Limited, *Sydney*
Prentice-Hall Canada Inc., *Toronto*
Prentice-Hall Hispanoamericana, S.A., *Mexico*
Prentice-Hall of India Private Limited, *New Dehli*
Prentice-Hall of Japan, Inc., *Tokyo*
Simon & Schuster Asia Pte. Ltd., *Singapore*
Editora Prentice-Hall do Brasil, Ltda., *Rio de Janeiro*

To ELAINE

Contents

Preface

Courses related to computer programming have been found in engineering curricula for over two decades. Textbooks used in early courses emphasized syntax of a particular programming language. These texts often included practical matters, such as how to fill out coding forms and how to punch IBM cards. Subsequent texts cover similar material but place more emphasis on formulation of algorithms and the general art of problem solving.

Currently, there are numerous freshman level programming texts available. For those satisfied with existing texts, there is no need for one more textbook. *Pascal for Engineers* was developed primarily for those seeking an alternative to the existing set of textbooks.

Pascal For Engineers is a freshman-level textbook for a course in computer programming. It is intended primarily for those majoring in engineering and related fields.

Freshman engineering students have good backgrounds in mathematics, but have not yet taken any engineering courses. The material in this text requires competence in algebra and trigonometry. This mathematical background is required for concepts related to solving engineering-type problems.

Learning programming concepts in Pascal helps students develop good programming and problem solving techniques. It facilitates learning other programming languages such as Ada and C. But many engineers are required to develop programs or to use software written in FORTRAN. The material in Chapter 10 is provided to satisfy these needs. We have found that freshmen students proficient in Pascal can easily learn to develop programs in FORTRAN. The material in Chapter 10 facilitates this transition.

The majority of American-born engineering students have had some exposure to computers and programming. Frequently programming is introduced in elementary school. A large number of students own their own computers. There is no need to devote large increments of time to introductory concepts of programming.

The following attributes differentiate *Pascal for Engineers* from currently popular programming texts:

1. Material is first introduced with examples. Then it is formally defined and reinforced with more examples. This appears to coincide with the way humans learn more closely than traditional logical presentations.
2. Current textbooks are becoming longer, and yet do not cover more material. We attempt to avoid unnecessary wordiness without sacrificing clarity.
3. We introduce certain *engineering* examples. These do not require knowledge of engineering principles.
4. Most current texts advocate modularity in program development. Yet, frequently the use of subprograms is not introduced until later chapters. We introduce use of subprograms in Chapter 2 and cover the topic in detail in Chapter 3.
5. Concepts that are deferred in other textbooks are introduced very early. In particular, concepts related to storage of data, input/output, transmission of arguments, pointers and recursive techniques are introduced near the beginning of the text. We have found that freshmen engineering students are capable of understanding and using these concepts at an early stage in the course.

Many of the examples and programs found in this text involve a significant amount of computation. Yet, use of this text does not requires massive computer facilities. Virtually all Pascal programs were run using TURBO Pascal.*

The United States was once the undisputed leader in manufacturing technology. This is no longer true. We are still the world leader in computer applications. I am concerned that we may lose this position.

Although there are many fine courses in programming offered to freshmen, I am somewhat pessimistic about the future. Many of our college-level programming courses have not changed significantly in the last two decades. Although there are a large number of textbooks available, there is not significant diversity in the type of texts available. Whereas there have been enormous changes in the computer industry, many college professors are dogmatic about computers programming "principles." Certainly good programming techniques are important. But good programming techniques, like other endeavors, involve many tradeoffs.

On the other hand, I am very optimistic about the future. If given the opportunity, freshmen can learn and master programming concepts that required years for their teachers to master. Based on my work with freshmen, I believe the future is very promising if teachers are willing to change with the times, and give our students the opportunity to develop to their full capacity.

William H. Jermann

* TURBO Pascal is a trademark of Borland International, Inc.

1

Introduction

Early civilizations probably developed numerical concepts by associating quantitative events with the fingers or toes. After more sophisticated numerical measures evolved, elementary computations were simplified through the use of aids such as knots in twine and beads mounted on wires.

Although such rudimentary aids have been popular even in the twentieth century—for example, the abacus, for business calculations, and the slide rule, for scientific calculations—the most modern computational tools—electronic calculators and computers—have truly revolutionized society. These devices not only perform numerical computations, they also process information, something done previously only by human beings.

1.1 DIGITAL COMPUTERS

The original idea for a general-purpose stored-program digital computer is frequently credited to Charles Babbage, who, in the nineteenth century, nearly completed construction of such a device. His assistant in this project, Ada Augusta Byron, a mathematician, is sometimes acknowledged as the first computer programmer. The modern programming language Ada is named in her honor.

Due to the difficulty in fabricating precision parts, Babbage's "analytical engine" was never completed. Even if it had been, its usefulness would have been limited because of the very slow speed at which mechanical devices are constrained to operate.

Early in the twentieth century, Lee De Forest invented the vacuum tube. That led, first, to the development of the radio industry, then to the electronics industry, and ultimately to the first electronic computers. In 1938, Claude Shannon applied the symbolic algebra developed by logician George Boole to the description of relay switching circuits. Although that was initially visualized as a tool for designing telephone switching circuitry, it has proved useful in the design and characterization of logic circuits required in stored-program digital computers.

Significant research and development involving electronic circuitry took place during World War II, and by the early 1950s commercial computers were available for general-purpose applications. UNIVAC, produced by Sperry-Rand, caught the imagination of the public. Shortly afterwards, IBM, the commercial business machine company, entered the computer market. At that time, much of the public viewed computers as extensions of special-purpose business machines. Even today, business applications constitute the most significant use of digital computers.

During the 1950s, transistorized circuitry replaced cumbersome vacuum tube circuits. During the 1960s, it became possible to incorporate a large number of transistors on a single silicon chip. These large-scale integrated circuits became the essential building blocks of modern computers. Furthermore, they enabled drastic reductions in both the size and the cost of computers.

By the end of the 1960s, entire computer central processing units were being fabricated on single large-scale integrated circuits. During the 1970s, these chips, called **microprocessors,** were used to develop a wide variety of general-purpose microcomputers. In 1981, IBM introduced its personal computer (PC) family. The PC and its clones became widely used in commercial applications.

As computer hardware was evolving, software packages were also being written. A variety of assemblers, compilers, and interpreters were developed to facilitate computer programming. In addition, numerous special-purpose packages were created, including word processing packages to facilitate typing and the preparation of text, and spread sheet packages to facilitate elementary bookkeeping and accounting. Microcomputer-based data-base management packages for a wide variety of applications were also produced.

This text is concerned with developing programs using high-level languages. To this end, it is helpful to understand how a computer functions. Consider the digital computer represented in Figure 1.1. The computer's **central processing unit (CPU)** contains an arithmetic and logic unit (ALU), a set of internal registers, and the computer's general control circuitry.

In small computers the CPU consists of a single large-scale integrated circuit (microprocessor).

The computer's memory consists of a small set of chips, or integrated circuits. A few of these chips are generally read-only memory (ROM) chips. Most of the memory chips can be either read by the CPU or written into by the CPU. These large-scale integrated circuits are referred to as RAM chips (for "random access memory"). Addresses on *both* RAM and ROM chips are accessed randomly. That

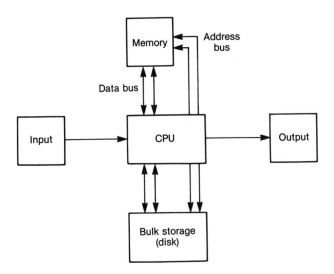

Figure 1.1 Representation of a digital computer

is, the address sent out on the address bus can be used to identify either a RAM or a ROM location.

Memory serves to store two types of information, **data** and **instructions.** A sequence of computer instructions is called a **computer program.** The computer instructions stored in memory are encoded in absolute, or machine, code. That is, they are encoded in a way that can be interpreted by the particular CPU or microprocessor.

Here is how a single computer instruction is executed: An internal register in the CPU keeps track of the address of the next instruction to be executed. This address is sent out on the **address bus.** Then a control signal is sent to memory, and this signal accesses the contents of the specified address and places the contents on the **data bus** to be brought back to the CPU. This instruction code is then translated by the CPU. We say that an instruction has been **fetched.**

Even though an instruction has been fetched, and even though the CPU "knows" what the instruction is, the instruction has not yet been **executed.** Suppose the instruction is to add together two numbers stored in memory. These two data words must first be retrieved from memory and added together. Then the answer must be placed in an appropriate memory location. Before instruction execution is completed, the address of the next instruction must be determined and placed in the appropriate CPU register.

Note that computer memory such as shown in Figure 1.1 is used to store both computer instructions and data. Furthermore, there is a variety of data types. Computer programming would be quite tedious if we had to program in machine language. Fortunately, most programming is done in English-type directives that are contained in high-level programming languages such as BASIC, FORTRAN, and Pascal.

Refer again to Figure 1.1. The two blocks identified as Input and Output provide mechanisms for external entities to communicate with computers. Numerous input and output devices can be used to communicate with the computer CPU and/ or memory. These include switch consoles, punched-paper-tape readers, card readers, line printers, magnetic tapes, and magnetic disks.

One of the most common input devices is the keyboard. Two of the most common output devices are CRT (cathode ray tube) screens and printers. These as well as other devices are connected to the computer using large-scale integrated-circuit interface chips. In small computer systems, the CPU chip, memory chips, and interfacing chips may all be mounted on a single board.

REVIEW

1. Even though Charles Babbage's concepts were sound, his computer projects were not very successful. Explain why.
2. What are the main components of a digital computer?
3. What is a microprocessor?

1.2 BINARY REPRESENTATION OF INFORMATION

Information stored in a computer CPU or computer memory or passing along a computer bus is represented by sets of binary, or two-state, signals. Each simple computer cell may be considered to be a switch having two possible states, On and Off. More frequently these states are represented as two distinct electrical voltage levels, High and Low.

It is convenient to represent sets of two-state signals using the binary number system. Frequently, these signals or the corresponding storage cells occur in groups of 8, 16, or 32. A set of 8 binary digits is called a **byte.** A set of 16 binary digits is frequently called a **word.** A set of 32 binary digits is sometimes called a *word* and sometimes a **long word.** Some computers address memory in such a way that each unique memory address contains a byte of information. In other computer systems, each memory address may represent a word or a long word of information.

Recall that computer memory contains two different types of information: instructions and data. Furthermore, there are many different types of data. Whereas the binary codes used for computer instructions depend on the type of computer central processing unit, data types are independent of the processor used.

For example, suppose the following byte of information is stored in computer memory:

0100 0111

What does this mean? We really do not know. If this is an instruction code and the CPU is an 8085 microprocessor, then the code is the command to move the contents of one CPU register (the B register) to another CPU register (the A register). But if the CPU is an M6800 chip, then the command is to divide by 2 the signed number in a register called the A accumulator.

On the other hand, the number may not be an instruction code. It may be a code representing a character corresponding to one of the keys on a standard keyboard. The most common code in current use is ASCII (American Standard Code for Information Interchange). In this code, the capital letter A is represented as the binary sequence

$$0100 \quad 0001$$

Subsequent capital letters are represented by binary codes having numerical values one larger than their predecessor. Thus, the code 0100 0111 represents the letter G if interpreted as character-type data.

Suppose the binary sequence 0100 0111 represents the value of a binary integer. Then this corresponds to the integer

$$1 \times 2^6 + 1 \times 2^2 + 1 \times 2^1 + 1 \times 2^0 = 71 \text{ (base-10)}$$

Thus, we say that the 8-bit representation of the integer 71 is 0100 0111.

But we can represent the number 71 by the keyboard or ASCII code for a 7 followed by the keyboard or ASCII code for a 1. This is called a **string representation.** The ASCII code for the numerical character 0 is 0011 0000. The ASCII code for each of the other nine characters has a value one greater than its predecessor.

Example 1.1

Represent each of the following character strings by the corresponding ASCII codes.
    (a) DOG   (b) GOAT   (c) 1234
Solution   (a) The code for D is the code for $A + 3$. Similarly, the code for O is the code for $A + 14$, and the code for G is 0100 0001 + 6. Thus, DOG is represented as

$$0100 \ 0100 \quad 0100 \ 1111 \quad 0100 \ 0111$$

(b) $GOAT$ is represented as

$$0100 \ 0111 \quad 0100 \ 1111 \quad 0100 \ 0001 \quad 0101 \ 0100$$

(c) The ASCII string 1234 is represented as

$$0011 \ 0001 \quad 0011 \ 0010 \quad 0011 \ 0011 \quad 0011 \ 0100$$

Characters and character strings are commonly used data types. There are several other data types in widespread use in programming languages, including the **integer.** Generally, the value of a positive integer is the value of the binary number represented by a set of zeroes and ones. Leading zeroes may be assigned to positive integers without changing their values. When integers are represented as **signed** numbers, positive integers must have at least one leading zero. For example, the positive number 7 may be represented either as 0111 or as 0000111. But the representation 111 is not valid, since there is no leading zero.

Different computer systems use binary words of different lengths to represent integers. Frequently, 32-bit words represent integers.

Example 1.2

If the ASCII string representing 1234 given in Example 1.1 were interpreted as an integer, what would be its value?

Solution   The value of this 32-bit positive integer would be:

$$2^{29} + 2^{28} + 2^{24} + 2^{21} + 2^{20} + 2^{17} + 2^{13} + 2^{12} + 2^9 + 2^8 + 2^5 + 2^4 + 2^2 = 825,373,492$$

Negative integers are generally represented as the two's complement of the corresponding positive integer. To get the two's complement of an integer expressed as a binary number, merely change the ones to zeroes, change the zeroes to ones, and add 1 to the number. It follows that the most significant bit of a negative integer is a 1 and that appending leading ones to a negative number does not change its value.

Let us consider a property of positive integers expressed in the binary number system. If we assume the binary point to be just to the right of the least significant digit, then multiplying the number by 2 raised to the nth power corresponds to moving the binary point n places to the right. Dividing the number by 2 raised to the nth power corresponds to moving the binary point n places to the left.

Example 1.3

Given the positive number

$$01100.$$

what number is obtained when this number is divided by 32? (Note: The binary point to the right of the least significant character is shown explicitly.)

Solution   Dividing by 32 corresponds to moving the binary point five places to the left. This yields

$$.01100$$

whose value is

$$0 \times 2^{-1} + 1 \times 2^{-2} + 1 \times 2^{-3} = 0.375 \text{ (base-10)}$$

This is an interesting representation of a number, since the binary point is not encoded as part of the binary string. Yet the value of the number depends on the location of this binary point. For computer applications, the user may decide arbitrarily where to locate this point. Thus, if a user locates the point to the right of the least significant number, the string 01100 represents the integer 12. On the other hand, if a user arbitrarily locates the binary point to the left of the most significant character, the string represented as 01100 has a value of 0.375.

It is easy to convert any positive base-10 integer to the corresponding binary representation. The following **algorithm,** or rule, may be used.

Rule 1.   To convert a positive base-10 number X to the corresponding binary representation:

0. Let $Y = X$.

1. Divide Y by 2. Write the remainder to the left of the last character written. Let $Y = $ the quotient.

2. If $Y = 0$, go to step 3. Otherwise, go to step 1.

3. Write a zero to the left of the last character written. Then the binary representation of X is the set of characters written. Note: The binary number written will always have a leading zero.

In computer applications it is often necessary to express a positive base-10 number less than 1 as a corresponding binary number. This requires that the binary point be just to the left of the most significant binary character. There is one other consideration. Just as the number $\frac{1}{3}$ cannot be expressed as a base-10 decimal without using an infinite number of characters, many decimal numbers that can be expressed exactly in base 10 can only be approximated in the binary number system. Thus, when making a conversion, we should specify the maximum number of binary characters we wish to represent the desired number. This is referred to as the **precision** of the specified number.

The following algorithm may be used to convert a positive number that is less than 1 to the corresponding binary number.

Rule 2.   To convert a positive base-10 number X that is less than 1 to the corresponding binary number:

0. Let $Y = X$. Choose a value of precision.

1. Multiply Y by 2. Let Y be the number to the right of the decimal point of this product. Write the character to the left of the decimal point. (Note: Absence of a character corresponds to a zero.)

2. If $Y = 0$ or if the number of characters written is equal to the specified precision, then quit.

3. Go to step 1.

Example 1.4

Convert each of the following base-10 numbers to the corresponding binary number.

(a) 13

(b) .375, with a precision of 16

(c) .6, with a precision of 8

Solution   Applying Rule 1:

Step no.	Value of Y	String written
(a)		
0	13	
1	6	1
1	3	01
1	1	101
1	0	1101
	0	01101
(b)		
0	.375	.
1	.75	.0
1	.5	.01
1	.0	.011
	.0	.011
(c)		
0	.6	.
1	.2	.1
1	.4	.10
1	.8	.100
1	.6	.1001
1	.2	.10011
1	.4	.100110
1	.8	.1001100
1	.6	.10011001
	.6	.10011001

Integers are just one way to represent numbers. Another data type is the **real number,** or **floating point.** In many versions of BASIC all numbers are represented as real numbers. The idea behind real number representation relates to what is commonly called *scientific notation*. For example, in scientific notation the number 12,345 may be represented as

$$1.2345 \times 10^4$$

Figure 1.2 shows the general form of a real number. The value of the number is

$$\text{Number} = + \text{ or } - \text{ Significand} \times \text{Base}^{\text{Characteristic}}$$

The number of bits in the floating point, the significand field, and the characteristic field depend on the type of floating point representation employed. One bit represents

Figure 1.2 Representation of a floating point

the sign of the number. Generally, a value of 1 represents a negative number and a 0 represents a positive number. The characteristic field generally is **biased,** meaning that a constant value is added to the true value of the characteristic. Although the **base** can be any number, commonly only two numbers are used: 16 and 2.

There are many different ways to represent real numbers. We will consider just one of these: the 32-bit representation of a floating point that is closely related to the standardized IEEE (Institute of Electrical and Electronic Engineers) floating point. In this representation, the sign field is one bit long, the biased characteristic is eight bits long, and the significand or mantissa is 24 bits long. We assume a binary point is just in front of the most significant character of the mantissa. The floating point is always normalized; that is, the value of the significand must always be within the following range:

$$.5 \leq \text{significand} < 1$$

Since the significand is always within this range, it follows that the most significant bit of the significand must always be 1. Because there are no exceptions to this rule, it is unnecessary to store the most significant bit of the significand. Only the twenty-three least significant bits of the significand are stored as part of the floating point representation. The unstored bit is sometimes called the **hidden bit.**

The 8-bit characteristic field of this floating point contains the true characteristic biased by 126. That is, the number 126 is added to the true characteristic. To represent a specified number as a floating point, merely express it in a form in which the significand is normalized, suppress the most significant character, add 126 to the true characteristic, and insert the sign bit.

Example 1.5

Express each of the following numbers as 32-bit floating points.
        (a) 365   (b) −0.4375   (c) 0.1
Solution   (a) Using Rule 1, it is seen that

$$365 \text{ (base-10)} = 101101101 \text{ (base-2)}$$

But

$$101101101 = .101101101 \times 2^9$$

The 23-bit significand, with the most significant bit suppressed, is

$$011\ 0110\ 1000\ 0000\ 0000\ 0000$$

The biased characteristic has a value of $9 + 126 = 135$, and the sign bit is 0. Therefore, this floating point is represented as

$$0100\ 0011\ 1011\ 0110\ 1000\ 0000\ 0000\ 0000$$

(b) Using Rule 2, it is seen that

$$.4375 \text{ (base-10)} = .0111 \text{ (base-2)}$$

But

$$.0111 = .111 \times 2^{-1}$$

The biased characteristic has a value of 125, and the floating point representation is

$$1011\ 1110\ 1110\ 0000\ 0000\ 0000\ 0000\ 0000$$

(c) Using Rule 2 and a precision of 28,

$$.1\ (\text{base-10}) = .0001\ 1001\ 1001\ 1001\ 1001\ 1001\ 1001\ (\text{base-2})$$

But

$$.0001\ 1001\ 1001\ 1001\ 1001\ 1001\ 1001$$
$$= .1100\ 1100\ 1100\ 1100\ 1100\ 1100\ 1000 \times 10^{-3}$$

Suppressing the most significant bit and adjusting the least significant bit by rounding the unused bits, the 23-bit significand is

$$100\ 1100\ 1100\ 1100\ 1100\ 1101$$

Since the biased characteristic has a value of 123, this floating point is represented as

$$0011\ 1101\ 1100\ 1100\ 1100\ 1100\ 1100\ 1101$$

REVIEW

1. Represent each of the following character strings by the corresponding string of ASCII codes
   (a) HORSE   **(b)** 5280   **(c)** TIGER99
2. Represent each of the following integers as a 16-bit binary number.
   (a) 5280   **(b)** -45 **(c)** 10560   **(d)** -90
3. Represent each of the following numbers as a 32-bit IEEE floating point number.
   (a) 5280   **(b)** -45 **(c)** 57.325   **(d)** 1.9
4. What real numbers are represented by each of the following IEEE 32-bit floating points?
   (a) 1100 0000 1010 0000 0000 0000 0000 0000   **(b)** 0100 0001 0100 0000 0000 0000 0000 0000

1.3 SCOPE AND OBJECTIVES OF THIS BOOK

This textbook is intended for use in an introductory college-level course in computer programming. The material has been selected for use by freshmen in engineering, computer science, or a closely related curriculum.

Although no previous programming experience is necessary, most students probably will have had some prior to entering college. In some school systems, students are introduced to BASIC programming as early as the first grade. But experience in BASIC programming is not a prerequisite for the material covered here. Lack of such experience will be in no way disadvantageous.

Although the material covered in the first two sections of this book is not related directly to programming, the concepts presented will be useful throughout.

Programming in Pascal is treated in Chapters 2 through 9, the primary objectives being to develop good skills in programming in particular, and in problem solving in general. Knowledge of Pascal is almost a prerequisite for learning other structured programming languages, such as C and Ada. Chapter 10 provides the necessary transition material for those who require a knowledge of FORTRAN.

Today's freshmen will spend most of their working lives in the twenty-first century. It is quite possible that programming languages such as Pascal and FORTRAN will no longer be needed then. Nonetheless, the organizational skills and problem-solving techniques developed by learning to program in these languages will undoubtedly still be valuable.

Learning programming techniques and problem-solving skills is probably not the most important reward from a course of this nature. Mahatma Gandhi spent part of each day weaving. This activity was useful because it constantly reminded him of his frailty as a human being and his propensity for making errors. A serious course in computer programming serves the same purpose. What we learn about ourselves from our activities in such a course is much more meaningful than the details we study.

EXERCISES

1. What is a computer CPU? What functions does it perform?
2. What types of information are stored in computer memory? Identify at least three data types.
3. Describe in detail what happens during the *fetch* portion of a computer instruction.
4. Suppose the following computer instruction is fetched and executed:

   Add two numbers that are stored in memory and place the sum back into memory.

   How many different words will be placed on the data bus as this instruction is being fetched and executed? Assume that the instruction width and the data width are the same as the width of the data bus.
5. Convert the following base-10 numbers to the corresponding 16-bit binary integers.
   (a) 25   (b) −59   (c) 3234
6. Convert the following base-10 numbers to the corresponding binary numbers.
   (a) .0375   b) .8125   (c) .651 (precision = 8)
7. Convert the following base-10 numbers to 32-bit floating points. Use the floating point representation given in Section 1.2.
   (a) 1.0   (b) 29.0   (c) −31.0
8. Convert the following base-10 numbers to 32-bit floating points. Use the floating point representation given in Section 1.2.
   (a) .0625   (b) −57.125   (c) 3234   (d) .3
9. Represent the number 1234 as:
   (a) a 4-byte ASCII character string
   (b) a 32-bit integer
   (c) a 32-bit floating point

10. Convert the number 0.0 to a 32-bit floating point. Note: With the technique described in Section 1.2, there is no way to represent this number exactly. Represent it as closely as possible. What is the "true" value of the number representing 0.0?
11. Modify Rule 1 in Section 1.2 so it can aid in converting base-10 numbers to base-8, or **octal,** numbers.
12. Modify Rule 2 in Section 1.2 so it can be used to convert base-10 numbers to base-8, or octal, numbers.
13. Modify Rule 1 in Section 1.2 so it can convert base-10 numbers to base-B numbers, where B is any integer greater than 1.
14. Modify Rule 2 in Section 1.2 so it can convert base-10 numbers to base-B numbers, where B is any integer greater than 1.
15. The following binary numbers are representations of 32-bit floating points. What number does each represent?
    (a) 1100 0000 1010 0000 0000 0000 0000 0000
    (b) 0011 1110 0000 0000 0000 0000 0000 0000
    (c) 0011 1110 0100 0000 0000 0000 0000 0000
    (d) 0100 0001 0100 0000 0000 0000 0000 0000
16. Who was Mahatma Gandhi? What was his most meaningful contribution? What was probably his biggest failure?

2

Programming in Pascal

A high-level programming language enables computer users to develop programs employing a set of simple, English-type statements. Dozens of popular programming languages have emerged over the past two decades. BASIC, or Beginners All-purpose Symbolic Instruction Code, is widely used by novices and owners of inexpensive personal computers. FORTRAN, which stands for FORmula TRANslation, has been used for scientific programming applications for over two decades. Similarly, COBOL, or COmmon Business-Oriented Language, has been used extensively for business applications for over two decades.

One of the more popular languages has been Pascal, which was developed by the Swiss computer scientist Niklaus Wirth during the late 1960s and early 1970s. *Pascal User Manual and Report*, by Kathleen Jensen and Niklaus Wirth (New York: Springer-Verlag, 1974), has served as a de facto standard for the language.

In 1983, a standard was developed for the Pascal programming language by the American National Standards Institute and the Institute of Electrical and Electronic Engineers. This ANSI/IEEE standard serves to define the programming language. Unfortunately, numerous versions of the language were developed prior to the publication of this standard. Furthermore, numerous versions of Pascal exist. And various vendors incorporate modifications, simplifications, and enhancements.

Some textbooks attempt to define capabilities of some of the various versions

13

of Pascal. We attempt to use syntax and commands that are common to most versions of this language. We encourage students to avoid any simplifications or "powerful" enhancements that are unique to their particular computer system. One of the biggest advantages of using standardized high-level programming languages is that the program, or source code, is "transportable." Use of features unique to a particular installation destroys the portability of a program.

2.1 A PASCAL PROGRAM

Pascal was developed by Niklaus Wirth as a language that would be a "good" first programming language. That is, it was intended to be a language in which novices could learn to develop good programming skills. Because Pascal has a rather limited number of capabilities, only a few concepts need be mastered. This not only facilitates learning, but results in relatively small and inexpensive Pascal compilers.

Unfortunately, Pascal frequently is not the first programming language learned. Most young people are introduced to at least BASIC before encountering Pascal. While relatively brief exposure to BASIC may actually be beneficial, those with extensive programming experience in that language sometimes have withdrawal symptoms when learning Pascal and have great difficulty abandoning the poor programming techniques that they have been using for a long time.

Pascal not only has a relatively small number of concepts, but it is a logical and a highly structured language. While these elements are formally defined in the following chapters, many of them are introduced in the programs in this chapter.

Consider the Pascal program given in Figure 2.1. When this program is actually executed, the phrase MY FIRST PASCAL PROGRAM will be printed on your output console. By inspecting the program code, it is easy to understand this program. Run this program on the computer facility available to you. (Running a program on an unfamiliar computer can be traumatic.) Once you have learned to run a program, then you have overcome a major hurdle and can concentrate on learning the programming language.

There are two types of statements in the program: **declaration statements** and **executable commands.** Although the first statement, the **program declaration statement,** is on the first line of the program code, a statement is not synonymous

```
program first_program(input,output);
begin
      writeln;
      writeln(' MY FIRST PASCAL PROGRAM');
      writeln
end.
```

Figure 2.1 A Pascal program

with a line. A line may contain several statements. Likewise a single statement may occupy several lines. This statement identifies, or declares, a program with the user-defined name "first_program." When writing Pascal programs, we frequently assign names to elements. The names we assign will generally begin with a letter and may include other letters, number characters, or the underscore character.

The user-defined name "first_program" is followed by a left parenthesis, a set of names, and a right parenthesis. The set of names between the parentheses is referred to as an **argument list.** The argument list must include an identifying name for all files used in the program. There are two special files, the INPUT file and the OUTPUT file. The INPUT file contains the text that is entered during program execution. The OUTPUT file contains the text that is printed during program execution.

In Figure 2.1, no text is entered as the program is run, so it is unnecessary to include the word "input" in the program argument list. But a character string is sent to the OUTPUT file as the program is being run. Therefore, inclusion of "output" in the program argument list is required.

The "begin" directive is a pseudo-directive to the compiler, indicating that executable instructions follow. The "end" statement is a pseudo-instruction that indicates the end of a related set of executable commands, and the period following the "end" directive indicates the end of the program code.

The other three statements are executable commands. There are two types of executable statements: Pascal commands and subprograms. The three executable statements in this program are calls, or invocations, to a subprogram. In particular, a subprogram called WRITELN is invoked three times.

Pascal has two different types of subprograms: **procedures** and **functions.** Subprograms may be classified as **system subprograms** or **user-defined subprograms.** The subprogram WRITELN is a system subprogram.

A subprogram is an independent program module. It may have been written in Pascal or in some other language. System subprograms may be accessed by user programs and do not have to be formally declared. When a subprogram is invoked, first it runs and then control reverts back to the invoking program.

Refer again to the program in Figure 2.1. The first time the subprogram WRITELN is invoked, it places a code for a "return and line-feed" in the OUTPUT file and then returns control to the invoking program. From the programmer's perspective, the WRITELN command merely skips a line on the output console.

After this is done, the next statement in the main program is executed. This statement, also a call to the subprogram WRITELN, is different from the previous one, for it contains an argument list. Clearly we want the WRITELN procedure to print the character string MY FIRST PASCAL PROGRAM. In order for WRITELN to do this, it must know what we want printed. We let it know by passing the information to the subprogram using the argument list.

Argument lists may be used to pass a variety of data types to procedures or functions. This argument list contains two apostrophies. Between the apostrophies are 24 characters, including four spaces. This set of characters is the information that must be passed on to the procedure. In particular, the set of binary codes, generally ASCII codes, representing this character string must be passed on to the entity in charge of printing the string.

There are two ways in which information in an argument list such as the one in this example may be passed on, or transmitted, to a subprogram. One is to directly give the subprogram the **values** of the arguments. That is, the codes representing each of the twenty-four characters may be transmitted directly to the subprogram being invoked. This is called **passing parameters by value.**

The internal logistics involved in passing twenty-four pieces of information to an independent program module are not trivial. This method of transmitting information related to character strings is certainly not the best method. More often the information is passed by **reference,** meaning that the character string is stored somewhere in consecutive memory cells, and a special internal code is used to identify the end of the character string. Then it is necessary just to pass to the subprogram a number that identifies the memory location of the first character in the string. A number that identifies the location of a memory cell is called a **pointer.** Transmitting information to subprograms by passing one or more pointers to the subprogram is called **passing parameters by reference.**

Let us summarize these concepts. A *subprogram* generally performs a specific task on one or more arguments or numbers. These arguments are said to be *passed* to the subprogram *by value* if only numerical values are transmitted to the subprogram. If the addresses of **memory locations** at which these numbers are stored are transmitted to the subprogram, the arguments are *passed by reference*. A *pointer* is a number that corresponds to a specific memory address.

In some high-level programming languages, passing parameters is always done by reference. In other languages it is done only by value. In Pascal, parameters may be passed either by reference or by value.

Refer again to the Pascal program in Figure 2.1. Though trivial, this program introduces a number of important concepts related to the Pascal programming language. These are:

1. The structure of a Pascal program
2. Files used in Pascal programs
3. Declaration statements
4. Executable statements
5. The use of subprograms
   a. functions
   b. procedures
6. Passing parameters to subprograms
   a. by value
   b. by reference
7. Pointers

These concepts will be discussed in more detail and illustrated in subsequent sections and chapters.

REVIEW

1. What two general types of statements are found in a Pascal program?
2. What are the two general methods of passing information to a subprogram?
3. Write and run a Pascal program that prints your name, your age, and the name of your favorite university.

2.2 RUNNING A PROGRAM

By now you have probably run the Pascal program in Figure 2.1. But what do we actually mean when we say that we have "run" a program? This depends a lot on the computer facility and the software we are using.

In general, running a program involves the following steps: The program code or the source code is entered into a text file, meaning that the characters entered on a console, such as a keyboard, are encoded in some binary code such as ASCII. Then this encoded information, which is accessible to the computer CPU, is processed.

Processing of source code generally starts by running one or more system programs, such as a **Pascal compiler.** Initially, the **text file** (a simple encoding of characters) containing your code is converted to a form that is further removed from your source code. Then the newly generated code is stored in a different file. This new file frequently is not a text file. That is, it may contain information that cannot be interpreted as simple encoding of characters.

Processing of code may pass through several stages. But eventually, program activity directly related to the commands in your source code must occur. There are two general ways in which this can take place:

1. After your source code has been processed it is placed in a data file, which is loaded into memory. Then an **interpreter** program is run, which reads the various elements of your data file, interprets them, and causes the directives specified in your source code to be implemented.

2. After successive steps in processing your source code, a file is produced that contains the binary codes for machine language computer instructions. This absolute, or executable, code is loaded into computer memory. Then the entry point, or starting address, of this machine language program is loaded into an appropriate CPU register. Finally, the machine language instructions related to your source program are fetched and executed.

The running of a user program appears to be a somewhat confusing process, because there are so many different ways the program can be "run." Instead of discussing this in general, let us examine one set of steps in running a Pascal program (see Figure 2.2).

0. First the program or Pascal source code must be stored in an accessible file.
1. Then the Pascal compiler is run. Since the compiler is a large program, the

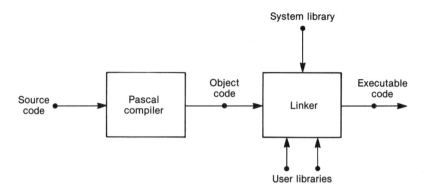

Figure 2.2   Compiling and linking a Pascal program

file containing the machine code for it (which is not a text file) must be loaded into memory before it is actually run. During execution of the Pascal compiler, this program gets input data from your source file. It translates these data into object code and places the object code in an object file.

2. Next, another large program, called a **linker** or a **linking loader**, must be loaded into memory and run. As this program is being run, it gets data from the object code file produced by the compiler. The program may invoke subprograms. Object codes for subprograms are stored in files called **libraries.** Object codes for system subprograms such as WRITELN are in the system library. The linker must get and combine the object codes for the main program and the various subprograms required for performance of the specified tasks.

Many implementations of Pascal also allow for **user libraries,** which contain object codes for subprograms that users such as yourself have already written, verified, and compiled. *If you have the capability of developing and utilizing user libraries, you should do so*, for they are highly important for good programming technique.

When the linker is run, it reads your object code file and accesses the various libraries. The linker produces a machine language program and places this program in a file called an **executable** or **absolute file.** Certain information about the absolute file must also be contained in the **header,** or preamble, of the file. In particular, the **starting address,** or entry point, to the absolute code must be identified.

In order to actually run your program, a systems program called a **loader** is run. This program places your executable code in memory, places the starting address of the program in a CPU register, and transfers control to your program. As your program is actually being run, data from the INPUT file may be required. If the data are not in this file, program execution will be suspended until you enter the data on your console.

The process of running a program appears to be quite complicated, since a number of files are involved, large programs such as compilers and linkers must be loaded and run, and new files are generated. In order to simplify matters, systems programs that manage the entire process are frequently developed. Then a sequence of system commands can be initiated by typing a single directive, such as RUN.

An essential step in running programs is the development of source files. We must convert the code that is written on a piece of paper to a file of source code by using a program called an **editor** or a **word processor.** These tools enable us to create and modify text files. Modern editor programs frequently contain at least a limited set of file-managing capabilities.

We have suggested that running a single program involves the use of systems programs such as editors, compilers, linkers, and loaders. Furthermore, different types of files must be created and managed. But before we do anything on a computer, certain programs must be running. For example, to access a word processor needed to create a source file, we must enter some type of request or command, which means that a program must already be running in order to service our request.

The program or set of programs that manages the operation of a computer is called an **operating system.** One of the tasks an operating system performs is to respond to user requests and directives. There are many popular operating systems. Two of the current more popular ones are **DOS** and **Unix.** DOS is an operating system frequently employed in personal computers. Unix is often found in multiuser and multitasking systems.

In order to run Pascal programs, you will need to know a few operating system commands on the computer system you are using. But you will not require much knowledge about the particular operating system. A good operating system is one that allows users to run desired software and to perform desired tasks with minimal difficulty. Yet the functioning of the operating system should be nearly transparent to the user.

REVIEW

1. Describe the difference between an *interpreter* and a *compiler*.

2. What is meant by each of the following terms?

   (a) source code   **(b)** object code   **(c)** a library

   (d) a linker   **(e)** an operating system

2.3 VARIABLES AND ASSIGNMENTS

The Pascal program in Figure 2.3 introduces several new concepts. Observe that:

1. Line numbers are used with this program. Frequently, line numbers are supplied by a text editor. Line numbers are ignored when the program is compiled.

2. Comments appear throughout this program. Observe that there are two ways in which comments may be specified. (a) Open with a left parenthesis followed

```
{100}      (* Example illustrating the use of
{110}                      Pascal variables *)
{120}   program variables_and_asgs(output);
{130}   { NOTE:
 140           1.  There are two ways to insert comments.
 150           2.  Comments may be inserted anywhere in the program. }
{160}   (*  Now we will DECLARE the variables that will be used! *)
{170}       var dog,cat: integer;  mouse: real;
{180}                              bird: char;
{190}   begin    (*  Start main program *)
{200}     { NOTE:  The assignment operator is        :=      !! }
{210}     dog := 1;   cat := 2;   mouse := 3.14;   bird := '1' ;
{220}     writeln(dog,cat,mouse,'     ',bird);
{230}     cat := dog;  writeln(cat);
{240}     mouse := cat;
{250}     writeln(' cat has a value of ',cat:1);
{260}     writeln(' dog is ',dog:1);
{270}     writeln(' the value of mouse is ', mouse:2:1);
{280}     writeln(' bird is ',bird:1);
{290}   end   (* END MAIN PROGRAM *)  .
```

Figure 2.3   A program illustrating variables and assignments

by an asterisk, insert the comment, and then terminate it with an asterisk followed by a right parenthesis. This is illustrated in lines 100 to 110 as well as in other places throughout the program. (b) Comments may also be enclosed by braces, as illustrated by the comment starting at line 130.

3. This program is written using lowercase letters. At one time it was common to write code using capital letters. Currently, most Pascal programs are written in lowercase letters.

In line 120 the program is declared and named. The files to be used are identified in the argument list. Only the file OUTPUT is required for this program.

In lines 170 and 180 the variables to be used in the program are formally declared. In Pascal programs, it is generally necessary to explicitly declare or define variables before they are used.

In Section 1.2 a variety of data types was illustrated. In particular, binary representations of characters, integers, and floating points, or real numbers, were illustrated. Recall that the binary representation for the character 1 was not at all like the binary representation for the integer 1. Likewise, the binary representation for the floating point 1 was much different from the integer representation of the number 1.

In Pascal, variable names must be associated with a particular type of variable. On line 170, *dog* and *cat* are declared as integer variables. Only integers are stored in memory locations identified as *dog* and *cat*. Any binary string assigned to the variables *dog* and *cat* must be an integer. Similarly, only *real* or floating point values may be assigned to *mouse*, and only *character* values may be assigned to *bird*. No other variables names may be used in the subsequent program, since no other variables are declared.

Next we will consider the *assignment* of values to variable names. In line

210, observe that the assignment operator in Pascal is a colon followed immediately by an "equals" sign. Refer in particular to the statement

$$dog := 1;$$

This line is part of a text file, or a file of character codes, frequently ASCII codes. This statement is an executable statement. When the sequence of machine language codes corresponding to this command is actually executed, the binary representation of the integer 1 is stored in a segment of computer memory identified by the integer variable name *dog*.

Similarly, when the machine language commands corresponding to the character string

$$cat := 2;$$

are executed, the binary representation of the integer 2 is stored in a segment of memory identified by the name *cat*. But when the directive

$$mouse := 3.14;$$

is executed, a significantly different data type is stored in the variable *mouse*. A floating-point representation such as described in Section 1.2 is stored in *mouse*.

When the command

$$bird := '1';$$

is executed, the character code, generally an 8-bit code, representing the character 1 is stored in a memory segment represented by the name *bird*. Note that the storage space required for a character variable is smaller than that required for an integer or a real variable.

Refer again to line 210. In the first two statements we specify values to be assigned to integer variables. But when we enter characters on a keyboard, we can only enter character codes into a source file. The compiler and supporting software must convert these codes to proper integer representations. Similarly, we specify the character string 3.14 as the number to be assigned to *mouse*. The compiler and its supporting software must convert this string to proper floating point format before the data can be stored in *mouse*.

We enter our source program code as well as our data by depressing keys on a keyboard. Since each key corresponds to a character code, we can *enter only character codes*. Supporting software must convert these codes to various machine language codes or data types. Similarly, *only character codes may be printed* on output devices. This is true regardless of which programming language is being used.

Line 220 invokes the WRITELN procedure and passes five arguments to the procedure. The first two arguments are the names of the integer variables *dog* and *cat*. The next argument is the name of a real variable. The following argument represents a character string that contains five spaces. This can be a set of five-character codes. But more often it is a *pointer* to the memory location in which the first character code of the string is stored. The last argument is the name of a character variable.

Most of the time we classify the five arguments as two integers, one real, a pointer, and a character. Now let us see what the WRITELN procedure does. First, it gets the integer variable that is currently stored in *dog*. Then it converts this integer to an appropriate sequence of character codes and sends them to the OUTPUT file. Note: Codes sent to this file are printed on the user's console. Next, a character string corresponding to the value of the integer in *cat* is formulated and printed. Then the floating point currently stored in *mouse* is represented as a character string and printed. The next argument is a pointer identifying a character string consisting of five spaces and a string terminator. The spaces are printed. Finally, the character corresponding to the character code stored in *bird* is printed.

Let us review what has been done by WRITELN. Two integers, one real, one pointer, and one character were passed to WRITELN. The procedure responded by printing five different character strings, which serve to identify the desired values. The process of converting integer data types to corresponding character strings is not trivial. Conversion of floating point data types to corresponding character strings is even less trivial. Fortunately, this is generally done by system software, and the process is transparent to the computer user.

Consider now the statements in line 230. The first statement,

cat := dog;

causes the integer currently stored in *dog* to be assigned to the variable *cat*. This is straightforward, since *cat* is an integer variable. The value assigned to *dog* is not changed, since no new assignment has been made to *dog*. The WRITELN command on the same line causes a character string corresponding to the value of the integer in *cat* to be printed. The integer in *cat* has a value of 1. What character string will be printed? There are several possibilities. Leading zeroes followed by a 1 could be printed. Just a single character 1 could be printed. Or leading spaces followed by a 1 could be printed. Many systems will print the value of 1 in a default format that consists of several spaces followed by a 1.

Observe the statement in line 240. When this command is executed, the integer stored in *cat* is fetched. Then a floating point data type having the numerical value of the integer stored in *cat* is formulated and assigned to *mouse*.

The statements in lines 250 to 280 are similar to each other. Each of these invocations to WRITELN has an argument list containing two arguments. The first argument is a pointer to the designated character string. The second is a variable name. But appended to each variable name is a colon followed by a number. There are two such attachments to the variable *mouse*.

Appending numbers to variable names in the argument list of WRITELN specifies the format in which the output string is to be printed. In this example, just one character is to be printed to identify the values stored in *dog*, *cat*, and *bird*. If we had specified 4 instead of 1, three leading spaces would have been printed. If the format we specified were not large enough to identify the value to be printed, our format specification would be ignored and a default format would be utilized.

Refer to line 270. There are two numbers appended to the variable name *mouse*. The first specifies the total number of characters to be printed, and the second specifies the number of characters that will be printed to the right of the decimal point. In most systems the decimal point will be printed, and we do not have to include space for this character in our specification of total characters to be printed. Once again, if our format does not allow sufficient space for the character string to be printed, it will be overridden and a default format used. The default format for floating point output generally closely resembles scientific notation.

When statements 250 to 280 are executed, the following strings will be printed on the extreme left of your output device:

> cat has a value of 1
> dog is 1
> the value of mouse is 1.0
> bird is 1

But recall that the integer representation for 1 is not at all like the floating point representation of this number. Similarly, the representation for the character 1 is significantly different from the integer or floating point representations.

When using high-level languages such as Pascal, there is generally no need to know exactly how the various data types are represented on the system being used. However, it is important to know that the various data types are represented differently.

REVIEW

1. Refer to Figure 2.3. Suppose line 110 is deleted. What effect will this have?
2. When we type input data on our keyboards, what type of data are we sending to the computer?
3. When the program in Figure 2.3 is being run, exactly how is the code that is assigned to the variable *mouse* actually represented?

2.4 NUMERICAL OPERATIONS

Pascal (as well as other programming languages) has capabilities for performing arithmetic operations. The arithmetic operations used in Pascal are:

Type	Symbol	Comment
Addition	+	Real or integer operations
Subtraction	−	Real or integer operations
Multiplication	*	Real or integer operations
Integer division	div	Returns quotient
Integer division	mod	Returns remainder
Real division	/	Returns real quotient

An arithmetic expression may contain a number of arithmetic operations, and it is important to know the order in which these operations are performed. The order is similar to the one in which we normally perform algebraic operations. For example, in the expression

$$A * B + C$$

we first multiply A by B and then add the result to C. On the other hand, in the expression

$$A * (B + C)$$

we first add B to C and then multiply the result by A.

Consider the following expression:

$$A * (B + (C * D + (E * F + G) - H) + I - J)$$

The subexpression $E * F + G$ is nested within three sets of parentheses. As the most deeply nested subexpression, it is evaluated first. Let $X = E * F + G$. The second most deeply nested subexpression, $C * D + X - H$, is enclosed, or nested, within two sets of parentheses and is evaluated next. Evaluation of expressions in Pascal programs follows the same general rules.

The following rules define the way in which numerical expressions are evaluated in Pascal programs.

1. When parentheses are used, expressions nested within a larger number of parentheses are evaluated before expressions nested within a smaller number of parentheses. Once a nested expression has been evaluated, the innermost parentheses surrounding the expression are no longer meaningful and should be considered as deleted.

2. When no parentheses are involved, or when inner parentheses have been conceptually removed, the operations *, div, mod, and / have a higher priority than + or − operations. Operations with a higher priority are performed first. When operations have the same priority, numerical operations proceed from left to right.

Often, numerical operations are performed on real numbers and the result assigned to a real variable. Similarly, arithmetic operations are frequently performed on integers and the result assigned to an integer variable. But sometimes we mix modes. That is, both integers and reals are involved in an expression. Then the following rule applies.

If a real number is involved in a numerical expression, the result returned is real.

Although the rules for evaluating numerical expressions are relatively simple, care must be taken when the minus sign is used. Sometimes it denotes the subtraction operation. But on other occasions the symbol denotes the sign of a constant or a negation command, and does not specify an arithmetic operation.

Example 2.1

What numbers are printed when the program in Figure 2.4 is run?

Solution   Dividing 7 by 4 produces a quotient of 1 and a remainder of 3. These numbers are written by the commands on lines 130 and 140. In line 150, the integer quotient is converted to real format and assigned to *cat*. A value of 1.0 is printed in scientific notation. In line 160, division between two real numbers is performed. Thus, the character strings 7 and 4 are first converted to floating points. The number 1.75 is printed in scientific notation.

The statement in line 180 is considerably more involved than the other statements. The argument of the WRITELN procedure is an expression rather than a variable name. The value of this expression is carried into the procedure, and a corresponding character string is printed.

The outermost parentheses in line 180 are not part of the arithmetic expression but merely serve to enclose the argument list. The argument list contains just one argument, the evaluated expression. The constant -1.5 is also enclosed within parentheses. This indicates unambiguously that the minus sign is part of the string defining the constant and not an arithmetic operator. When evaluating the expression, we can ignore these parentheses. The innermost subexpression, enclosed by three sets of parentheses, is

$$3.0 + \text{dog}$$

This evaluates to 6.0. Enclosed by two sets of parentheses is

$$\text{bird} * 2.0 - \text{mouse} * 6.0$$

This subexpression evaluates to -12.0. The remaining expression within parentheses is

$$1 + -12.0 * -1.5$$

```
(100) program numerical_ops(output);
(110) var dog,mouse:integer;  bird,cat: real;
(120) begin
(130)     dog := 7 div 4;      writeln(dog);
(140)     dog := 7 mod 4;      writeln(dog);
(150)     cat := 7 div 4;      writeln(cat);
(160)     cat := 7 / 4  ;      writeln(cat);
(170)     mouse := dog;     bird := dog;
(180)     writeln(cat + mouse*(1+(bird*2.0-mouse*(3.0+dog))*(-1.5)))
(190) end.
```

Figure 2.4   Program for Example 2.1

which has a value of 19.0. The value of the expression carried into the procedure writeln is

$$cat + mouse * 19.0 = 1.75 + 3.0 * 19.0 = 58.75$$

Thus, a character string representing a value of 58.75 is printed.

REVIEW

1. What number will be printed by each of the following statements?
   (a) writeln(12 + 21 div 3);
   (b) writeln (12 + 21 div 3 * 7);
   (c) writeln (12 + 21 div (3 * 7));
   (d) writeln (12 + (21 + 3) mod 7);
2. What number will be printed by each of the following statements?
   (a) writeln(3 + 4 * 5 * (6 * 2) mod 3 * 4);
   (b) writeln(3 * 4 * 5/6 + (4.0 + 4/(7 div 2))/2);
3. What number is printed by each of the WRITELN statements in the following program?

```
program review(input,output);
    var a,b,c: integer;   x,y,z: real;
    begin
      a := 1; b := 2; c := 3;
      x := 2.0; y := 3.0;
      z := b/a + x;
      writeln(z/x+y);   (* QUESTION 1 *)
      writeln(b div c - a);   (* QUESTION 2 *)
      writeln(b * (a + c*b+(a*(b mod (c + (b-a))+2)+a)));
                      (* QUESTION 3 *)
    end.
```

2.5 INTRODUCTION TO LOOPING

One benefit of modern programming languages is that they enable us to perform a large number of computations with a short program. This is accomplished with commands to "loop" through a sequence of instructions many times. Each time the loop is passed through, the program changes one or more of the parameters that appear in our calculations.

There are several ways of implementing loops in Pascal. (See Chapter 5.) Perhaps the most popular method for performing repetitive operations is the WHILE command, whose format is

while (condition)   do   statement

The condition is an expression that must evaluate to one of two possible values: True or False. If the condition is false, the statement is skipped. If the condition is true, the statement is executed and the WHILE loop is reentered. Let us consider the following program segment (assume i is an integer variable):

```
i := 4;
while (i < 10) do i := i + 2;
writeln(i);
```

The first time the WHILE statement is encountered, the condition is true, since 4 is less than 10, so the statement is executed. Now i has a value of 6. Then the WHILE statement is executed again. Once again the statement $i := i + 2$ is executed, and the WHILE loop is reentered. After the statement in the WHILE loop has been executed three times, i has a value of 10. The WHILE loop is reentered, but now the condition is false, since 10 is not less than 10. The statement is not executed, and program control passes on to the WRITELN command.

The program segment shown above seems to have no practical application, for only one statement can be performed in the WHILE loop. However, in Pascal a group of statements is considered to be a single statement if the group is bracketed by a ''begin'' and an ''end.'' Consider the following program segment:

```
i := 1;
while (i <> 10) do
          begin
                writeln(' Merry Christmas');
                writeln(' and Happy New Year!!!');
                i := i + 1;
          end;
(*   program continues *)
```

The condition here means that i *is not equal* to 10. As long as this condition is true, the statement bracketed by ''begin'' and ''end'' will be executed. Once the condition is false, program control exits from the WHILE loop. In this program segment, eighteen lines of text will be printed.

Suppose, however, that the line

```
i := i + 1
```

is changed to

```
i := i + 2
```

Then, the condition i is less than or greater than 10 will always be satisfied. This means the loop will never be left and the two messages will never stop printing. The program will be in an infinite loop, and external methods will be needed to break out of the loop. Virtually everyone who writes programs will at some time make errors that place program control in an infinite loop. (People who write programs that result in infinite loops are sometimes referred to as normal human beings!)

Example 2.2 illustrates a practical use of a WHILE loop.

```
(100)  (  An investor is to deposit $1000.00 on the first day of each
(110)     year into a money market fund.  This fund pays a fixed
(120)     interest rate of 9.65%.  Interest is computed on the last day
(130)     of each year, and is deposited back into the fund.  The inves-
(140)     tor makes her first deposit in 1990.  This program computes
(150)     both annual interest earned, and the total amount in the fund
(160)     at the end of each year from 1990 to 2010.   )
(170)  program get_rich(output);
(180)  var         year:  integer;
(190)              yearly_deposit,rate,interest,total: real;
(200)  begin
(210)      rate := 0.0965;   year := 1990;   total := 0.0;
(220)                        yearly_deposit := 1000.00;
(230)      {  Prepare heading for output data }
(240)      writeln; writeln('     YEAR            INTEREST              TOTAL');
(250)      writeln;
(260)      {  Initialization done.  Begin loop.   }
(270)      while (year <= 2010) do
(280)          begin
(290)              total := total + yearly_deposit;
(300)              interest := total * rate;
(310)              total := total + interest;
(320)              writeln(year:8,interest:17:2,total:17:2);
(330)              year := year + 1;
(340)          end { end of loop };
(350)      writeln; writeln; {skip two lines}
(360)  end.
```

Figure 2.5   Solution to Example 2.2

Example 2.2

Suppose an investor is to deposit $1000 into a money market fund on the first day of each year, beginning in 1990. The fund pays an annual interest rate of 9.65%. Interest is computed on the last day of each year and deposited back into the fund. Develop a Pascal program that computes and prints annual interest and total balance at the end of each year from 1990 to 2010.

Solution   A solution is given in Figure 2.5. Observe the use of the WHILE loop.

REVIEW

1. Refer to the following program:

```
program review(input,output);
    var i: integer:
    begin
        i := 0;
        while (i <= 30) do
                begin
                    writeln(i,' ', i*i,' ', i*i*i);
                    i:= i+5;
                end;
    end.
```

(a) When this program is run, how many lines are printed?

(b) How many numbers are printed?

(c) What numbers appear on the last line that is printed?

2. Suppose that on the first day of January 1990 you deposit $1000 into a savings account that pays interest at an annual rate of 5.75%, and no more deposits are made. Write and run a program that prints the total amount in your account at the end of every year from 1990 to 2050.

3. Repeat Review Exercise 2 for the following case: The annual interest rate remains the same, but interest is paid and compounded quarterly.

2.6 INPUT AND OUTPUT

We have already illustrated use of the WRITELN command to produce program output at the user's console. We will now introduce techniques for reading input data into a program.

At one time computer programs were run in a **batch** mode. Typically, a computer program was punched onto IBM cards, and periodically these decks of cards were read into the computer system. If data were to be entered, it was necessary to punch a complete data deck and have this deck read into a data file. Then when a program was actually being executed, requests for input data would be referred to this data file.

It is still very common and often advantageous for computer programs to read input data from one or more data files. However, sometimes it is advantageous, even necessary, for a program to run in a conversational mode. That is, the user interacts with the program as the program is being executed.

Computer systems handle data entered from the console pretty much like they handle data read from other data files. In fact, we consider these data to be read from an INPUT file. Niklaus Wirth developed Pascal in a manner that facilitates handling of input data. Input and output are discussed in detail in Chapter 4. However, we will introduce the major concepts in this section.

Refer to the program in Figure 2.6. Observe that both of the default files, INPUT and OUTPUT, are specified in the program declaration statement on line 120. The program that follows requests a number to be entered. After this number is entered, a WHILE loop is used to enter a set of test scores. After all the scores are entered, the average test score is computed and printed.

Line 190 shows the command

```
readln(number);
```

which is a call to the READLN procedure. In this case there is just one parameter in the argument list. In most popular implementations of Pascal, this is the method used for entering data in a conversational mode of operation. Note: In older versions of Pascal, those originally designed for batch operation, this command may not

```
{100}  (* This program illustrates entry of input data from
{110}          a user console!   *)
{120}  program console_input(input,output);
{130}  { This program computes and prints the average of N test scores.}
{140}  var  number,count,score,total: integer;  average: real;
{150}  begin
{160}        count := 1;    total := 0;
{170}        writeln(' Enter the number of test scores to be averaged.');
{180}        writeln;  writeln;
{190}        readln(number);   (* End initialization *)
{200}        while (count <= number) do
{210}              begin
{220}                  writeln(' Enter score number ',count:3);
{230}                  readln(score);
{240}                  total := total + score; { Add scores together }
{250}                  count := count + 1;
{260}              end; { End WHILE loop }
{270}        (* Compute and print average  *)
{280}        average := total / number;
{290}        writeln; writeln(' The average score is ', average:5:2);
{300}  end.
```

Figure 2.6   A program illustrating input from console

function as expected. If you are employing one such implementation, it will probably be necessary to replace a command such as

readln(number);

with the two commands

readln;
read(number);

The command READLN(number) allows the user to enter a character string representing an integer, converts this character string to proper integer format, and assigns this integer to the variable "number." The following sequence of events occurs in response to the procedure call READLN(number):

0. Data generally cannot be read from files, even from the INPUT file. Data are read from memory. Therefore, a portion of a text file must first be transferred to computer memory before it is read. A set of memory cells, referred to as a **buffer,** is associated with each file used in a program. The buffer stores one line or one record of text. A **line** is a set of character codes terminated by a Newline code. Typically, the Newline code is the character code resulting from pressing a Return, Enter, or Transmit key on the console keyboard.

1. Now, suppose the READLN procedure has been invoked with the single argument "number." This command to read characters from the INPUT buffer is implemented as follows: (a) A pointer identifying the next cell to be read from the INPUT buffer is used to get the next character from the INPUT buffer. (b) The character code is read and the pointer value advanced to identify the next cell in the buffer.

If the character code read is the code for a space, step b is repeated. (c) If valid data have been entered, a character code corresponding to a character between 0 and 9 is read and saved when this step is first entered. The pointer value is advanced to identify the next character in the input buffer. Step c is then repeated until a character code is read that corresponds to a character that is not between 0 and 9.

2. An internal subprogram is used to convert the character string to the corresponding integer. This integer is then assigned to the variable "number."

3. If the argument list contains more than one variable, the sequence of instructions identified in step 1 is repeated.

4. After the assignment or assignments are made, the remaining characters in the INPUT buffer are abandoned. That is, the command is interpreted to read a new line into the INPUT buffer. When we are using the keyboard console that corresponds to the INPUT file and INPUT buffer, a new line of information is not loaded at that time. The INPUT buffer is not loaded until it is necessary to read characters from the buffer.

Refer once again to the statement in line 190. When the procedure is invoked, there will be nothing in the INPUT buffer. Therefore, program operation ceases until a line is entered from the keyboard console. Suppose the operator wishes to find the average of twenty-four test scores. At this time, the operator may enter the character string

                                   24

and then press a Newline key, such as Return or Enter. This causes a 3-character record to be placed in the INPUT buffer. The character string 24 is read, converted to the integer 24, and assigned to the integer variable called "number." But this is not the only way in which the data may be entered. One can also enter the same data by typing either of the following strings:

        24 is the number of test scores that I wish to average.

or

                        24 NUTS to YOU!!!!!

After these data have been entered, the WHILE loop located between steps 200 and 260 is used to read in the twenty-four test scores. Line 230 is the actual line that enters test scores. Suppose the first score is 100. At this point we may type the line

                                  100

But it is also permissible to type a line such as

100 is the first test score.

Students who have programmed in BASIC may initially find console input operations in Pascal to be somewhat confusing. Actually, input in Pascal is quite similar to the corresponding operations in BASIC. But BASIC is often taught at primary or elementary school levels, when students have neither the maturity nor the need to understand the functioning of these operations. However, for college-level work, it is often helpful to understand the functioning of the various commands and procedures.

When significant amounts of data are to be processed, it is not practical to enter the values from a console during program execution. In such cases, data should be read from files that are already available on the system being used. Example 2.3 illustrates a Pascal program in which data are read from an existing file.

Example 2.3

A file called GRADEFILE contains many lines of data. Each line contains five different character strings representing integers. The first string in each line is a student ID number. The second, third, and fourth string in each line represent grades on tests 1, 2, and 3, respectively. (Maximum score = 100.) The final number on each line represents the student's grade on the final exam. (Maximum score = 200.) (Note: A file GRADEFILE is included in Appendix A.)

Develop a program that requests a number such as N to be entered, where N is equal to or less than the number of lines in GRADEFILE. The program computes and prints the average score of test no. 2 obtained by the first N students listed in GRADEFILE.

Solution A solution is given in Figure 2.7. Note that this program is very similar to the one given in Figure 2.6. The major difference is that data are read from GRADEFILE rather than from the console. There is no special significance in the use of capital letters to represent GRADEFILE. This is only to emphasize new material.

Observe that in line 120 the file GRADEFILE is included in the program argument list. File names, like other variables, must be formally declared. In line 150, GRADEFILE is declared as a text file. Although Pascal permits the use of other types of files, text files (files of characters) are the most commonly used type.

The RESET statement in line 170 opens the file identified as the argument, loads the first line of this file into the GRADEFILE buffer, and sets a pointer that references the first character in the GRADEFILE buffer.

The only other statement in this program that is different from statements in the program of Figure 2.6 is the call to the READLN procedure on line 230. The first argument in the argument list is GRADEFILE. Since this is the name of a file identified in the program declaration, input data will be read from the GRADEFILE buffer rather than from the INPUT buffer. The first three integer character strings in the GRADEFILE buffer will be read, converted to integer format, and assigned, respectively, to the variables "id," "test1," and "score." Then the remainder of the data in the GRADEFILE buffer are discarded and the next line of the file GRADEFILE is loaded into the INPUT buffer.

```
{100} { This program illustrates entry of input data from
 110               a file called GRADEFILE }
{120}  program file_input(input,output,GRADEFILE);
{130} { Program computes average of N test scores on test #2)
{140} var number,count,score,id,test1,total:integer;average:real;
{150}     GRADEFILE: text;
{160} begin
{162} (*** The following command is needed if TURBO Pascal
{164}         is used ***)     assign(GRADEFILE,'GRADEFILE');
{170}  count := 1;  total := 0;   reset(GRADEFILE);
{180}  writeln(' Enter the number of test scores to be averaged.');
{190}  writeln;  writeln;
{200}  readln(number); (** End initialization  **)
{210}  while (count <= number) do
{220}     begin
{230}        readln(GRADEFILE,id,test1,score);
{240}        total := total + score; ( Add scores together )
{250}        count := count + 1;
{260}     end {End WHILE loop );
{270}  (** Compute and print average **)
{280}     average := total/number;
{290}     writeln; writeln(' The average score is ',average:5:2);
{300} end.
```

Figure 2.7   Solution to Example 2.3

Example 2.4

Write a program that computes and prints the average grade for test no. 2 in the information contained in GRADEFILE. We do not know how many lines are stored in GRADEFILE.

Solution   Since we do not know how many lines of information are in GRADEFILE, we cannot use the program given in Figure 2.7. To find the average score on test no. 2, every time we add a score to the running sum, we add 1 to the total count. We keep doing this until we come to the end of the file.

In order to identify when we come to the end of the file, we will use the standard Pascal function EOF. Refer to line 180 in Figure 2.8. The function

eof(GRADEFILE)

returns a True when an end-of-file symbol is in the GRADEFILE buffer. The function returns a False when other information is in the GRADEFILE buffer. Observe the NOT operation just in front of the EOF function. The NOT command converts a False to a True, and vice versa. Thus, if the file contains N lines before it is terminated with an appropriate end-of-file symbol, the statements in the WHILE loop will be executed exactly N times.

The way this program is written, when control passes out of the WHILE loop, the variable called "count" will contain a number that is 1 larger than the number of data lines in the file. The statement in line 250 assigns the correct value to the variable called "number."

```
(100) { This program illustrates entry of input data from
 110      a file called GRADEFILE and use of the EOF function }
(120)  program file_input(input,output,GRADEFILE);
(130)  { Program computes average of ALL test scores on test #2}
(140)  var number,count,score,id,test1,total:integer;average:real;
(150)      GRADEFILE: text;
(160)  begin
(162)  (*** The following command is needed if TURBO Pascal
(164)          is used ***)    assign(GRADEFILE,'GRADEFILE');
(170)    count := 1;   total := 0;   reset(GRADEFILE);
(180)    while (not eof(GRADEFILE)) do
(190)       begin
(200)          readln(GRADEFILE,id,test1,score);
(210)          total := total + score; { Add scores together }
(220)          count := count + 1;
(230)       end {End WHILE loop };
(240)    (** Compute and print average **)
(250)       number := count - 1;
(260)       average := total/number;
(270)       writeln; writeln(' The average score is ',average:5:2);
(280)  end.
```

Figure 2.8   Solution to Example 2.4

REVIEW

1. Suppose line 230 in Figure 2.7 is replaced with the following line:

readln(gradefile,test1,score);

What then will be computed by this program?

2. Write and run a program that computes the average percent grade on the final exams stored in GRADEFILE (Appendix A).

3. What modification would have to be made to the program in Figure 2.8 so line 250 could be eliminated?

2.7 STRUCTURE OF A PASCAL PROGRAM

Pascal is sometimes considered a highly structured language. For instance, there are well-defined rules related to declarations of the various elements in a program. Furthermore, it is generally necessary to explicitly declare a program element before it is used. The following list defines the general structure of a Pascal program.

1. Program declaration
2. Label declarations
3. Type definitions
4. Constant definitions
5. Variable declarations
6. Subprogram declarations
7. Main program

All of the example programs so far introduced include a *program declaration*. Recall that the argument list in the declaration statement must include the names of *all* files used in the program.

Following the program declaration statement is the *label declaration statement*. Labels are numerical values that precede a program statement. Do not confuse labels with the line numbers that are frequently supplied by a text editor: Line numbers are *not* passed on to a Pascal compiler. Labels, in contrast, are part of the program and must be processed by the compiler. Labels that require declarations are seldom found in Pascal programs. Label definitions and usage are illustrated in Figure 2.9. Note: Labels that require declarations will *not* appear in any other examples in this textbook.

Type definition statements, the next segment of a Pascal program, are used extensively. There are certain standard Pascal variable types, such as integers, reals, and characters. Pascal enables users to define other variable types that satisfy their specific needs.

Constants may be defined with a user-supplied name. Frequently the name is in capital letters, but this is not required. Representing constant values by meaningful names improves the readability of a program. It also simplifies the modifying of a program. However, we should remember that a constant name is *not* the same as a variable, so we cannot assign values to a constant name during program execution.

In the next segment of a Pascal program, *variables* are declared, each as a specific type, either standard or user-defined.

After variable declarations, *user-defined subprograms* must be declared. The two types of subprograms found in Pascal are functions and procedures. Subprograms may include label declarations, type definitions, constant definitions, variable declarations, and declarations of other subprograms. In computer installations that permit the user to store previously compiled subprograms in user libraries, it may be sufficient just to explicitly declare the subprograms desired. If the programs are unavailable in the library, they must be both declared and defined. By *defining* a subprogram, we mean writing the entire source code for the program.

The *main program* follows the subprogram declarations. It starts with the word "begin," is followed by the program statements, and is terminated by the "end" directive.

The program in Figure 2.9 illustrates the general structure of a Pascal program. The numbers shown in the left-hand column are merely comments that represent line numbers. The label declaration is in line 2, where the numbers 50 and 30 are declared as labels. Only one of these labels is used in the program: The label 30 is employed (a) to identify the first statement on line 37; (b) in conjunction with the GOTO statement in line 35, which causes the two statements in line 36 to be by-passed. Thus, even though these two statements are valid assignment statements, they will not be executed when the program is run. The GOTO statement in line 35 is seldom found in Pascal programs. It is employed here merely to illustrate the use of labels and will not appear again in this textbook.

In the type definition statement in line 3, we formulate a user-defined data

```
{  1}    program pascal_structure(output);
{  2}    label 50,30;
{  3}    type tiger = packed array [1..4] of char;
{  4}    const    pie = 3.14159;
{  5}             AVAGADRO = 6.02E23;
{  6}    var      x,y: real;
{  7}             a,b: integer;
{  8}             t: tiger;
{  9} procedure dumb(n: integer);
{ 10}             const    ONE = 1;
{ 11}             var i: integer;
{ 12}             begin
{ 13}                 i:= ONE;
{ 14}                 while (i <= n) do
{ 15}                     begin
{ 16}                         i := i + 1;
{ 17}                         writeln(' Have a nice day! ');
{ 18}                     end;
{ 19}             end;   (* dumb ends *)
{ 20} function cube(n:integer):integer;
{ 21}             begin
{ 22}                 cube := n*n*n;
{ 23}             end;
{ 24} procedure dog(cat:tiger);
{ 25}             var number: integer;
{ 26}             begin
{ 27}                 number := cube(2);
{ 28}                 while (number <> 0) do
{ 29}                         begin
{ 30}                             number := number - 1;
{ 31}                             writeln(cat);
{ 32}                         end;
{ 33}             end (* dog *) ;
{ 34} begin
{ 35}     goto 30;
{ 36}     x := pie;   y := AVAGADRO;
{ 37} 30: t[1] := 'H'; t[2] := 'e'; t[3] := 'l'; t[4] := 'p';
{ 38}     dumb(3);
{ 39}     dog(t);
{ 40} end.
```

Figure 2.9   Structure of a Pascal program

type. We choose the name "tiger." The definition as given means that "tiger" is declared as a string of four characters. Tiger-type variables may now be declared. A string of four character values may be assigned to a tiger-type variable. A single character value may be assigned to any one of the four fields of a tiger-type variable.

In the variable declarations in lines 6 to 8, observe that two integer variables and two real variables are declared. But note also that the variable *t* has been declared as a tiger-type variable!

Lines 9 to 33 are used for subprogram declarations and definitions. Two procedures and one function are declared and defined. In Pascal, elements generally must be declared before being used. Thus, it is necessary to declare the function CUBE before the procedure DOG is defined. The procedure DOG invokes the function CUBE.

Consider the procedure DUMB, which is defined between lines 9 and 19. The argument list contains one variable, *n*. When the procedure is invoked, a value is carried into the procedure and stored in the local variable *n*. Observe that within the procedure a constant definition is made, and another local variable, *i*, is defined. We refer to these as "local variables" because they are defined only when this procedure is being executed. Each time this procedure is invoked, it will cause the message, "Have a nice day" to be printed *n* times.

A function is like a procedure except that functions generally can return just one value to the invoking program. The function CUBE returns just one value, which is an integer. This particular function has a call list containing just one variable, the integer *n*. The function returns the cube of *n*.

In the procedure DOG, the argument list contains just one variable: "cat." Note that "cat" is a tiger-type variable. When DOG is invoked, a 4-character string is carried into the local variable "cat." Now refer to line 27, the first executable line in the procedure DOG. The function CUBE is invoked with an argument having a value of 2. Cube returns the integer 8, which is assigned to "number." Then the string carried into procedure DOG is printed eight times.

Line 34 identifies the beginning of the main program. The first statement following this line is the entry point to the program. This is where program execution begins. Everything preceding this statement is just a declaration or a definition. The subsequent statements may invoke the user-defined functions and procedures many times. Similarly, the program statements may never invoke the functions or procedures that have been defined. The user-defined subprograms are executed only when they are explicitly invoked.

Line 35, the entry point to the program, passes program control to line 37. In this line, character values are assigned to the four-character variables, *t*[1], *t*[2], *t*[3], and *t*[4]. Thus, the tiger variable *t* contains the string "Help." In line 38, procedure DUMB is invoked, and a value of 3 is carried into DUMB's local variable *n*. This procedure prints "Have a nice day!" three times before program control reverts back to line 39. Then procedure DOG is invoked. The value "Help" stored in *t* is now assigned to local variable "cat" in procedure DOG. Then this string is printed eight times before control reverts back to the main program.

We have introduced user-defined functions and procedures. Developing subprograms that perform well-defined and relatively simple tasks is perhaps the most important part of programming. We will address this topic in more detail in Chapter 3.

REVIEW

1. Why are constant declarations so common in Pascal programs?
2. Why are user-defined functions and procedures used in Pascal programs?
3. When the program in Figure 2.9 is run, what is the first line that is actually executed?

EXERCISES

1. Why should we avoid the enhancements or improvements that are frequently added to high-level programming languages?
2. Describe a typical process involved in compiling and running a program written in a high-level language. What type of supporting software is generally required?
3. Which two types of statements comprise a Pascal program?
4. Define or describe each of the following terms or phrases.
   (a) Subprogram
   (b) Argument list
   (c) Procedure
   (d) Function
   (e) Passing parameters by value
   (f) Passing parameters by reference
   (g) Pointers
5. Write and run a Pascal program that prints your name, social security number, and age.
6. What is meant by each of the following?
   (a) Source code
   (b) Object code
   (c) Absolute code
   (d) Operating system
   (e) Library
7. What is the function of a *linker*, or *relocatable linking loader*?
8. The arguments in the call list of the WRITELN procedure may include integers, reals, characters, pointers, and packed arrays of characters. What is the only type of coded information that is printed by WRITELN?
9. Refer to lines 250 to 280 in Figure 2.3. How are the quantities assigned to the variables "cat," "dog," "mouse," and "bird" actually encoded? Assume the various data types are encoded as described in Section 1.2.
10. What numbers are printed when the program in Figure 2.10 is run?
11. What numbers are printed when the program in Figure 2.11 is run?
12. Write a Pascal program that prints the values of *I*, *I*-squared, and *I*-cubed for values of *I* between 0 and 100 inclusive.

```
program ex2_10(output);
var a,b,c,d: integer;  w,x,y,z: real;
begin
      a := 2; b := 3; c := 4; w := 5.0; x := 6.0;
      d := a + (b+2*c) mod b;
      y := 2.0 + w -x/1.5 * 2.0;
      z := 2.0  + w -x/(1.5 * 2.0);
      writeln(d,'  ',y,'  ',z);
end.
```

Figure 2.10   Program for Exercise 2.10

```
program ex2_11(output);
var a,b,c: integer;  x,y,z: real;
begin
      a := 2; b := 3; c := 1;  y := 2.0;  z := -2.5;
      writeln(3 +a*(c-2*(b-1)) div 4);
      writeln(x + y -2.0*z);
      writeln(' The discriminant is ', b*b - 4*a*c);
end.
```

Figure 2.11   Program for Exercise 2.11

13. Refer to the program in Figure 2.5. Suppose line 330 is deleted. What happens when this modified program is run?
14. Modify the program in Figure 2.5 so it prints the current balance every second year. Interest values are not to be printed.
15. Modify the program in Figure 2.5 so it uses the same values as shown but computes and awards interest quarterly instead of annually.
16. Modify the program in Figure 2.5 so that prior to entering the loop, values of rate, starting year, and terminating year are requested and entered as data.
17. Refer to the program in Figure 2.6. Modify this program so it also prints the variance and standard deviation of the grades entered. Note: **Variance** is the average of the squares of each grade minus the average grade squared. **Standard deviation** is the square root of the variance.
18. Refer to Figure 2.7. Modify this program so it prints the average of the first N scores on test no. 1 in GRADEFILE.
19. Refer to Figure 2.8. Modify this program so it prints:
    (a) The number of lines in GRADEFILE.
    (b) The average scores on tests 1, 2, and 3.
20. Refer to Figure 2.9. Suppose lines 38 and 39 are replaced with the following line:

    dog(t); dog(t); dumb(2); dumb(3); dumb(4);

    How many lines will be printed when this modified program is run?
21. Write and run a Pascal program that requests you to enter an integer N and four character values. The program will print a four-letter name corresponding to the characters you entered exactly N times.
22. Write and test a function that returns the square of the number transmitted in the argument list.
23. Write and test a function that accepts three arguments corresponding to the integers A, B, and C. The function returns the value of the discriminant $B * B - 4 * A * C$.
24. Write and run a Pascal program that computes and prints the value of the following function F as X varies from 0 to 10 in steps of 1:

$$F = 3.0\,(X^3) - 4.5\,(X^2) + 6.4\,(X) - 12.0$$

25. What will be printed when the program in Figure 2.12 is run?

```
program ex2_25(output);
type  fox = packed array [1..2] of char;
const   CAKE = 2.71;    A = 'HELLO';
        B = 7;     CAT = 'D';
var     x: integer;  y: real;   z: fox;
begin
      writeln(A);  writeln(A);
      x := (2 + B) div 5;
      writeln(x);
      y := CAKE;  z[2] := 'g';  z[1] := 'o';
      writeln(y:2:1);
      writeln(cat:1,z:2);
end.
```

Figure 2.12   Program for Exercise 2.25

3

Introduction to Subprograms

Suppose we plan to be the chief operating officer of a major corporation. Or suppose we are a student taking several courses, working part time, and engaged in a variety of social activities. Or suppose we are in charge of managing a household. In any of these situations we will have similar problems: A variety of tasks must be performed; one task often will differ significantly from the others; and each individual task or subtask will require us to pay attention to particular details. The details may seem unimportant as far as the overall duties are concerned, but they will be essential for successful completion of each subtask.

There are other factors involved in managing our responsibilities. We may need assistance from others. If so, we must specify clearly what is to be done, and should expect the job to be done properly. But we may be unconcerned with exactly how the job is done. Furthermore, we must try to perform sequences of relatively simple and independent tasks. If we try to feed the baby while simultaneously painting the ceiling and washing the car, it is unlikely that any of the subtasks will be performed properly. Similarly, if our accounting department tries to train sales help to satisfy accounting requirements, and our salespeople decide to control the manufacturing process, our company will soon be filing for bankruptcy.

The same principles that help manage other human endeavors apply to the development of computer programs. In particular, we should subdivide our problems into a set of simpler tasks. Then we should further subdivide each of these until we have a set of relatively simple tasks to perform. Finally, an appropriate manager must decide how each of the simple tasks will actually be implemented.

When developing computer programs, we develop subprograms corresponding to each well-defined level of management. Subprograms at higher levels merely invoke lower-level routines to perform tasks. Eventually, work is done by a relatively simple set of "working" routines. Main programs that control extremely long and complicated programs are generally very simple. A typical **main program** may look something like the following:

```
        DECLARATION STATEMENTS
  begin
              initialize;
              run_program;
              terminate;
  end.
```

In this example, three very high-level procedures are invoked. We have given them names INITIALIZE, RUN_PROGRAM, and TERMINATE. Of course, each of these must invoke lower-level subprograms. Eventually, working routines that perform relatively simple tasks will be invoked.

3.1 STANDARD PASCAL FUNCTIONS

It is unnecessary for a Pascal user to develop all the subprograms that are needed. We have already used two of the powerful standard procedures, READLN and WRITELN.

Function name	Type of argument	Type returned by function	Comment
ABS	integer or real	integer or real	Returns absolute value
ARCTAN	integer or real	real	Arctangent, in radians
COS	integer or real	real	Cosine. Argument in radians
EXP	integer or real	real	Raises transcendental number e (2.7182 . . .) to specified power
LN	integer or real	real	Logarithm to base e
ROUND	real	integer	Rounds to closest integer
SIN	integer or real	real	Sine. Argument in radians
SQR	integer or real	integer or real	Squares argument
SQRT	integer or real	real	Square root
TRUNC	real	integer	Truncates; returns whole part of number

Figure 3.1 Some standard Pascal functions

```
program functions(output);
(*  Illustrates use of functions in Figure 3.1 *)
const PI = 3.14159265;
var a,b:integer;  x,y,z: real;
    begin
        x:=PI/4.0; y:= cos(x); z:=sin(x); a:=-2; b:=round(sqrt(81));
        writeln(abs(a),' ',y:6:3, ' ',round(z), ' ',trunc(z));
        x:=arctan(1.0)*180.0/PI;  y:=exp(0.0);  z:= ln(1.0);
        writeln(x:4:1,y:4:1,z:4:1,' ',sqr(-3),b:4);
    end.
```

Figure 3.2 Use of standard Pascal functions

There also are a number of standard Pascal functions. Furthermore, many installations have libraries of functions and procedures available to system users.

Figure 3.1 tabulates a set of standard, or predefined, Pascal functions. Other standard functions will be introduced at appropriate places in this text. Observe that each of the functions in Figure 3.1 has just a single argument. In general, functions as well as procedures may have extensive argument lists.

The program in Figure 3.2 illustrates the use of all the standard functions listed in Figure 3.1. When this program is run, the first line printed will display the numbers 2, 0.707, 1, and 0. The second line printed will display 45.0, 1.0, 0.0, 9, and 9.

REVIEW

1. Write and run a Pascal program that prints values of X, cosecant(X), and secant(X) for values of X between 30° and 60° in 1° increments.
2. Write and run a Pascal program that prints values of the hyperbolic functions SINH(x) and COSH(x) as x varies from 0.0 to 3.0 in increments of 0.1.

3.2 USER-DEFINED FUNCTIONS

A **function** is a subprogram that returns just one value to the invoking statement. In addition to the standard, or predefined, functions, Pascal users may define their own functions. Suppose we wish to solve a quadratic equation. It is impractical to write a function that will solve a quadratic equation, since such an equation has *two* roots, which may not even be real numbers (they may be complex numbers).

Suppose we are given the quadratic equation

$$AX^2 + BX + C = 0$$

In order to solve this equation, we must first evaluate the discriminant, which is defined as

$$B^2 - 4AC$$

```
( 1) program more_functions(input,output);
( 2)    var a,b,c,d: real;  p,q,r: integer;
( 3)    function discriminant (a,b,c:real): real;
( 4)         var d,e,f: real;
( 5)         begin
( 6)            (*  The following two lines are used just for
( 7)                    illustrative purposes  *)
( 8)                f := 0.0;  f := cos(f);
( 9)                f := arctan(f);
(10)            (* Now we will find the discriminant *)
(11)            d := sqr(b);
(12)            e := 4*a*c;
(13)            discriminant := d - e;
(14)         end;
(15) begin (* main program *)
(16)    writeln(' Enter values of A,B and C');
(17)    readln(a,b,c);
(18)    while (a <> 0.0 ) do begin
(19)                        d:=discriminant(a,b,c);
(20)                        writeln(d);
(21)                        writeln(' Enter new values of A,B,C');
(22)                        readln(a,b,c);
(23)                        end;
(24)    writeln(discriminant(b,c,b));
(25) end.
```

Figure 3.3   A user-defined function

The program in Figure 3.3 employs a user-defined function to evaluate the discriminant. However, some unnecessary steps have been added to both the program and
the function, to help introduce certain concepts fundamental to functions.

There are seven variables in Figure 3.3 that are defined in the main program:
a, b, c, d, p, q, and r. Space to store values for these variables must be available
in computer memory when this program is running. In Pascal, space for such variables
is allocated to a data structure called a **stack** (see Figure 3.4(a)). An internal CPU
register is used to identify the current *top* of the stack. All variables used by a
program must be *below* the top of the stack.

When line 17 in Figure 3.3 is executed, we must enter values for A, B, and
C. Suppose we type in the following line of data:

$$1.0 \qquad 7.0 \qquad 12.0$$

Then 1.0 will be assigned to variable a, 7.0 to b, and 12.0 to c. This is shown in
Figure 3.4(a).

The procedure DISCRIMINANT is invoked in line 19 of Figure 3.3, and the
argument list contains three entries. When using Pascal functions, *values* are generally
carried into the function by the invoking statement. In the function DISCRIMINANT
(defined between lines 3 and 14), since values are to be passed into the function,
the formal parameters are used to define *local* variables in the function. We could
have selected any variable names for these local variables. We chose a, b, and c,
which happen to be valid variable names in the main program. When we first
invoke DISCRIMINANT in line 19, the value stored in main variable a is passed on to

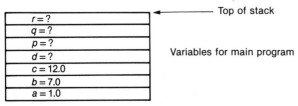

(a) Just before DISCRIMINANT is invoked for the first time

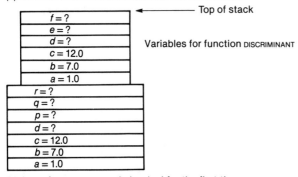

(b) Just after DISCRIMINANT is invoked for the first time

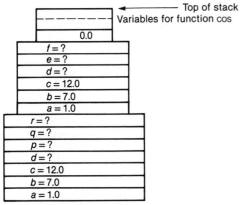

(c) Just after cos is invoked for the first time

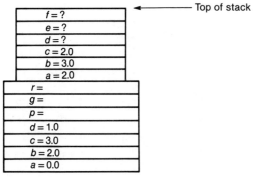

(d) Just after DISCRIMINANT is invoked for the second time

Figure 3.4 Example of a run-time stack for the program in Figure 3.3

the first local variable in DISCRIMINANT, which also happens to be called *a*. Likewise, 7.0 is assigned to local variable *b* and 12.0 to local variable *c*.

Observe from line 4 of the procedure that three other local variables are also defined. Figure 3.4(b) illustrates the variables accessible to the function DISCRIMINANT just after it has been entered. In general, a Pascal subprogram can access any variable below the top of the stack. But observe that at this time there are two variables called *a*, two called *b*, and two called *c*. The following rule always applies:

When a subprogram is being executed, and when the run-time stack contains more than one variable with the same name, the multiply named variable closest to the top of the stack will be used.

Program control is now in the subprogram DISCRIMINANT. In line 8, this subprogram invokes the system function COS. The value 0.0 is assigned to a variable local to COS. Likewise, COS may employ other local variables. This is illustrated in Figure 3.4(c). After the system function COS computes the cosine of 0.0, program control reverts back to line 8, and the value of 1.0 is now assigned to variable *f*. The run-time stack once again looks like that shown in Figure 3.4(b), except a value of 1.0 is now assigned to variable *f*.

In line 9, another system function is invoked. The stack space previously used by COS is now used by ARCTAN. A similar situation occurs when system function SQR is invoked.

In line 13, the value of the discriminant, which is 1.0, is computed. Program control then returns to line 19, and the value 1.0 is assigned to variable *d*. The run-time stack now looks like that shown in Figure 3.4(a), except that 1.0 is now assigned to *d*. In line 20, procedure WRITELN is invoked. The same stack space previously used to store DISCRIMINANT's local variables is now used to store WRITELN's local variables.

When line 22 is executed, new values for *a*, *b*, and *c* are entered. Suppose the following line is entered:

$$0.0 \qquad 2.0 \qquad 3.0$$

Then the program will leave the WHILE loop, and DISCRIMINANT will be invoked in line 24. When program control is passed to this function, the run-time stack will contain values shown in Figure 3.4(d). Observe that the values stored in the local variables *a*, *b*, and *c* are not the same as those stored in the main program variables *a*, *b*, and *c*.

At first glance it appears that variable storage and access in Pascal is somewhat complicated. However, grasping the concepts illustrated in Figures 3.3 and 3.4 will serve as a major step in facilitating understanding of the sophisticated use of Pascal subprograms. The following two examples should further clarify how to employ user-defined functions.

Example 3.1

Formulate a Pascal function that accepts the value of a positive integer N and returns the sum of all the positive integers from 1 to N.

Solution   In developing the function, one approach is to add N to the sum of all positive integers up to $N - 1$. But how can this function find the sum of all the positive integers up to $N - 1$? It can invoke itself with an argument of $N - 1$. This circular reasoning is referred to as a **recursive technique.** Recursion may be used in Pascal, but we must be careful when writing recursive subprograms.

The program in Figure 3.5 is a solution to Example 3.1. The program contains a new statement in line 5, the IF-THEN-ELSE statement, whose form is:

```
if condition then statement1 else statement2;
```

Observe that there is no semicolon after statement1. If the condition is true, statement1 will be executed. If not, then statement2 is executed. If we wish to use a sequence of statements instead of a single statement, we can bracket the sequence of statements between a "begin" and an "end" directive.

Refer to the function SUM defined between lines 3 and 6. Observe that unless the argument has a value of 0, SUM will invoke itself. Now consider the test program that starts at line 9. In line 10, SUM is invoked and a value of 3 is carried into the local variable k. From line 5, since k is not equal to 0, SUM is again invoked, with an argument of 2. But since the condition is still false, SUM is again invoked, with an argument of 1. Then SUM is invoked once more, with an argument of 0. At this point, SUM has been invoked four times but has not been completed even once. The run-time stack corresponding to this point in time is shown in Figure 3.6(a).

Now the condition specified in line 5 is true. Therefore, the value of 0 is assigned to SUM, the function SUM reaches its "end" directive, and program control reverts back to the program that last invoked SUM. When we first return from SUM, the value of 0 is returned to the invoking statement on line 5, and the run-time stack is as shown in Figure 3.6(b). The value returned is added to the value of k, which is 1. This again completes SUM, and control reverts to the invoking statement, which again is on line 5. Then 2 is added to 1, and the sum of these numbers is again returned to the invoking statement on line 5. At this time, the run-time stack is as shown in

```
{ 1} program recursion(output);
{ 2} var n: integer;
{ 3} function sum(k:integer):integer;
{ 4}        begin
{ 5}            if (k = 0) then sum := 0 else sum := sum(k-1) + k;
{ 6}        end;
{ 7} (* test program *)
{ 8} begin
{ 9}        n:=3;
{10}        writeln(sum(n));
{11} end.
```

Figure 3.5   Solution for Example 3.1

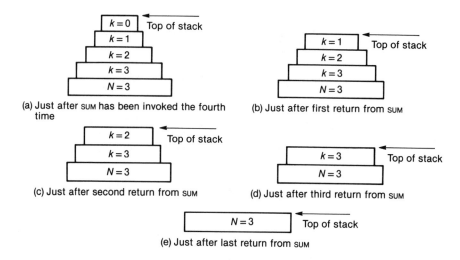

Figure 3.6 Run-time stack for Example 3.1

Figure 3.6(d). The sum of 3 + 3 is computed, program control returns to line 10, and the number 6 is printed.

Let us summarize this sequence of events:

1. SUM is called from line 10, with an argument 3.
2. SUM is called from line 5, with an argument 2.
3. SUM is called from line 5, with an argument 1.
4. SUM is called from line 5, with an argument 0.

Up until this time, the function SUM has never been completed. Now each time sum is completed, control reverts to the statement that last invoked it. Thus,

5. SUM returns 0 to line 5.
6. SUM returns 1 to line 5.
7. SUM returns 3 to line 5.
8. SUM returns 6 to line 10.

At first introduction, recursive techniques may appear somewhat difficult to comprehend. But they are popular with programmers because they can significantly ease the development of certain types of programs (see Section 9.2).

Example 3.2

Referring to the file GRADEFILE discussed in Section 2.6 and illustrated in Appendix A, recall that this file contains many lines, each with a student ID number and the scores the student obtained on test nos. 1, 2, and 3 and the final exam. Write a function that accepts the value of an ID number. If the number carried into the function is the same as one of the ID numbers in GRADEFILE, the ID number is returned and the corresponding student's test scores are placed in the GRADEFILE buffer. If the ID number is not in the file, a value of 0 is returned and an end-of-file mark is placed in the GRADEFILE buffer.

Solution   A function satisfying the specification as well as a test program are shown in Figure 3.7. Two new concepts are introduced. A **boolean** variable is declared in line 4. A boolean variable may be assigned just two possible values: True or False. An IF-THEN statement is used in line 22. The statement following the condition is executed only if the condition is true. Observe that program control remains within the WHILE loop of the function until either the ID number carried into the function is located or there are no more lines in the file.

```
{ 1} program search_file(input,output,gradefile);
{ 2} var m,n,t1,t2,t3,final: integer;  gradefile:text;
{ 3} function search(id:integer):integer;
{ 4}     var x:integer; flag:boolean;
{ 5}  (* This function searches GRADEFILE to see if the requested
{ 6}     identification number is in the file.  If it is, the
{ 7}     function returns the requested ID and leaves the grades
{ 8}     obtained by that individual in the GRADEFILE buffer.  If the
{ 9}     requested ID is not in GRADEFILE, the function returns a val-
{10}     ue of 0, and leaves an EOF mark in the GRADEFILE buffer.  *)
{11}   begin
{12}     reset(gradefile); flag := true;  search := 0;
{13}     while (flag) do
{14}       begin
{15}         read(gradefile,x);
{16}         if (x =id) then begin
{17}                         flag := false;
{18}                         search := id
{19}                     end
{20}                 else begin
{21}                         readln(gradefile);
{22}                         if eof(gradefile) then flag:=false;
{23}                     end;
{24}       end;
{25}   end;
{26}   (* test program *)
{27} begin
       (*** The following command is needed if TURBO Pascal
               is used ***)    assign (gradefile,'GRADEFILE');
{28}     writeln(' Enter an identification number.');
{29}     readln(n);
{30}     m := search(n);
{31}     if (m=0) then writeln('ID number ',n, ' is not in GRADEFILE!')
{32}             else begin
{33}                     read(gradefile,t1,t2,t3,final);
{34}                     writeln(' The test scores for ID # ',n,' are:');
{35}                     writeln(t1:8,t2:8,t3:8,final:8);
{36}                 end;
{37} end.
```

Figure 3.7   Solution for Example 3.2

REVIEW

1. Write and test the following two functions:
   (a) A function that accepts a real argument and returns the hyperbolic sine of the argument.
   (b) A function that accepts a real argument and returns the hyperbolic tangent of the argument.
2. Write and test a function that accepts two arguments, a character and a real number. If the character is *R*, the function converts the real number from degrees to radians. If the letter is *D*, the function converts the number from radians to degrees. For any other letter, the function prints an error message and returns a value of 0.
3. Refer to the following program segment:

```
program main (input,output)
    var a,b,c,d,x,y,z: integer;
        function dumb ( n,m : integer); integer;
            var i,j,a,b: integer;
            . . . . . . . . . . . . . . . . . . . . . .
```

   (a) How many local variables are available to the function DUMB? That is, how many variables can be used only by the function DUMB?
   (b) The function also has access to some of the main program variables. How many variables in all is the function able to access?
4. Refer to the program in Figure 3.5 (p. 47). Suppose line 9 is changed from

$$n := 3$$

   to

$$n := 9$$

   When the new program is executed:
   (a) How many times will the function be invoked?
   (b) What number will be printed when line 10 is executed?
5. Write a recursive function that accepts an even integer *N* and returns the sum of the squares of all even integers up to and including *N*.

3.3 PROCEDURES

A Pascal procedure is quite similar to a Pascal function. But a procedure does not return a value. Therefore we may not assign a procedure call to a variable or use a procedure call as part of an arithmetic expression.

We have mentioned that there are two ways of passing arguments to subprograms, by value or by reference. Arguments passed to functions are almost always passed by value. Concepts related to passing arguments by *value* have already been illustrated: The values get placed on a run-time stack and become local variables in the subprogram that is invoked. When arguments are passed by *reference*, a *pointer* to an existing variable is placed on the stack. When the subprogram uses the formal parameter corresponding to this variable, operations are performed not on the pointer but on the variable identified by the pointer.

It may seem to make little difference how parameters are passed to subprograms. But if we want information returned from a procedure, we must pass at least one parameter by reference. In general, it is safe to use the following guidelines:

Variables that are to be changed in the invoking program must be passed by reference. All other variables in the call list should be passed by value. Numbers must be passed by value.

The method chosen to pass parameters is defined by declaration statements in the argument list of the subprogram. If a declaration statement in this list is preceded by the word *var*, then these parameters are to be passed by reference.

The Pascal programs in Figures 3.8, 3.9, and 3.10 illustrate how to pass parameters by reference and by value. These programs are identical except for the manner in which the procedure's formal parameters are declared. That is, the programs are identical except for the argument list in line 5.

From the argument list in line 5 in Figure 3.8, we can see that parameters are to be passed by value. When this procedure is invoked in line 12, values of 3

```
{ 1} (* Introduction to user-defined procedures *)
{ 2} program procedures(output);
{ 3} var x,y: integer;
{ 4} (* Procedure is to compute cube of first input argument *)
{ 5} procedure cube(a,b: integer);
{ 6}        begin
{ 7}             a := a*a*a;
{ 8}             b := a;
{ 9}        end;
{10} begin
{11}      x := 3;   y := 0;
{12}      cube(x,y);
{13}      writeln(x:10,y:10);
{14} end.
```

Figure 3.8 Passing parameters by value

```
{ 1} (* Introduction to user-defined procedures *)
{ 2} program procedures(output);
{ 3} var x,y: integer;
{ 4} (* Procedure is to compute cube of first input argument *)
{ 5} procedure cube(var a,b: integer);
{ 6}        begin
{ 7}             a := a*a*a;
{ 8}             b := a;
{ 9}        end;
{10} begin
{11}      x := 3;   y := 0;
{12}      cube(x,y);
{13}      writeln(x:10,y:10);
{14} end.
```

Figure 3.9 Passing parameters by reference

```
( 1) (* Introduction to user-defined procedures *)
( 2) program procedures(output);
( 3) var x,y: integer;
( 4) (* Procedure is to compute cube of first input argument *)
( 5) procedure cube(a: integer; var b:integer);
( 6)        begin
( 7)              a := a*a*a;
( 8)              b := a;
( 9)        end;
(10) begin
(11)        x := 3;   y := 0;
(12)        cube(x,y);
(13)        writeln(x:10,y:10);
(14) end.
```

Figure 3.10   Passing parameters by value and by reference

and 0 are assigned to local variables *a* and *b*. Before execution of the procedure is completed, a value of 27 is assigned to both *a* and *b*. But once execution of the procedure is completed, control reverts back to line 13, and information stored in the local variables is lost. The statement in line 13 prints the values 3 and 0.

From line 5 in Figure 3.9, we can see that both parameters are to be passed by reference. When this procedure is invoked in line 12, pointers to variables *x* and *y* are carried into the procedure. Thus, all assignments within the procedure are made to variables *x* and *y*. When program control leaves the procedure and reverts back to line 13, both *x* and *y* have been assigned values of 27.

From line 5 in Figure 3.10, we see that the first parameter in the call list is passed by value but that the second one is passed by reference. Just before program control leaves the procedure, local variable *a* and variable *y* will be assigned values of 27. But the value of *x* is never changed. The WRITELN statement in line 13 will cause the numbers 3 and 27 to be printed. If we wish to have a procedure that computes the cube of a number, we would probably wish to transmit arguments by the method shown in Figure 3.10.

Example 3.3

Write and test a procedure that accepts the coefficients of a quadratic equation and returns the roots.

Solution   A quadratic equation has two roots. If the discriminant is nonnegative, the roots are real. If the discriminant is negative, the roots are complex. But suppose we know one complex root, such as

$$P + Qi$$

where P and Q are real numbers and i is the square root of -1. Then the other real root is the complex conjugate, or

$$P - Qi$$

Thus, our procedure must return three pieces of information: two real numbers and whether the roots are real or complex.

A solution is given in Figure 3.11. A procedure called ROOTS, defined between

```
( 1) (* Find roots of a quadratic equation *)
( 2) program find_roots(input,output);
( 3) var a,b,c,x,y: real;   complex: boolean;
( 4)      function discriminant(a,b,c: real): real;
( 5)          begin
( 6)              discriminant := sqr(b) -4.0 * a * c;
( 7)          end;
( 8)      procedure roots(a,b,c:real; var p,q:real; var flag:boolean);
( 9)              var d: real;
(10)          begin
(11)              d:= discriminant(a,b,c);
(12)              if (d >= 0.0) then
(13)                      begin
(14)                          p := (-b+sqrt(d))/(2.0*a);
(15)                          q := (-b-sqrt(d))/(2.0*a);
(16)                          flag := false
(17)                      end
(18)                          else
(19)                      begin
(20)                          p := -b/(2.0*a);
(21)                          q := sqrt(-d)/(2.0*a);
(22)                          flag := true;
(23)                      end;
(24)          end;
(25) (* Start test program *)
(26) begin
(27)     writeln(' Enter values of a,b and c on a single line');
(28)     readln(a,b,c);
(29)     while(a <> 0.0) do
(30)         begin
(31)             roots(a,b,c,x,y,complex);
(32)             if (not complex) then
(33)                     writeln(x:20:2,y:20:2)
(34)                         else
(35)                     begin
(36)                         writeln(x,' + ',y,' i');
(37)                         writeln(x,' - ',y,' i');
(38)                     end;
(39)             writeln(' Enter coefficients. Exit by entering zeroes');
(40)             readln(a,b,c);
(41)         end;
(42) end.
```

Figure 3.11   Solution to Example 3.3

lines 8 and 24, performs the desired task. From the argument list in this procedure (line 8), observe that pointers to two real variables and one boolean variable are to be carried into this procedure. That is, three parameters are to be carried into this procedure by reference. The other parameters are carried in by value.

REVIEW

1. Write and test a procedure that accepts a real number that is between -89.0 and $+89.0$, treats this number as an angle (in degrees), and returns the sine, cosine, and tangent of the angle.

2. Write a procedure that accepts three real values and returns the largest and smallest of these three numbers.
3. Write a procedure that accepts a real number and returns the hyperbolic sine and hyperbolic cosine of this number.

3.4 DEVELOPING PROGRAMS

There are several key characteristics associated with a good program. It is essential, of course, for the program to work, for it to do what it is supposed to do. There are several phases in developing programs:

1. Specification of program requirements
2. Development of program code
3. Testing and debugging
4. Program maintenance

Specifying program requirements is the most important phase and often requires the greatest amount of time. We must thoroughly understand what tasks we want performed by our programs. Unfortunately, these tasks often are only partially specified by the originator (manager, boss, teacher, etc.). Nonetheless, we must thoroughly and satisfactorily define what is to be done.

Once program requirements have been thoroughly specified, it is relatively easy to develop source code for our program.

Having developed source code, we must then thoroughly test it. This step of program development is often tedious. Furthermore, at this stage we may find we have not yet satisfactorily defined program requirements.

It may seem that, once our program is thoroughly tested and debugged, the programming task has been completed. But the requirements of any system change, often before we have even completed the task at hand. Modifications of working programs that are necessary to meet changing specifications are referred to as **program maintenance.** For commercial programs, the number of hours required for program maintenance can frequently be twice as great as the number required for initial program development!

Developing program code is similar to solving other problems. First the problem is divided into a small set of independent tasks. Then each of these subtasks is subdivided into a small set of simpler tasks. Subdivision and refinement of tasks eventually leads to a set of very simple tasks. Each of these simple tasks is then converted to program code and thoroughly tested. Then the higher-level routines are written and tested. These higher-level routines merely invoke the working routines that have already been written, in order to accomplish a more general task. This general approach to problem solving is referred to as a **top-down bottom-up** approach.

When defining tasks and subtasks, it may be useful to express requirements in a combination of conversational language and programming language syntax, a

1. Set TOTAL and COUNT to 0
2. Get a NUMBER
3. TOTAL = TOTAL + NUMBER
4. COUNT = COUNT + 1
5. Repeat steps 2 to 4 until there are no more numbers
6. AVERAGE = TOTAL/COUNT

Figure 3.12   Pseudocode for averaging a set of numbers

combination known as **pseudocode.** A pseudocode algorithm for averaging a set of numbers is presented in Figure 3.12. A program giving two different implementations of the pseudocode is shown in Figure 3.13.

We have introduced techniques and tools for developing programs. But we want to write *good* programs. The following list enumerates some attributes associated with good programs.

```
(*   Find average of a set of positive integers.   Terminate
     set by entering a negative integer.   *)
program ave(input,output);
var ans1, ans2: integer;

function average1: integer;      (* First Method *)
    var count, total, number : integer;
       begin
             count := 0;  total := 0;
             readln(number);
                repeat
                    total := total + number;
                    count := count + 1;
                    readln(number);
                until number < 0;
             average1 := total div count;
       end;

function average2: integer;
       var count, total, number:  integer;
          begin
                count := 0;  total := 0;
                readln(number);
                while number >= 0 do
                        begin
                              total := total + number;
                              count := count + 1;
                              readln(number);
                        end;
                average2 := total div count;
          end;

begin
    ans1 := average1;    ans2 := average2;
    writeln(ans1, '        ', ans2);
end.
```

Figure 3.13   A program that shows two implementations of the pseudocode in Figure 3.12

1. The program should *work*. It should function properly for any set of valid input data and for any of the possible options.

2. The program code should *be efficient* so that the corresponding machine code requires minimal memory space.

3. The program should *execute rapidly*.

4. The program should *be well documented*. In-program comments should clearly specify the task being performed, but not how the statements of a particular programming language function. The purpose of each separate module should be described. Proper documentation may include appropriate user manuals and training modules.

5. Programs should *be readable*. That is, a user who is not a programmer should be able to comprehend what tasks various modules are performing. Good readability means that variable and subprogram names are meaningful, loops within modules clearly indented, and modules clearly separated from other modules.

6. Programs should *be maintainable*. That is, program modules as well as the general program organization should be planned so the program is relatively easy to expand or modify. This requires modular development of code.

7. Programs should *be transportable*. Programs generally should not be written for a specific machine. Most programs should be written using a standardized high-level language. The programmer should not take advantage of the idiosyncracies of a particular system. Programmers should be cautious in using ''powerful enhancements'' of standard programming languages. Computers and operating systems are frequently changed or updated. Sometimes it becomes necessary to discard massive programs developed by such ''clever'' programmers.

8. Programming tasks should *be completed in a reasonable length of time*, always before the specified deadline.

It is impossible to develop meaningful programs that optimize all of the above requirements—tradeoffs are always necessary. Although it is impractical for students to develop ''commercial-quality'' programs, students still need to cultivate reasonably good programming habits, particularly if they aspire to jobs involving some programming activity.

Perhaps the most important aim in developing programs is to create program code in small, independent modules. But how small is ''small''? A good guideline is to limit the size of a module so the meaningful lines of code are all visible simultaneously on the console monitor.

Example 3.4

A data file called SALFILE (see sample file included in Appendix A) comprises information on a number of people. Each line of the file contains:

16-character name   ID number (integer)   Salary (real)

Develop a program that does the following: reads the "change" portion of each person's salary, then prints the name of every individual in the file, followed by the amount of change she or he is to receive, specified as the numbers of quarters, dimes, nickels, and pennies required for that particular amount.

Solution   A solution is given in Figures 3.14, 3.15, and 3.16. In Figure 3.14, the program, file names, and main program variables are declared. The simple subprograms START, GET_NAME, GET_SAL, and GET_CHANGE are also declared and defined. In Figure 3.15, three additional subprograms are declared and defined. Included in this set is the high-level routine RUN. The main program is shown in Figure 3.16. Note that this program has been developed so it can be easily modified and expanded.

```
(**** This program module reads a salaries from a file.  A line of
the file contains the following  information:

 16-letter name     ID number (integer)    Salary (real)

This program extracts the change portion of the salary.  Then for each
line in the file, it prints the individuals name and the number of
quarters, dimes, nickels and pennies the individual is to receive. **)

program findchange(input,output,datafile);
type name = packed array[1..16] of char;

var datafile: text;

procedure start;
   begin ·
     reset(datafile);
     writeln('  Name             Quarters     Dimes     Nickels     Pennies');
   end;

function get_change(total:real):integer;
      var x: integer;  y: real;
      begin
          x :=trunc(total);
          y := x;  total:= 100. * (total -y);
          get_change := round(total);
      end;

procedure get_name(var n:name); (* Reads name from datafile*)
      var i: integer;
      begin
          i:=1;
          while (i<=16) do
               begin
                   read(datafile,n[i]);
                   i := i + 1;
               end;
      end;

procedure get_sal(var x: real);
      var id: integer;
      begin
          readln(datafile,id,x);
      end;
```

Figure 3.14   Program and some subprogram declarations for Example 3.4

```
procedure get_denomination(denom: integer; var tot,amount: integer);
 (*  Enter denomination and total.  Returns new total and
        number of the specified denomination *)

    begin
        amount := tot div denom;
        tot := tot mod denom;
    end;

procedure run;
  const QUARTER = 25;
        DIME = 10;
        NICKEL = 5;
        PENNY = 1;
  var sal: real; change,q,d,n,p : integer; na: name;
    begin
        while not eof(datafile) do
            begin
                get_name(na);
                get_sal(sal);
                change := get_change(sal);
                get_denomination(QUARTER,change,q);
                get_denomination(DIME,change,d);
                get_denomination(NICKEL,change,n);
                get_denomination(PENNY,change,p);
                writeln(na,q:10,d:10,n:10,p:10);
            end;
    end;

procedure stop;
    begin
        writeln;
        writeln(' ----------     END OF RESULTS ----------- ');
        writeln;
    end;
```

Figure 3.15   Some procedures for Example 3.4

```
begin
 (**** The following statement is used in TURBO PASCAL only.
        It should be deleted for other versions!    ****)
 assign(datafile,'salfile');
 (** In other systems, file is defined with operating system
        directives. **)
 start;
 run;
 stop;
end.
```

Figure 3.16   Main program for Example 3.4

REVIEW

1. What are some key characteristics of a good program?
2. Discuss the steps involved in developing a program.
3. Refer to the text file SALFILE used in Example 3.4 and given in Appendix A. Suppose all individuals with odd ID numbers are male and those with even numbers are female.

(Note: The standard Pascal function ODD(*n*), returns True if *N* is an odd integer and False if it is even.) Develop software that prints the names of all men listed in SALFILE.
4. For the situation in Review Question 3, develop software that prints the names of each woman whose salary is at least $500.

EXERCISES

1. Outline a general plan for managing a major project.
2. Referring to Figure 3.2, what type of units are used for arguments of the SIN and COS functions?
3. **(a)** Write and test a function that converts a number representing *degrees* to the corresponding angular measurement in *radians*.

   (b) Write and test a function that converts *radians* to *degrees*.
4. Write and test a function that accepts an argument expressed in degrees and returns the tangent of the argument. Assume the value of the argument is greater than $-89.5°$ but less than $89.5°$.
5. The ARCTAN function specified in Figure 3.1 returns an angle that is in a principal quadrant (first or fourth). Develop a function called ATAN2 that accepts two arguments corresponding to the ordinate and abscissa of a tangent function. Your function is to return the arctangent, expressed in degrees, and in the correct quadrant.
6. Develop and test a function that accepts five arguments and returns the average of these values.
7. Develop a function that accepts five arguments and returns the standard deviation of the arguments.
8. When the following program is run:
   (a) How many times will BIRD be printed?
   (b) What is the value of DOG that is printed?
   (c) Just after MOUSE has been invoked for the last time, how many different variables called CAT will be on the run-time stack?

```
PROGRAM DUM(OUTPUT);
VAR DOG,CAT: INTEGER;
    FUNCTION   MOUSE(CAT:INTEGER) : INTEGER;
        BEGIN   WRITELN('BIRD');
                IF (CAT< 30) THEN MOUSE := 3
                    ELSE MOUSE := MOUSE(CAT + 7) + CAT DIV 3;
        END;
BEGIN
        CAT := 8;    DOG := MOUSE( -5);    WRITELN(DOG);
END.
```

9. Develop a recursive function that accepts an odd integer *N* and returns the sum of all the odd integers up to and including *N*.
10. Develop a recursive function that returns the value of the factorial of some relatively

small integer. Use this function to find 9! (9 factorial). NOTE: If your system uses 16-bit integers, 7! is the largest factorial you can compute using integer data types.

11. Refer to Example 3.2 and Figure 3.7. Write a function called FIND that accepts an integer corresponding to an ID number in GRADEFILE. If the ID number is located, the average grade (real) is returned; otherwise, a value of −1.0 is returned. (Note: Your function FIND may invoke the function SEARCH_FILE given in Figure 3.7.)

12. Develop and test a procedure that accepts an average test score and lists the ID numbers of all individuals in GRADEFILE who obtained an average score greater than or equal to the specified average.

13. Develop and test a procedure that accepts two arguments, a real and an integer. The procedure prints the ID numbers of each individual in GRADEFILE whose average test score is greater than the first argument and whose final exam score is greater than the second argument. Use this procedure to identify every student whose average is greater than 89.9% and whose final test score is greater than 179.

14. Write a procedure that accepts six values and returns the largest and smallest of these values.

15. Write a procedure that accepts six values and returns the average of the values, the average of the squares of the values, the variance of the values, and the standard deviation of the values.

16. Discuss some of the attributes of a good program as well as tradeoffs that are made when developing programs.

17. When developing programs on modern computers, memory space required and execution speed are not nearly as important as some other desirable attributes. Why?

18. Referring to the data file SALFILE discussed in Example 3.4 and given in Appendix A, develop a procedure that returns the name, ID number, and salary of the highest-paid person listed in this file.

19. Refer to the program given in Figure 3.5. Modify the procedure RUN so it returns the *total* number of quarters, dimes, nickels, and pennies required to satisfy the change requirements of the payroll.

20. Refer to SALFILE as specified in Example 3.4. Suppose you are now concerned with paying the "dollar" part of each person's salary. Develop software, or modify existing software, to print each person's name as well as the number of bills of each of the following denominations that each person is to receive: hundreds, twenties, tens, fives, and ones. Your software should also print the total number of each denomination needed to satisfy the dollar requirements of the payroll.

21. Develop software, or modify existing software, to read SALFILE and produce the following output:
    (a) A list containing each person's name followed by his or her salary. Following the salary figure is a list that specifies the numbers of hundreds, twenties, tens, fives, ones, quarters, dimes, nickels, and pennies each person is to receive.
    (b) A tabulation of the total numbers of hundreds, twenties, tens, fives, ones, quarters, dimes, nickels, and pennies required to pay all employees listed in SALFILE.

22. Modify the software developed in Exercise 21 to include $50 bills and 50¢ coins in the denominations used to pay salaries.

4

Input and Output

Section 2.6 introduced input and output of data, including the entry of data from a user's console and an illustration of how to read information from existing data files. This chapter discusses input and output of information in more detail.

4.1 GENERAL CONCEPTS

We have illustrated two general methods for entering data as a program is being executed: (1) in a conversational mode from the console, and (2) from one or more files that have already been created. Either method has advantages and disadvantages. Entering information from the console permits the program user to make decisions as the program is being run. That is, the particular information entered may depend on program output already printed. **Placing a person in the loop** provides a high degree of flexibility. Furthermore, a human being is a very good information processor, and is very difficult to emulate with computer code.

On the other hand, a human being is not good at performing tedious tasks without error. For example, if a thousand data points are to be entered, it is extremely unlikely a person could do so without making a number of errors.

Therefore, when a large amount of data is to be entered, the data generally should be placed in a data file *before* the program is run. Then the editing tools for developing programs can be used to enter the data into files and to correct any errors made while creating those files.

What is meant by a *file*? A file is a set of information stored on a robust, or permanent, storage medium, such as a flexible diskette (floppy disk), fixed or hard magnetic disk, or magnetic tape. To store information on such a device, the information must first be encoded in some two-state, or binary, code. Then the encoded elements are stored sequentially.

Let us consider the most common type of file, a text file. From a broad, functional viewpoint, a *text file* is a file of binary-encoded characters. (A more precise definition is given in the following section.)

Suppose we wish the following information to be stored in a text file:

DATA1	25.25	123
DATA2	91.3	400
DATA3	15.67	45

The contents of the corresponding text file is illustrated in Figure 4.1. The binary codes for each character are generally stored in a single byte (8 bits, or binary digits) of storage space. Frequently, ASCII codes, such as described in Section 1.2, are used. Each block in Figure 4.1 represents a byte of storage space. Note that storing a space requires just as many binary characters as storing any other character code. Further, observe that an N/L (Newline) code must be stored to represent the end of each line. The code representing N/L may be the standard code for a Carriage Return, a Line Feed, or any arbitrary 8-bit code. Likewise, a file must contain a code representing EOF, or the End of File. In text files, this code is preceded by an N/L code.

Thus, the three lines of data displayed above are actually stored as a sequence of character codes on some secondary storage device. But recall that both instruction codes and data are read from computer memory. Thus, reading from a file requires two steps:

1. A subset of the file is transferred from secondary storage to computer memory. This subset is placed in a set of contiguous memory registers called a *buffer*. (Each file used in a program has its own memory buffer.) Then an indicator, or *pointer*, must be defined so as to point to, or identify, the first element in the buffer.

2. Values that are to be read and assigned to appropriate variables are always read from one or more buffers. After an element is read and assigned, the pointer advances to the next element in the buffer.

In the Pascal programming language defined in the de facto standard written by Kathleen Jensen and Niklaus Wirth, the two-step process involved in input (or output) operations was clearly defined. Command capabilities were provided such that one command could be used for loading buffers and a separate command for

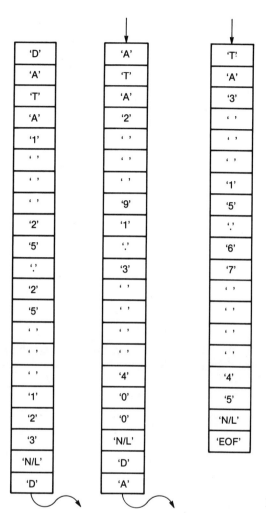

Figure 4.1   Contents of a text file

reading elements from a buffer. The use of separate commands to implement these two tasks can provide a programmer with a clear understanding of the input process, and avoid possible errors in handling input operations.

But commands also exist that combine these two different functions. In particular, most modern systems incorporate input commands that "facilitate" console input for novice users. Unfortunately, these do not all function in precisely the same manner. As a result, examples using console input given in any textbook may not function just as they do on the system you are using. However, the two-step process described above is typical of most systems.

```
(100)   program input_out(output,myfile);
(110)   var a,b,c,d,e,f: char;
(120)       myfile: text;
(130)   begin
(135)       assign(myfile,'myfile'); (** TURBO Pascal **)
(140)       reset(myfile); (* LOAD FIRST LINE INTO myfile BUFFER *)
(145)       readln(myfile); (* LOAD NEXT LINE INTO myfile BUFFER *)
(150)       read(myfile,a,b,c,d,e,f);
(160)       read(myfile,a,b,c,d,e,f);
(170)       writeln(d:1,e:1,c:1);
(180)   end.
```

```
DATA1    25.25    123
DATA2    91.3     400
DATA3    15.67     45
```

Figure 4.2 Program and data file for Example 4.1. (Note: There are no leading or trailing spaces.)

Example 4.1

What number is printed when the program in Figure 4.2(a) is run using the data file in Figure 4.2(b)?

Solution In line 140, the first line of the file is read into the file buffer. In line 145, the second line is read into the MYFILE buffer. In line 150, character values of D, A, T, A, 2, and space are assigned respectively to variables a, b, c, d, e, and f. In line 160, new values of space, space, 9, 1, ".", and 3 are assigned to variables a, b, c, d, e, and f, respectively. In line 170, the character string

1.9

is printed.

The contents of the MYFILE buffer just after the reset command has been executed is illustrated in Figure 4.3(a). The contents of this buffer just prior to the end of the program is illustrated in Figure 4.3(b).

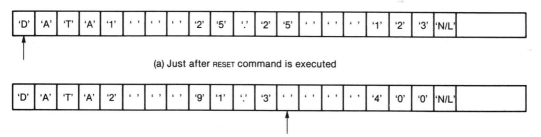

(a) Just after RESET command is executed

(b) Just prior to end of program

Figure 4.3 Position of pointer in MYFILE buffer

REVIEW

1. (a) How many bytes of storage are required to store the following information in a text file?

dog8 c99at
99cat

(b) How many integers are stored in the file?
2. What are buffers? Why are they required for reading input data?

4.2 USE OF TEXT FILES

A text file frequently is defined as a file of characters or as a file of character codes. It is better to consider a text file as a file of lines, where a *line* is defined as a set of character codes followed by a Newline code. Figure 4.1 illustrates a typical text file. In this file there are three lines followed by an EOF, or End-of-file, code. Note that a Newline code precedes an EOF code.

We have already discussed input from files, and have commented that records from files are first transferred to INPUT buffers that reside in computer memory. This is consistent with the way most input/output operations actually function and closely related to the de facto Pascal standard published by Jensen and Wirth. However, in current literature, input/output operations often are defined independent of the buffers actually used.

Let us consider two Pascal procedures used with text files:

readln(FILENAME,argument list);

and

writeln(FILENAME,argument list);

Neither a file name nor an argument list is required for either of the above procedures. Invoking the function READLN merely causes the INPUT file pointer to identify the first character past the next Newline mark. Most of the time, a programmer need not be aware that actual data transfers are made between a file and its INPUT buffer. Similarly, the command READLN(filename) merely causes the FILENAME pointer to point to, or identify, the first character after the next Newline code.

Let us now consider the general READLN statement

readln(dog,cat,mouse,bird,fish);

The arguments in this procedure must be valid Pascal variable names. If the first variable is a declared file name, then input will be read from this file. Otherwise, input will be read from the default file INPUT, which represents data entered from the console. In either case, after information has been read and values have been assigned to all variables in the argument list, the file pointer is advanced to the first character past the next Newline code.

The remaining variables in the variable list must be declared Pascal variables. Furthermore, they must be one of the following variable types:

> char   (character variable)
>
> real   (floating point variable)
>
> integer   (integer variable)

If the variable is a *char* variable, then the character or character code identified by the file pointer is assigned to the variable and the pointer is advanced to the next character.

Suppose the variable is an integer. Then a sequence of events such as the following is performed.

1. If the pointer identifies a space, it is advanced to the next character. This step is repeated until the file pointer identifies a character that is not a space, at which time the character is read and the pointer advanced.

2. If the character is not between 0 and 9, the program halts and an error message is printed.

3. The character is appended to the internal character string and the file pointer advanced. Next, the character is read and the pointer advanced. If the next character is neither a space, Newline, or between 0 and 9, the program halts and an error message is printed.

4. If the last character read is between 0 and 9, the program branches back to statement 3.

5. The internal character string is converted to the binary number corresponding to the desired integer and assigned to the corresponding variable.

The above sequence of events is not specifically related to Pascal; it occurs when entering data in any programming language. Only character codes can be entered, so an internal subprogram must convert this code string to the corresponding representation of a number.

Entering strings corresponding to real numbers is very similar to entering strings corresponding to integers. A similar set of rules, or algorithm, can be formulated for entering real numbers. However, the format for entering real numbers in Pascal is somewhat different. Some valid representations for input of real numbers are

$$1.2 \qquad 365.0 \qquad 1.06e-19 \qquad -437.2 \qquad 6.02E23$$

Note that scientific notation is used to represent numbers with very large or very small magnitudes, such as 6.02×10^{23} and 1.06×10^{-19}.

Example 4.2 in Figure 4.4 illustrates console input. The program ignores data entered to the right of the character strings representing the real numbers. This information is passed over, since after the READLN procedure has assigned values to all variables in the argument list, the file pointer is advanced to the first character past the next Newline code.

The system procedures READLN and WRITELN are used only with text files, including the default text files INPUT and OUTPUT. A number of other system subprograms are also frequently used with text files. These are:

1. READ(   ); This performs the same task as READLN, except that after values have been assigned to variables, the file pointer is *not* advanced past the next Newline code.

2. WRITE(   ); Performs same as WRITELN, except that the output sequence is not terminated with a Newline code. Note: Neither READ nor WRITE may have a void argument list.

3. RESET(filename); Opens filename for reading.

4. REWRITE(filename); Opens filename for writing. Note: If this file already exists, execution of the REWRITE command sets the byte count of the file to zero, meaning the existing file is essentially destroyed! RESET and REWRITE may *not* be used with the two default files.

5. EOF(filename); This function returns a True if and only if the file pointer identifies an End-of-file code. The default argument is INPUT.

6. EOLN(filename); This function returns a True if and only if the file pointer identifies a Newline code. The default argument is INPUT. Note: Neither the EOF code not the Newline code may be assigned to any Pascal variable!

There are slight variations in the way different Pascal compilers implement input and output of text files, particularly when those files are input from a console.

```
program input(input,output);
var a: integer; b:real;
      begin
            while (a<>16) do begin
                              readln(a,b);
                              writeln(a,'     ',b);
                        end;
      end.
```

(a) Program

```
12       1.2        this is my data!
13       365.0      Note:  Text is ignored
1        1.06e-19        1 2 3 4 5
115      -437.2     abcde
45       6.02E23
16       1.0        This is the end!!!
```

(b) Data entered from console

Figure 4.4 Example 4.2

```
(100)  (* Program that counts the number of lines in a textfile.
          The LOGICAL name of the file is dog_file *)
(120)  program count_lines(output,dog_file);
(130)  var       n:integer;
(140)            dog_file: text;
(150)            c: char;
(160)  begin
(162)  (** In TURBO Pascal assignment of true file name to
          logical file name is made DURING program execution **)
(164)       assign(dog_file,'mydata'); (** TURBO Pascal **)
(170)       n := 0;   c:='A';
(180)       reset(dog_file);
(190)       while not eof(dog_file) do
(200)         if eoln(dog_file) then begin
(210)            n:= n+1;  readln(dog_file)
(220)                                    end
(230)                             else read(dog_file,c);
(240)       writeln('  The number of lines in the file is ',n);
(250)  end.
```

(a) Program

```
hello 1.9821
Voltage is 1.025 volts.   Current is 18 AMPS!
12 345 6.534
Dogs like to eat fleas!!
```

(b) Contents of file MYDATA

Figure 4.5   Solution to Example 4.3

We have tried to define input and output operations as most commonly implemented. However, readers may observe some differences in the system they are using.

Example 4.3

Develop a program that counts and prints the number of lines in a text file.
Solution   A solution is given in Figure 4.5(a). The logical name for the file is DOG_FILE. The true file name must be assigned to this Pascal variable either before or during program execution. The result is obtained by counting the number of Newline marks contained in the file. But care must be taken not to assign the "value" of a Newline mark to any Pascal variable. Lines 200 to 230 contain the necessary statements.

REVIEW

1. Refer to the algorithm described earlier in this section for reading a character string corresponding to an integer value. This algorithm is not general enough to describe input of integers because it does not permit entry of negative values. Generalize the algorithm.
2. Formulate a set of statements that describes what is done by the WRITELN(   ) system subprogram.
3. Develop a program or a subprogram that counts the number of bytes in a file. The byte count should include the EOF mark. Test your program using the file shown in Figure 4.5(b).

4.3 GENERAL FILE COMMANDS

Most programming languages use text files for input and output operations. The Pascal programming language permits the use of a broader class of files. In general, a file is a set of elements stored sequentially on some secondary storage device. The elements may be any type of element, and may be assigned to the corresponding type of variable.

Consider the following set of numbers:

    1234
    2222
    12
    987634

Suppose these elements are stored sequentially on a secondary storage medium. This would constitute a text file, since clearly the elements are sets of characters terminated by Newline codes. Although a novice might consider this a file of integers, it most definitely is not. Integer data types consist of sequences of binary characters such as illustrated in Section 1.2. Furthermore, only character strings can be printed, *not* integers.

Generating files that are not text files is illustrated in Figure 4.6. Reading data from files that are not text files is illustrated in Figure 4.7.

When the program in Figure 4.6(a) is run, two files are created, and numbers are stored in those files. Five hundred integers are stored in the file identified as INTS, and 500 real numbers are stored in the file identified as FLOATS. Recall that these names are logical or Pascal names for the files. The true file names must be associated with these variable names before the program is run.

Figure 4.6(b) illustrates the same program written in **turbo** Pascal. This version provides the ASSIGN subprogram for assigning logical names to true file names. When the program is run, two files are created, INTS and MYFLOATS. Observe also that when using this version of Pascal, it is necessary to *close* the files before the program is terminated.

In both versions of this program, files are created that are not text files. Elements are written into the files using the WRITE command. The files contain neither valid character codes nor Newline marks. The files are terminated with EOF marks in the same way text files are terminated with EOF marks.

The function LOOKUP in Figure 4.7 reads the file MYFLOATS. LOOKUP reads the first K elements in the file and returns the Kth element. This function illustrates TABLE LOOKUP. In this example, the square root of a number is found by entering the table contained in the file MYFLOATS. This is not the way square roots are generally found, but it is presented to illustrate a table-lookup technique.

Four Pascal procedures for handling nontext files have been illustrated:

```
                          READ(      );
                          WRITE(     );
                          RESET(     );
                          REWRITE(   );
```

In addition, the function EOF(filename) may be used in the same way as with text files. There are two other Pascal subprograms commonly used with files that are not text files:

```
                          GET(filename);
                          PUT(Filename);
```

The procedure GET(filename) merely loads the next element of the file into the file's INPUT buffer. If this element is not the end-of-file mark, it may then be assigned to a variable of the same type using the command

$$x = filename^\wedge\ ;$$

```
{100}  program files(ints,floats);
{110}     var ints:    file of integer;
{120}         floats: file of real;
{130}         i: integer;   x: real;
{140}     begin
{150}        rewrite(ints);  rewrite(floats);
{160}        for i := 1 to 500 do begin
{170}                          x := i; (* Convert integer to real *)
{180}                          x := sqrt(x);
{190}                          write(ints,i);
{200}                          write(floats,x);
{210}                             end;
{220}     end.
```
(a) Standard Pascal version

```
    program files(ints,floats);
       var ints:    file of integer;
           floats: file of real;
           i: integer;   x: real;
    begin
    (* NOTE:  This program is developed in TURBO Pascal.  True file
    names are assigned to logical file names using the following
    Turbo Pascal Procedures:  *)
           assign (ints,'ints');
           assign (floats,'myfloats');
    (*******                              *******)
           rewrite(ints);  rewrite(floats);
           for i := 1 to 500 do begin
                             x := i; (*Convert integer to real *)
                             x := sqrt(x);
                             write(ints,i);
                             write(floats,x);
                          end;
           close(ints);  close(floats);  (** Turbo Pascal **)
    end.
```
(b) Turbo Pascal version

Figure 4.6   Creating files that are not text files

```
(***   READING FROM A FILE OF REALS   ***)
program lookup(input,output,herfloats);
const MESSAGE = ' Enter a number between 0 and 500:    ';
var   herfloats:  file of real;
      i: integer;    x: real;
function lookup(k:integer): real;
      var p:  integer;   y: real;
      begin
              reset(herfloats);
              for p := 1 to k do
                   read(herfloats,y);
              lookup := y;
      end;
begin
      assign(herfloats,'myfloats');   (* Turbo Pascal *)
      write(MESSAGE);    readln(i);
      while (I<>0) do begin
                      x:=lookup(i);
                      writeln(i:10,x:20:10);
                      write(MESSAGE);   readln(i);
                  end;
end.
```

Figure 4.7   Accessing data from a file of reals

The variable filename^ is used to access the contents of the file's INPUT buffer and is sometimes referred to as a file pointer.

The PUT(filename) command writes the contents of the file's OUTPUT buffer to the file. The OUTPUT buffer may be loaded by specifying the assignment

$$\text{filename}^{\,}:=x$$

where x is a variable of the appropriate type.

The subprograms PUT and GET are not really necessary, since the same tasks can be performed using WRITE and READ. Even though these subprograms are defined in the de facto Pascal standard, they are not included in some modern implementations of Pascal.

Example 4.4

Write a Pascal program that copies a file of reals to another file of reals.

Solution   A solution is given in Figure 4.8(a). An alternative solution is given in Figure 4.8(b).

REVIEW

1. Identify three standard Pascal functions that may be used with text files but not with any other type of file.
2. Suppose a user-defined variable is called a FOUR-type variable and is defined by the following statement:

             type   FOUR =   array[1..4] of char;

```
(*  Program that copies a file of reals. *)
program copy(floats,newfloats);
var floats,newfloats: file of real; x:real;
    begin
        assign(floats,'myfloats');        (* Turbo Pascal *)
        assign(newfloats,'newfloats'); (* Turbo Pascal *)
        reset(floats);   rewrite(newfloats);
        while not eof(floats) do
                begin
                        read(floats,x);
                        write(newfloats,x);
                end;
        close(newfloats); (* Turbo Pascal *)
    end.
```

(a) Using READ and WRITE

```
(*  Program that copies a file of reals. *)
program copy(floats,newfloats);
(* Will not run on Turbo Pascal *)
var floats,newfloats: file of real; x:real;
    begin
        reset(floats);   rewrite(newfloats);
        while not eof(floats) do
                begin
                        x := floats^; get(floats);
                        newfloats^ :=x;  put(floats);
                end;
    end.
```

(b) Using PUT and GET

Figure 4.8   Solution to Example 4.4

Write a program that will create a file of FOUR-type elements, that is, four-letter words.

3. The file created in Review Question 2 is not a text file. Explain the difference between that file and a similar text file.

4.4 FILE-HANDLING EXAMPLE

Most computer files are text files. Many programming languages use only text files for input and output of data. But there are some advantages in employing a broader class of files.

The use of files of integers and files of reals has already been illustrated. But such files are seldom involved in real-world applications. In the program in Figure 4.9(a), a file of four-letter words is created. Although this appears similar to a text file, it is not a text file. There are no Newline marks in the file. Each element of the file that is created is a set of bits corresponding to a four-letter word. The Pascal subprograms READLN and WRITELN cannot be used with this file.

```
(* This program creates a file of four-letter words.  Lines
   are read from a textfile.  The first four letters of each line
   are read and stored in a file of FOUR. *)

program make_file(mydata,names);
    type four = packed array[1..4] of char;
    var mydata: text; names: file of four;
    procedure create_file;
        var c:four; i: integer;
        begin
          reset(mydata);  rewrite(names);
          (*  NOTE:  Each line of the file mydata must contain
                     at least four characters. *)
          while not eof(mydata) do begin
                                 for i := 1 to 4 do
                                        read(mydata,c[i]);
                                 readln(mydata);
                                 write(names,c);
                                  end;
        end;

  begin(* main program *)
    assign(mydata,'filedata');    (* Turbo Pascal*)
    assign(names,'FOUR');         (* Turbo Pascal*)
    create_file;
    close(names);                 (* Turbo Pascal*)
  end.
```

(a) Program

```
          Lisa Jones
          Mary Smith
          Lucy Brown
          Mark White
          Jill Green
          Lisa Smith
          Bill Brown
          John Pink
          Bill Herman
          Jose Gonzalez
```

(b) Data in 'filedata'

Figure 4.9 Program that creates a file of four-letter words

The program in Figure 4.10 reads elements from the file created in the program of Figure 4.9. Note that an entire element, that is, a four-letter word, is read using just one statement. If we were reading from a text file, only one character at a time could be read! Clearly the same is true if we are reading 20-letter names or even much larger arrays of characters as single elements of a file. A practical application of this is illustrated in Example 4.5.

```
(* This program reads the name from a file of four-letter
   words.  The names are counted and printed.  *)
program get_names(herfile,output);
    type four = packed array[1..4] of char;
    var herfile: file of four;  n:integer;
        function read_file: integer;
            var i: integer; x:four;
            begin
                reset(herfile); i :=0; writeln;
                while not eof(herfile) do
                    begin
                    read(herfile,x);
                    writeln(x);
                    i:=i+1 ;      (* Increment name count *)
                    end;
                read_file:=i;
                writeln;
            end;

begin(* main program *)
  assign(herfile,'FOUR'); (* TURBO Pascal *)
  n:=read_file;
  writeln(' There are ', n:3,' names in the file!');
end.
```

Figure 4.10   Reading data from a file of four-letter words

Example 4.5

Develop a program that creates a file of student records, where a student record is defined as an array of 50 characters whose fields are as follows:

FIELD	DEFINITION
1–16	Student's name
17	Gender: M or F
18–22	Five-digit zip code
23–33	Social security number
34–35	Class: i.e., FReshman, SOphomore, etc.
36–37	Age
38–43	Annual income: To nearest dollar. Must be right-justified!
44–47	GPA (number, dot, number, number)
48–50	Credit hours completed

Solution   A solution is given in Figure 4.11. A small set of data is included with the solution. A much larger data set is given in Appendix A.

The file of STUDENT_RECORDS created in Example 4.5 may be considered to be a data-base or part of a data-base. A **data-base** is a file or a set of files containing pertinent information.

Suppose we wish to write a program or a set of programs that lets us search this file for information. For example, we might want to know the names of all

```
(*  This program creates a file of student records, where each element
    is an array of 50 characters, and the fields are defined as:
            Field              Use
          1 - 16             Name
            17               Gender:  M or F
         18 - 22            Zip code
         23 - 33            Social security number
         34 - 35            Class
         23 - 36            AGE
         38 - 43            Annual income (Right justified)
         44 - 47            Grade point average
         48 - 50            Credit hours completed            *)
program stu_rec(data_in,STUDENT_RECORDS);
type student_record = array[1..50] of char;
     var data_in:text;   STUDENT_RECORDS: file of student_record;
         i:integer; x: student_record; c:char;
begin
     assign(data_in,'sdata');    (** TURBO **)
     assign(STUDENT_RECORDS,'recs');
     reset(data_in);  rewrite(STUDENT_RECORDS);
      while not eof(data_in) do
         begin
           for i := 1 to 16 do if eoln(data_in) then x[i]:=' '
                             else begin
                                      read(data_in,c);
                                      x[i] :=c;
                                    end;
           readln(data_in);
           readln(data_in,c); x[17]:=c;
           for i:=18 to 22 do begin
                                      read(data_in,c);
                                      x[i] :=c;
                                 end;
           readln(data_in);
           for i:=23 to 33 do begin
                                      read(data_in,c);
                                       x[i] :=c;
                              end;
           readln(data_in); read(data_in,x[34]); readln(data_in,x[35]);
           read(data_in,x[36]); readln(data_in,x[37]);
           for i:= 38 to 43 do begin
                                      read(data_in,c);
                                      x[i]:=c;
                              end;
           readln(data_in);
           for i:=44 to 47 do begin
                                      read(data_in,c);
                                      x[i]:=c;
                              end;
           readln(data_in); read(data_in,x[48]);
           read(data_in,x[49]); readln(data_in,x[50]);
           write(STUDENT_RECORDS,x);
         end;
      close(STUDENT_RECORDS);    (* TURBO Pascal *)
  end.
```

Figure 4.11(a)   Solution to Example 4.5

```
            Doe,Jane
            Female
            38117
            410-90-4320
            JUnior
            20
              1000      NOTE:   Right justified!!!
            2.93
              82        NOTE:   Right justified!!!
            Carver,George Washington
            Man
            38409
            000-01-1234
            GRaduate student
            97            Field is not large enough for true age!
             11500
            3.98
            425
            Jackson,Michael
            Male
            10002
            555-55-5555
            SOphomore
            29
            999999  Field is not large enough for true income!!
            2.80    Must contain trailing zero!!
             42     Right justified!!
```

Figure 4.11(b)   Some data for the text file used in Figure 4.11(a)


```
program search(STUDENT_RECORDS,output);
type name = array[1..16] of char;
     ssnum = array[1..11] of char;
     student_record = array[1..50] of char;
var STUDENT_RECORDS: file of student_record;
     procedure look(x:name);
        var n:name; i:integer; rec:student_record; ss: ssnum;
        begin
            reset(STUDENT_RECORDS);
            while not eof(STUDENT_RECORDS) do
               begin
                   read(STUDENT_RECORDS,rec);
                   for i := 1 to 16 do n[i] := rec[i];
                   if x = n then
                           begin
                               for i := 1 to 11 do ss[i] := rec[i+22];
                               writeln; writeln(n:20,ss:20);
                           end;
               end;
        end;
(*** Start test program ***)
begin
    assign(STUDENT_RECORDS,'recs');    (*  TURBO PASCAL *)
    look('Jackson,Michael ');
    look('Horse,Herman    ');
    look('Doe,Jane        ');
end.
```

Figure 4.12   Solution for Example 4.6

students who reside within a certain zip code. We might want a list containing names and phone numbers of all female students with GPA greater than 3.0 and annual income of at least $50,000. Or we might wish to have the name and social security number of the oldest male with income greater than $100,000.

Once we have a file such as a file of STUDENT_RECORDS, it is relatively easy to develop subprograms that permit us to search the file for the desired information. In Example 4.5, we created a file of character arrays. Various fields of each array contain specific information. (In Section 6.4, a more general type of "record" variable is defined that enables us to create more general files of user-defined records.)

Example 4.6

Develop a procedure that accepts a sixteen-letter name. If this name is included in a file of STUDENT_RECORDS, the name and corresponding social security number will be printed.

Solution   A procedure and a test program are shown in Figure 4.12.

REVIEW

Note: In order to make the following Review Exercises more meaningful, it is suggested that you create a file of STUDENT_RECORDS *using the program shown in Figure 4.11(a) and* the corresponding data given in Appendix A.

1. Write and test a function that returns the number of STUDENT_RECORDS in a file of STUDENT_RECORDS.
2. Write and test a subprogram that prints the name and age of all males listed in a file of STUDENT_RECORDS.
3. Develop and test a procedure that accepts a social security number. The procedure searches a file of STUDENT_RECORDS. If the social security number is found in the file, the record student_records containing the social security number is returned. If the social security number is not found, a student_record containing all blank spaces is returned.

EXERCISES

1. What is a *text file*? How does a text file differ from a file that is not a text file? What type of files are the default files INPUT and OUTPUT?
2. Under what conditions should data be read from a previously constructed file rather than entered from the console during program execution?
3. What is the difference between the READLN procedure and the READ procedure? What are the advantages of having both of these procedures?
4. What are *buffers*? How are they used in relation to computer input and output operations?
5. How many bytes of storage space are required to store the following text file? (There are no leading or trailing spaces. Include the EOF mark in your byte count.)

Volts	Amps	Ohms
4.0	1.0	4.0
6.0	3.0	2.0
12.0	4.0	3.0

6. Develop and test a function that returns the number of Newline or End-of-line marks in a text file whose logical name is MYFILE.

7. Develop a function that returns the total number of bytes (including the EOF mark) contained in a text file called MYFILE. Use a file containing the data shown in Exercise 5 to test the function.

8. Refer to the following program:

```
program ex8(input,output);
var dog,cat,mouse,bird,fish: char;
    rat: integer;  cow: real;
begin
        readln(dog,cat,mouse,bird,fish,rat,cow);
        writeln(rat:4,cow:6:2);
end.
```

When this program is run, the following line of data is entered:

3.14159 1.2 8.01e-15 6.24 dogs have fleas!

What two numbers will be printed?

9. Refer to the algorithm given in Section 4.2 for reading a character string corresponding to an integer. Formulate a similar algorithm for reading a character string corresponding to a real number.

10. Suppose a text file has the following format: A character string corresponding to a positive integer is in the first six columns of a line and a six-letter name is stored between columns 7 and 12. The remaining characters on each line contain no meaningful information. Two sample lines are:

100 REAGAN
234 HERMAN

The numbers and names are all unique.

Develop and test a procedure that accepts an integer as an argument. If one of the integer strings in the file has the same value, then the corresponding name is printed. If not, an appropriate message is printed.

11. For the text file described in Exercise 10, develop and test a procedure that accepts a six-letter name. If the name is in the file, the corresponding integer value is printed. If the name is not in the file, an appropriate message is printed.

12. Develop and test a procedure that copies most of the lines of ONE_FILE to ANOTHER_FILE. Lines of ONE_FILE that contain an asterisk in the first column should not be copied.

13. Write a program that creates a file containing 100 elements. Each element of the file is a real. This is not a text file! The elements of the file should be real values corresponding to the approximate cube roots of the whole numbers between 1 and 100.

14. Using the file created in Exercise 13, write and test a function that accepts an integer argument between 1 and 100. The function "looks up" the value of the cube root in the designated file and returns this real value.

15. Refer to the file created when the program shown in Figure 4.9(a) is run. Write and test a procedure that accepts a character value as an argument, reads the specified file, and prints all four-letter words beginning with the specified character.

16. Referring to Exercise 15, write and test a function that accepts a character value as an argument, reads the specified file, and returns an integer corresponding to the number of four-letter words beginning with the specified character.

Note: In order to make exercises 17–20 more interesting, it is suggested that you create a file of STUDENT_RECORDS *using the program shown in Figure 4.11(a) and the corresponding data given in Appendix A.*

17. Develop and test a function that accepts a character corresponding to one of the genders. The function reads a file of STUDENT_RECORDS and returns an integer value corresponding to the number of the specified gender in the file.

18. Develop and test a procedure that accepts a minimum GPA specification, reads a file of STUDENT_RECORDS, and prints the name and social security number of each student with GPA at least as good as the specified GPA.

19. Modify the procedure developed in Exercise 18 so both a minimum GPA and a gender specification are contained in the argument list of the procedure.

20. Modify the procedure developed in Exercise 18 so the argument list contains three values: a minimum GPA specification, a minimum annual income specification, and a gender specification. Use this procedure to obtain a list of all females in STUDENT_RECORDS with a GPA of at least 2.60 and an annual income of at least $45,000.

5

Control Statements

Use of high-level computer languages such as Pascal lets programmers perform a large number of simple tasks using short programs, by utilizing control statements that enable a sequence of commands to be performed repetitively.

We have already used several Pascal commands involving repetitive operations or controlled loops. In this chapter, we formally define some of the control statements we have already used and introduce some related topics.

5.1 BOOLEAN EXPRESSIONS

When performing repetitive operations, a program generally remains within a specified loop until the value of some Boolean expression is False. The expression may be very simple, such as:

X	Where X is a boolean variable
$x < 100.00$	Where x is a real variable
EOF (input)	Where EOF is a standard Pascal function

Or the expression may be a complex one involving logical operations. The three logical operations in Pascal are defined and illustrated in Figure 5.1.

Recall that relational operations return boolean values. A complex boolean expression may contain a number of relational operations connected by logic opera-

Operation	Use of operation	Comment
NOT	not exp1	The result is True if and only if the value of exp1 is False.
AND	exp1 and exp2	The result is True if and only if both exp1 and exp2 evaluate to True.
OR	exp1 or exp2	The result is True if either exp1 or exp2 evaluates to True.

Figure 5.1   Logic operations

tions. In order to evaluate the result of complex expressions, we must know the order of precedence in which subexpressions are evaluated. Subexpressions contained within innermost parentheses are always evaluated first. Operations with higher priorities are performed before those with lower priorities. Operations having the same priority are evaluated from left to right. The precedence of the various operations is given in Figure 5.2. (The IN operation is defined in Section 6.5.)

Note: We should be cautious using the EQUAL or NOT EQUAL operators with real values. Recall that real numbers or floating points in general cannot be expressed exactly. Thus, expressions such as

$$100.0 * 0.01 = 1.0$$

may not return a value of True.

Relational operators may be used with variables or expressions that involve neither integers nor reals. For example, if x is a character variable and A is assigned to x, then the expression

$$x <= \text{'B'}$$

will return True, since the binary code for an A is always a number having a smaller value than the binary code for a B.

Suppose variables x and y are packed arrays of five characters, and suppose "mouse" has been assigned to x and "money" to y. Then the expression

$$x < y$$

Operation	Priority
NOT	Highest
*, DIV,/, MOD, AND	Next highest
+, −, OR	Next highest
<, <=, >, >=, =, < >, IN	Lowest

Figure 5.2   Precedence of operations

will return a value of False, since the binary code for *u* is numerically greater than that for *n*.

Example 5.1

Consider the following boolean expressions. If an expression is invalid, modify it so it will be valid. If an expression is valid, indicate what boolean value is returned. The variables *a* and *b* are character-type variables, and *x* and *y* are integer variables. Assume the following assignments have been made:

$$a := 'P'; \quad b := 'W'; \quad x := -15; \quad y := 3;$$

(a) a < b and (x <= y)
(b) (y < abs(x)   ) and not(x < y −30)
(c) (y < abs(x)   ) and not(x < y −3) or not odd(y − x)
(d) not a > b

Solution   Expressions a and d are invalid. Since AND has a higher priority than <, an attempt will be made to perform a logical operation between a character value and a boolean value. This is invalid. In expression a, the operation

$$a < b$$

should be replaced with

$$(a < b)$$

In expression d, replace

$$a > b$$

with

$$(a > b)$$

Both of expressions b and c return a value of True. In expression b, the function

$$abs(x)$$

is first evaluated. Then

$$y < abs(x)$$

is True, and

$$not(x < y −30)$$

is also True. In expression c,

$$not(x < y - 3)$$

is False. This False ANDed with a True produces a False. But the expression

$$not\ odd(y - x)$$

is True, since the function ODD with an argument of 18 returns a False.

Example 5.2

Develop a function that accepts two boolean values and returns a True if and only if exactly one of the arguments is true.

Solution   A solution is given in Figure 5.3. The main program tests this function for all possible conditions.

```
program test(output);
    function eor(a,b:boolean):boolean;
    (* Exclusive ORs two boolean values *)
    begin
        if a and not b or b and not a then eor := true
                                      else eor := false;
    end;
(***** Start test program *****)
begin
    if eor(false,false) then writeln(' dog');
    if eor(false,true)  then writeln(' cat');
    if eor(true,false)  then writeln(' mouse');
    if eor(true,true)   then writeln(' bird');
end.
```

Figure 5.3   Solution to Example 5.2

REVIEW

1. Refer to Example 5.1. What value will each of parts a and d return after they have been modified?
2. What words will be printed when the program in Figure 5.3 is run?
3. What words will be printed when the program in Figure 5.4 is run?

```
program review(output);
var a,b:char;  x,y:integer;
begin
    a:='P'; b:='C'; x:=-15; y:=13;
    if (a <> b) and (x <= y) then writeln(' cat');
    if (x<>abs(x)) or not(x<y-3) and not odd(y-x) then writeln(' dog');
    if((x<>abs(x)) or not(x<y-3)) and not odd(abs(x-y)) then
                                    writeln(' mouse');
end.
```

Figure 5.4   Program for Review Question 3

5.2 USING THE WHILE COMMAND

We have already used the WHILE control statement a number of times. Recall that the syntax for this statement is

while <CONDITION> do STATEMENT;

A sequence of statements appears to be a single statement if it is bracketed by a ''begin'' and an ''end.''

The WHILE statement is probably the most commonly used statement in implementing Pascal loops. Other mechanisms may be convenient but are not required. Complex boolean expressions, such as those introduced in Section 5.1, enhance the power of the WHILE statement.

Example 5.3

In Example 4.6, we developed a procedure that accepts a sixteen-letter name. If the name was found in a file of student records, the name and the corresponding social security number were printed. Refer to the solution given in Figure 4.12. Observe that even when we locate the specified name, the file continues to be read until the End-of-file mark is encountered. Modify this solution so that program control exits from the loop when the requested name is located.

```
program search(STUDENT_RECORDS,output);
type name = array[1..16] of char;
     ssnum = array[1..11] of char;
     student_record = array[1..50] of char;
var STUDENT_RECORDS: file of student_record;
    procedure look(x:name);
        var n:name; i:integer; rec:student_record; ss: ssnum;
            found: boolean;
        begin
            reset(STUDENT_RECORDS);  found:=false;
            while not eof(STUDENT_RECORDS) and not found do
                begin
                    read(STUDENT_RECORDS,rec);
                    for i := 1 to 16 do n[i] := rec[i];
                    if x = n then
                            begin
                                found := true;
                                for i := 1 to 11 do ss[i] := rec[i+22];
                                writeln; writeln(n:20,ss:20);
                            end;
                end;
        end;
(*** Start test program ***)
begin
    assign(STUDENT_RECORDS,'recs');    (*  TURBO PASCAL *)
    look('Jackson,Michael ');
    look('Horse,Herman    ');
    look('Doe,Jane        ');
end.
```

Figure 5.5   A solution to Example 5.3

Solution   A solution is given in Figure 5.5. Note that the solution is similar to that shown in Figure 4.12, the differences being that in Figure 5.5 a boolean variable "found" is declared and initialized as False, the condition in the WHILE statement is modified, and the value of "found" is set to True when the name is located in the file.

REVIEW

1. Use a WHILE loop to generate a conversion table between Fahrenheit and Celsius temperatures. Recall, to change from Fahrenheit to Celsius, we subtract 32.0 and multiply by 5.0/9.0. Your table should extend from $-300°$ to $500°$ in increments of $20°$.
2. Refer to the file of student records created by the program in Figure 4.11(a). Develop and test a procedure that accepts values of a specified gender and a minimum GPA. The procedure reads the file until it locates a record satisfying the specification, prints the corresponding name and social security number, and then passes control back to the invoking program.

5.3 THE REPEAT-UNTIL STATEMENT

The syntax for this statement is

```
repeat
        statement 1
        . . . . . . . . . .
        statement n
until <CONDITION>
```

The major difference in implementing loop structures using a REPEAT-UNTIL instead of a WHILE statement is the point at which the condition is checked. The WHILE statement checks the condition at the beginning of the loop, whereas the REPEAT-UNTIL statement checks it at the end of the loop. Thus, the statements in a REPEAT-UNTIL loop are always executed at least once.

REVIEW

1. Rewrite the LOOK procedure in Figure 5.5 using the REPEAT-UNTIL statement in lieu of the WHILE statement.
2. Use a REPEAT-UNTIL loop to generate a table of conversions between Fahrenheit and Celsius temperatures. Your table should extend from $-300°$ to $500°$ in increments of $20°$.
3. Refer to Review Question 2 in Section 5.2. Develop the specified procedure using a REPEAT-UNTIL loop rather than a WHILE loop.

5.4 THE FOR STATEMENT

The syntax of the FOR statement is

```
for var:= expl to exp2 do STATEMENT;
```

where the following hold:

1. "Var" is a previously declared variable, sometimes referred to as a **loop variable.** (a) The loop variable must be either an integer type or a type that has the same attributes as an integer. In particular, each value of the variable, except possibly the last, must have a well-defined successor. For example, the successor of -25 is -24, and the successor of 8 is 9. Any subset of the integers, as well as character variables, possess this property. For example, the successor of '*j*' is '*k*', and the successor of '7' is '8'. Real-type variables do *not* possess this property. (b) The statement cannot assign a value to the loop variable. (c) If a FOR statement is part of a function or procedure, the loop variable must be a local variable.

2. Exp1 and exp2 are expressions that evaluate to the same type as the loop variable. The simplest expressions are just constants.

3. Exp2 has a value at least as great as exp1.

4. A sequence of statements is considered to be a single statement if it is bracketed by a "begin" and an "end."

5. If we wish to execute a FOR loop in which exp2 has a value less than exp1, then we must replace the word *to* with *downto*.

The FOR loop has equivalence to a longer sequence of commands. That is, the statement

```
for var := exp1 to exp2 do STATEMENT;
```

is equivalent to:

```
var := exp1;
  while var <= exp2 do
              begin
                   STATEMENT;
                   var := succ(var);
              end;
```

The standard Pascal function SUCC returns the value that is the successor of the current value. A similar Pascal function, PRED, returns the predecessor or the adjacent smaller value. If the FOR statement is implemented by the above sequence of commands, some of the constraints on the loop variable are no longer applicable.

```
program cube_root(input,output);
const CUBE_ROOT = 0.3333334;
var i:integer; a:real;
    function power(n,x:real):real;
    (*  this function returns the nth power of x.   The values
        of both x and n must be non-negative! *)
        begin
            if abs(x) < 0.00001 then power := 0.0 else
            power:= exp(n*ln(x));
        end;
begin
      for i:=0 to 50 do
            begin
                a := 10*i;
                writeln(a:10:0,power(CUBE_ROOT,a):10:4);
            end;
end.
```

Figure 5.6   A solution to Example 5.4

Example 5.4

Develop a program that prints the real cube root of whole numbers between 0 and 500 in increments of 10.

Solution   A solution is given in Figure 5.6. A FOR loop is used to select the desired arguments, and the function POWER is used to get the cube roots. The function utilizes the property

$$\log x^n = n * \log x$$

The EXP function is used to get the inverse natural logarithm.

Example 5.5

Develop and test a function that prints all characters between two specified character values.

Solution   A solution is given in Figure 5.7.

```
program for_example(input,output);
var c1,c2:char;
    procedure print(var x,y:char);
    var c:char;(* loop variable must be LOCAL *)
        begin
            if  x<=y then
                        for c :=x to y do write(c)
                    else
                        for c := x downto y do write(c);
            writeln;
          end;
  begin (*  test program *);
      writeln(' Enter 2 characters.  Then press RETURN key.');
      readln(c1,c2);  print(c1,c2);
      writeln(' Enter 2 more characters.  Then press RETURN.');
      readln(c1,c2);  print(c1,c2);
end.
```

Figure 5.7   A solution to Example 5.5

REVIEW

1. Consider a FOR statement in which exp2 returns a smaller value than exp1. Implement the FOR statement with a different sequence of statements that will perform the same operations.
2. Develop a program that uses a FOR loop to compute and print values of $\sin(x)$, $\cos(x)$ and $\tan(x)$, where x varies from 0 to 1 radian in increments of 0.01.
3. What will be printed when each of the following Pascal commands is executed?
   (a) writeln(succ(succ(−1)));
   (b) writeln(pred(pred('3')));
   (c) writeln(pred('P'):1,succ(succ('L')):1,succ(pred('E')):1);

5.5 IF-THEN-ELSE COMMANDS

The format for the Pascal IF-THEN command is

if <CONDITION> then statement;

where the condition is a boolean expression. The statement is executed if and only if the condition is true. The format for the IF-THEN-ELSE command is

if <CONDITION> then STATEMENT1 else STATEMENT2;

If the condition is true, statement1 is executed. Otherwise, statement2 is executed. Statement1 may *not* be terminated with a semicolon. Of course, any sequence of statements bracketed by a "begin" and an "end" is considered a single statement.

The statements may be any Pascal statements, including IF-THEN statements or IF-THEN-ELSE statements. But this can lead to ambiguous situations, for instance, which ELSE goes with which THEN? The rule is that the ELSE goes with the most recently used THEN.

If we do not want a particular ELSE condition to go with the most recent THEN, we can bracket one or more statements with a "begin" and an "end," as illustrated in Figures 5.8(a), (b), and (c). The word ' dog' will be printed when the program in Figure 5.8(a) is run. When 5.8(b) is run, ' mouse' will be printed. When 5.8(c) is run, ' cat' will be printed.

Example 5.6

Develop and test a function that accepts minimum values for grades of A, B, C, and D. The function also accepts a number corresponding to a student's average. The function returns the letter grade corresponding to the average.

Solution A solution is given in Figure 5.9. The function is tested for the grade standards identified in the CONSTANT statement.

```
program if_then(output);
var    x:integer;
begin
        x:=10;
        if x < 5 then
                    writeln(' bird');
        if x > 9 then writeln(' dog')
              else if x > 7 then writeln(' cat')
                            else writeln(' mouse');
end.
```

(a) Output is 'dog'

```
program if_then(output);
var    x:integer;
begin
    x:=10;
    if x < 5 then
                begin
                   writeln(' bird');
                   if x > 9 then writeln(' dog')
                         else if x > 7 then writeln(' cat')
                end
            else writeln(' mouse');
end.
```

(b) Output is 'mouse'

```
program if_then(output);
var    x:integer;
begin
    x:=10;
    if x < 5 then
                begin
                   writeln(' bird');
                   if x > 9 then writeln(' dog')
                end
            else if x > 7 then writeln(' cat')
                          else writeln(' mouse');
end.
```

(c) Output is 'cat'

Figure 5.8   Illustrations of IF-THEN-ELSE statements

REVIEW

1. Refer to the STUDENT_RECORDS file generated by the program in Figure 4.11(a), Section 4.4. Develop a procedure that searches the file and prints the names and social security numbers of all individuals of a specified gender with salary greater than a specified minimum but less than a specified maximum, and with GPA at least as great as a specified minimum. Test this procedure by having it list the names and social security numbers of all males with GPA greater than 2.5 and salary between $20,000 and $250,000.

2. What three words will be printed when the program in Figure 5.10 is run? Identify the order in which they are printed.

```
program grades(output);
const A = 89.9;
      B = 79.9;
      C = 69.9;
      D = 64.5;
function get_grade(a,b,c,d,ave:real):char;
     begin
       if ave >= a
         then get_grade:='A'
         else if ave >= b
                 then get_grade:= 'B'
                 else if ave >= c
                         then get_grade := 'C'
                         else if ave >= d then get_grade := 'D'
                                          else get_grade :='F';
       end;
(**** Start test program!!!!   ****)
begin
     writeln(get_grade(A,B,C,D,64.9));
     writeln(get_grade(A,B,C,D,94.5));
     writeln(get_grade(A,B,C,D,75.0));
     writeln(get_grade(A,B,C,D,64.1));
     writeln(get_grade(A,B,C,D,80.0));
end.
```

Figure 5.9   A solution to Example 5.6

```
program review_22(output);
var p,q: char;
    i: integer;
    x: real;
     begin
       p := '5' ;  q := p;
       for  i :=1 to 3 do
           begin
                   x:= i;
                   x := x + 0.5;
                   if (x > 1.6) and (x < 2.1)
               then
                   writeln(' Lana')
               else
                   begin
                        p := succ(succ(p));
                        q := pred(q);
                    end;
           if p = '9' then writeln(' Lisa')
                      else if q ='4'  then writeln(' Lori')
                                      else writeln(' Lucy');
           end;
     end.
```

Figure 5.10   Program for Review Question 2

5.6 USING CASE STATEMENTS

The IF-THEN-ELSE statement provides a condition, or a **selector,** that directs program control to one of two possible statements. The CASE statement permits program control to branch to one of a larger set of alternatives. The format for a CASE statement is

```
case <SELECTOR> of
     label list 1:   STATEMENT1;
     label list 2:   STATEMENT2;
     . . . . . . . . . . . . . . . . . . . . . . . .
     label list n:   STATEMENTn;
end;
```

The selector is an expression that evaluates to an integer or to a type that has the same attributes as integers. The value should be identified in one and only one of the label lists that follow the case declaration. Most modern implementations of Pascal merely ignore the CASE statement if the value of the selector is not included in one of the label lists. Frequently, the selector is the simplest kind of expression: just a variable name.

Each label list contains one or more values of the specified selector type: If the value of the selector is in label list k, then STATEMENTk will be executed. Use of the CASE statement is illustrated in the following two examples.

Example 5.7

Develop a program that allows a user to enter letter grades and the appropriate number of credit hours for each course taken. After all data have been entered, the total number of hours attempted, hours earned, and grade point average are printed.

Solution   A solution is given in Figure 5.11. The eight different letter grades used are defined in the program. Observe how the CASE statement facilitates implementing this program.

Example 5.8

Up until now we have used either the READLN or the READ procedure to convert a string of numerical characters to the corresponding integer value. In this example, we will read a string of numerical characters from a file INPUT buffer and convert the string to its corresponding numeric value.

Solution   The CONVERT function shown in Figure 5.12(a) is used to convert a string of numeric character values to the corresponding integer value. The value of an integer variable is initially set to 0. Then a character is read and a CASE statement used to obtain the corresponding numerical value. The integer variable is multiplied by 10 and the numeric value of the most recently read integer added to this variable. Another character is read, and the process continues until a nonnumeric character is read. The set of data shown in Figure 5.12(b) may be used in conjunction with the test program.

```
program get_qpa(input,output);
    var x,y,z:   real;
    procedure qpa(var hrs_attempted,hrs_earned,gpa:real);
    (*  grades are defined as follows:
                    A           4 quality points
                    B           3 quality points
                    C           2 quality points
                    D           1 quality point
                    F           0 quality points.  Credit hours not completed.
                    I           Incomplete
                    T           Transition.  Like an incomplete but have an
                                            indefinite period to complete
                                            course requirements.
                    P           Pass.  Course taken on Pass-fail basis.  Credit
                                hour are not used in computing GPA. *)
        var tot,hours,points:real; grade:char;
        begin
            points:=0;
            tot:= 0.0; hrs_attempted:=0.0; hrs_earned:=0.0;
    writeln ('  Enter data.  Each line of data consists of ',
             ' a letter grade');
    writeln ('   followed by the number of credit hours in',
    '   that course.');
    writeln(' To terminate data enter a  Q  followed by 0.0.');
    writeln(' A typical set of data is shown below:');writeln;
            writeln('A        3.0');
            writeln('C        4.0');
            writeln('B        1.5');
            writeln('Q        0.0');   writeln;
                    readln(grade,hours);
                    while grade <> 'Q' do begin
                        hrs_attempted:=hours + hrs_attempted;
                        tot:=tot+hours;
                        hrs_earned := hours + hrs_earned;
                        case grade of
                            'A':   points:=points+4.0*hours;
                            'B':   points:=points+3.0*hours;
                            'C':   points:=points+2.0*hours;
                            'D':   points:=points+hours;
                            'F':   hrs_earned := hrs_earned-hours;
                    'I','T','P':   begin
                                    tot:=tot-hours;
                                    if grade <> 'P' then
                                        hrs_earned:=hrs_earned-hours;
                                   end;
                        end; (* end CASE statement *)
                    readln(grade,hours);     end;
        if abs(tot) < 0.0001 then gpa := 0.0 else
                        gpa:= points/tot;
    end;
begin   (**** Start test program ****)
    qpa(x,y,z);  writeln; writeln;
    writeln('Hrs attempted: ',x:5:1,
            '  Hrs earned: ',y:5:1,'  GPA: ',z:5:1);
end.
```

Figure 5.11 A solution to Example 5.7

```
program convert(output,data);
var
        data: text;    x,y:integer;
function convert:integer;
    (**** This function converts a character string in the input
        buffer of a file called DATA to the corresponding
        integer value.                    ****)
    var c: char; sign,n,num:integer; flag:boolean;
        begin
        num:= 0;  read(data,c);  sign :=1;   flag:= false;
        while c = ' ' do read(data,c);
        (**** Skips leading spaces  ****)
        if c = '-' then
                    begin
                        sign := -1;
                        read(data,c);
                    end;
        while(c>='0') and (c <='9') and not flag do
            begin
                case c of
                    '0': n:=0; '1': n:=1; '2': n:=2; '3': n:=3;
                    '4': n:=4; '5': n:=5; '6': n:=6; '7': n:=7;
                    '8': n:=8; '9': n:=9;
                end; (* case ends *)
            num := 10 * num + n;
            if eoln(data) then flag:= true else read(data,c);
            end;
        num:=sign * num;
        convert:=num;
        end;
    begin(***** Start test program  ****)
    assign(data,'data');  (* TURBO Pascal *)
    reset(data);
            while not eof(data) do
            begin
                    writeln; x:=convert;  y:=convert;
                    write(x:20);  writeln(y:20);
                    readln(data);
            end;
    end..
```

(a) Program

```
       12345                -8765
       0                     482
       -26T                  X
       -5                    23456
```

(b) Contents of file 'data'

Figure 5.12   A solution to Example 5.8

REVIEW

1. Referring to the program in Figure 5.11, what three numbers will be printed for each of the following data sets?

(a) A   3.0
    C   2.0
    I   4.0
    P   1.0
    Q   0.0

(b) F   6.0   COMP 1001   Mr. Rotten
    C   3.0   ENGL 1201   Ms. Hard
    A   3.0   MATH 1111   Mr. Nice
    B   2.0   PHED 1234   Coach Lucy
    T   1.0   Freshman Seminar
    Q   0.0

2. What numbers will be printed when the program in Figure 5.12(a) is run using the data file in Figure 5.12(b)?
3. Modify the function CONVERT in Figure 5.12(a) so it will convert numbers expressed in octal (base-8 character set). Test this new function using the same test program but the following data file:

        746   −777
        0001   36543
        16   −5 APPLES

EXERCISES

1. What boolean value is returned by each of the following expressions? Both x and y are integer variables, and
   (a) succ(x) > x div 2 + abs(y)
   (b) ((x mod 2) > x div 2) and not(y < x)
   (c) ((x mod 2) > x div 2) or not (y < x)
2. Develop and test a boolean function called EVEN. The function accepts a single integer value and returns a True if and only if the argument is even.
3. Develop and test a boolean function that accepts three boolean values and returns a True if and only if exactly one of the arguments is True.
4. Develop and test a boolean function that accepts three boolean values and returns a True if exactly two of these values are True.
5. Develop and test a boolean function that accepts three values and returns a True if and only if the majority of the arguments are True.
6. Use a WHILE statement to create a table of conversions between Celsius and Fahrenheit temperatures. Celsius temperatures should vary between −100° and 300° in increments of 10°.
7. Do Exercise 6 using a REPEAT-UNTIL loop instead of a WHILE loop.
8. Do Exercise 6 using a FOR loop instead of a WHILE loop.
9. Using a WHILE loop, develop and test a procedure that accepts an initial value of x, a final value of x, and an increment. The arguments are all real. The procedure prints values of x, sinh(x), cosh(x), and tanh(x) (hyperbolic functions) as x is varied from its

initial value to its final value in step sizes corresponding to the specified increment. Test your procedure by invoking it with the following argument list: (0.0,1.0,0.01).

10. Do Exercise 9 using a REPEAT-UNTIL loop instead of a WHILE loop.

11. Do Exercise 9 using a FOR loop instead of a WHILE loop.

Note: Exercises 12, 13, 14, and 15 relate to the file of student records created using the program in Figure 4.11(a) (p. 75).

12. Develop and test a procedure that searches a file of student records and prints the names, social security numbers, and GPAs of all students of a specified gender whose social security number begins with the specified three characters that are carried into the procedure.

13. Develop and test a procedure that searches a file of student records and prints the names and social security numbers of all students of the specified gender whose GPA is less than the specified value.

14. Develop and test a procedure that searches a file of student records and prints the names of all individuals within specified age limits living within specified zip code limits.

15. Develop and test a procedure whose argument list includes local variables that will accept the following values:

specified gender
minimum age
maximum age
minimum GPA
maximum GPA
minimum salary
maximum salary
minimum zip code
maximum zip code

The procedure searches a file of student records and prints the name, age, salary, social security number, and zip code of each individual satisfying the specifications.

16. Consider the following type variable:

type salary = array[1..6] of char:

Suppose that each of the six characters in the array has a value between '0' and '9' inclusive. Develop and test a function that accepts a salary-type argument and returns the corresponding integer.

17. Consider the following type variable:

type gpa = array[1..4] of char;

Supposing the second character must be a '.' and the other characters are numeric, develop and test a function that accepts a gpa-type argument and returns the corresponding real value.

18. Modify the function developed in Exercise 17 so an appropriate message is printed unless the gpa value is between 0.00 and 4.00, inclusive.

19. Suppose the INPUT buffer of a text file contains a string of numeric characters followed by a dot, followed by another string of numeric characters. Develop and test a function that converts this string to a real value and returns the real value.

20. Suppose the INPUT buffer of a text file contains a string of binary characters. Develop and test a function that returns the corresponding integer value.

21. Suppose the INPUT buffer of a text file contains a string of hexadecimal characters; that is, values of the characters must be within one of the following intervals:

$$'0' = < c <= '9'$$
$$'A' = < c <= 'F'$$

Develop and test a function that returns the corresponding integer values.

22. Suppose the INPUT buffer of a text file contains a numeric character followed by a dot, followed by a string of numeric characters, followed by an 'E', followed by two more numeric characters. For example, the string might look like one of the following:

$$6.02E23 \qquad (** \ 6.02 * 10^{23} \ **)$$
$$3.14149E00$$
$$0.314159E01$$

Develop and test a function that converts the string to the corresponding real value.

23. Modify the function developed in Exercise 22 so a minus sign can precede either the characteristic or the mantissa.

6

Structured
Data Types

We have used four standard data types: integers, reals, characters, and binary or boolean. We have also used a structured data type, in particular, *arrays* and *packed arrays* of characters. We have created user-defined data types with statements such as

```
type string = packed array[1..16] of char;
     four = array[1..4] of char;
```

An **array** of characters is a set of character codes that are stored sequentially. Some Pascal systems permit more efficient storage of the character set if the data type is declared to be a **packed array.**

In this chapter, a wide variety of data types are introduced, and examples illustrating their use are presented.

Given the type declarations displayed above and some variable x: if x is declared to be a *four*-type variable, then it is a *user-defined* variable. If x is declared to be an array[1..4] of characters, it is a *structured* variable. Standard variables and user-defined variables (except files) may be used in declaring either local variables or formal parameters that appear in argument lists of Pascal subprograms. But variable names in call lists of subprograms may *not* be declared as structured variables. For example, the following declaration of variable y in procedure SAMPLE is valid:

```
type vec = array[1..4] of integer;
procedure sample(y:vec);
```

But the following, apparently logically equivalent, declaration of local variable *y* is *not* valid:

```
procedure sample(y:array[1..4] of integer);
```

6.1 USER-DEFINED DATA TYPES

Pascal offers considerable flexibility in creating user-defined data types. In this section, we illustrate two classes of these data types: **enumerated** and **subrange.**

A subrange may be defined on integers, or on types that have the same attributes as integers. For example, in the type declarations

```
type caps = 'A'..'Z';
     age = 0..110;
```

The type *caps* includes any character value between '*A*' and '*Z*', and the type *age* may have any value between 0 and 110. If a value outside the specified range is assigned to a cap-type variable or to an age-type variable, an appropriate error message will be printed.

The following declaration statement illustrates how to define an enumerated data type:

```
type class = (freshman,sophomore,junior,senior);
var x: class;
```

The only values that may be assigned to the variable *x* are freshman, sophomore, junior, and senior, and these values have the same property as any finite subset of integer values—that is, they are well ordered. For example, junior is greater than sophomore, and the successor of junior is senior.

Use of both a subrange type and an enumerated data type is illustrated in the program in Figure 6.1(a). A subrange is used for type *hours*, since any value less than 0 or greater than 24 is not meaningful. The enumerated *days* data type is used primarily to improve the readability of the program.

Values of enumerated types cannot be read from a text file. Nor can they be printed in the same way characters, integer strings, or real strings are printed. Some of the functions shown in Figure 6.2 are useful with enumerated variable types.

For the ORD, or ordinal, function given in Figure 6.2, if we are using a *class* type as defined previously, then

```
ord(freshman)
```

```
program example(input,output,time_sheet);
   type hours =  0..24;         (***** Subrange   *****)
        days = (mon,tue,wed,thur,fri,sat,sun); (* Enumerated*)
   const  RATE = 4.25;
   var pay:real; time_sheet:text;
   function compute_pay(rate:real):real;
   (*  This function reads seven integers from the input buffer
       of a file called time_sheet.  The numbers are the hours
       worked each day, Monday through Sunday.  According to
       the current labor contract, a fixed rate is payed each
       weekday.  Time-and-a-half is payed for hours worked
       on Saturday and double time for hours worked on Sunday
       *)
   var tot,x:real; hrs: hours; day:days;
   begin
        tot:=0.0;
        for day := mon to sun do
        begin
             read(time_sheet,hrs); x:= hrs;
             case day of
             mon,tue,wed,thur,fri:  tot:=tot + x*rate;
             sat: tot :=tot + 1.5*x*rate;
             sun: tot := tot + 2.0*x*rate;
             end;(*end case *)
        end;
        compute_pay:=tot;
   end;
begin(*** Start test program  ***)
   assign(time_sheet,'time');  (* TURBO Pascal *)
   reset (time_sheet);
   pay:=compute_pay(RATE);  writeln(pay:6:2);
   readln(time_sheet);
   pay:=compute_pay(RATE);  writeln(pay:6:2);
end.
```

(a) Program

```
4  4  0  6  0  3  12
8  8  8  8  8  0  0
```

(b) Contents of file 'time'

Figure 6.1 Use of user-defined data types

returns a value of 0, and

ord(senior)

returns a value of 3.

When the argument of the ORD function has a character value, a number corresponding to the position of the character in a finite character set is returned. This
number depends on the way Pascal is implemented on your system. However, the
CHR function is the inverse of the ORD function when the ORD function uses a character-
type argument. This set of functions is powerful for manipulating character data.
Examples 6.1 and 6.2 illustrate use of the ORD function.

Function name	Type of argument	Type returned by function	Comment
SUCC	enumerable*	same type as entered	Returns next higher value
PRED	enumerable	same type as entered	Returns next lower value
ORD	enumerable	integer	If argument is an integer, value is returned. Otherwise, number corresponding to position, starting with 0, is returned
CHR	integer	character	When argument of ORD is a character, CHR is the inverse function
ODD	integer	boolean	Returns true when argument is odd

*Note: An *enumerable* set is one in which elements can be mapped in one-to-one correspondence with a subset of integers.

Figure 6.2 More standard Pascal functions

Example 6.1

Develop a procedure that copies to the screen a file whose logical name is MYDATA. Characters in MYDATA that have values between '*a*' and '*z*' are to be printed as the corresponding capital letters.

Solution   A solution is given in Figure 6.3. The expression

$$c := chr(ord(c) -ord('a') +ord('A'))$$

is used to convert lowercase letters to the corresponding capital letters. The program shown in Figure 6.1 is stored in a file called FIG61.PAS. When the test program is run, this program is printed with all the lowercase letters replaced by the corresponding capital letters.

Example 6.2

Develop and test a function that accepts integers corresponding to the current month and day and returns the number of whole days left in the year.

Solution   A solution is shown in Figure 6.4. If the specified month is either January or February, the number returned depends on whether or not it is a leap year. For the months of January and February, additional information is requested from the user.

```
program pr_file(mydata,output);
   var mydata:text;
   procedure print_file;
   (*  This procedure copies the file, mydata, to the screen.
       Whenever a small letter appears in mydata, the correspond-
       ing capital letter is printed instead. *)
   var c:char;
   begin
           reset(mydata);  writeln;
           while not eof(mydata) do
            begin
              if eoln(mydata)
                 then
                    begin
                       readln(mydata); writeln
                    end
                 else
                    begin
                       read(mydata,c);
                       if (c < 'a') or ( c > 'z' )
                           then write(c)
                           else
                           begin
                             c := chr(ord(c)-ord('a')+ord('A'));
                             write(c);
                           end;
                    end;
            end;
      end;
begin(**** Start test program  ****)
     assign(mydata,'fig61.pas'); (* TURBO Pascal *)
     print_file;
end.
```

Figure 6.3   A solution to Example 6.1

REVIEW

1. Refer to the program and data given in Figure 6.1. What two numbers will be printed when the program is run?
2. What numbers will be printed when the program in Figure 6.4 is run, if the response to the query is YEP?
3. Refer to the CONVERT function shown in Figure 5.12, which converts a string of numeric characters to the corresponding integer value. Rewrite this function so the CASE statement is replaced with an expression that utilizes the ORD function.
4. Develop and test a function that accepts a character argument corresponding to one of the hexadecimal characters '0' to '9' or 'A' to 'F'. The function returns an integer value between 0 and 15, depending on the value of the argument.

```
program fig64(input,output);
var x: integer;
   function days_left(month_number,day:integer):integer;
            (* This function returns the number of whole
               days left in the year *)
         type month = (null,Jan,Feb,Mar,Apr,May,Jun,Jul,
                        Aug,Sept,Oct,Nov,Dec);

         var mo: month; c:char; n,tot:integer; leap: boolean;
         begin
              tot:=0; leap:=false;
              if month_number <= 2 then
                   begin
                       writeln(' Is this a leap year? ');
                       readln(c);
                       if (c ='Y') or (c = 'y') then
                                         leap:=true;
                   end;
                   for mo := Jan to Dec do
                       begin
                          case mo of
                          Apr,Jun,Sept,Nov: n:=30;
                          Jan,Mar,May,Jul,Aug,Oct,Dec: n:=31;
                          Feb: if leap then n:=29 else n:=28;
                          end (* case *);
                          if ord(mo) = month_number then
                                   tot := n - day;
                          if ord(mo) > month_number then
                                   tot := tot + n;
                       end;
                 days_left := tot;
         end;
begin (* Start test program *)
   x := days_left(6,29);  writeln(x);
   x := days_left(1,1);   writeln(x);
   x := days_left(12,31); writeln(x);
end.
```

Figure 6.4   A solution to Example 6.2

6.2 ARRAYS

We have used arrays of characters in several examples. Recall that an *array of characters* is just a contiguous set of characters. It is convenient to visualize an array of characters as a finite set of characters stored in consecutively numbered memory locations.

In general, an *array of elements* may be defined as a contiguous set of elements. This data structure may be visualized as a finite set of elements stored in consecutive memory blocks.

Most of the time when using arrays, we declare a user-defined data type associated with an array. The type declaration has the form

```
type some_name =array[<INDEX LIST>] of type;
```

The **index list** contains one or more indices. Each index is a subrange of an enumerable data type. After the word *of*, the type of element in the array is specified. This may be any standard Pascal type or any previously specified user-defined type.

If just one index range is specified, the array is a one-dimensional array. If *n* index ranges are specified, the array is said to be *n*-dimensional.

Four data types involving arrays are specified in Figure 6.5. The *st* data type is just a string of four characters. A *mul* data type is a three-dimensional array of integers. Each of the three indices in this data type is a subrange of integers. When we declare a variable to be a mul-type variable, we are defining twenty-seven integer variables.

The *other* data type declared in Figure 6.5 is also a three-dimensional array of integers. The first index is a subrange of integers, the second is a subrange of characters, and the third is a subrange of the user-defined *days*-type variable. When a variable is declared as an *other* type, fifty-four contiguous integer variables are defined.

The data type *names* defined in Figure 6.5 is an array of packed arrays of characters. A data structure of this type is useful if we wish to store an array of names. Consider the following type declarations:

```
type vector = array [1..10] of real;
     her_matrix = array [1..10] of vector;
     his_matrix = array [1..10, 1..10] of real;
```

Data structures such as these are found widely in engineering and scientific work. A one-dimensional array of *n* real numbers is often called a vector. The data types referred to as *his_matrix* and *her_matrix* are generically the same. They are each a two-dimensional array of real numbers commonly called a **matrix.** (Matrices are discussed in Section 8.1.)

Arrays facilitate the manipulation of large data sets. For example, it is convenient to store in an array of reals a set of voltage values measured at different points in

```
program t7(input,output);
    type st =  packed array[1..4] of char;
         mul = array[ 1..3,1..3,1..3] of integer;
         days = (sun,mon,tue,wed,thur,fri,sat);
         other = array[1..3,'A'..'F',tue..thur] of integer;
         names = array[1..50] of st;
    var x:st; y:mul; z:other; n: names;

    begin
    y[1,2,3]:=4;    writeln(y[1,2,3]);
    readln(x[1],x[2],x[3],x[4]);
    writeln(x:30);
    z[1,'B',wed] := 5; writeln(z[1,succ('A'),pred(thur)]);
    n[5] := x;
    writeln(n[70 div 12]);
end.
```

Figure 6.5   Array declarations

a network. Or we might wish to store in an array of real numbers the force measurements obtained at various points along a beam. Or we might want to store in an array of character arrays the names of everyone in our class. Once data have been stored in such a manner, it is often possible to process the data using only a few computer instructions.

When we define an array, we should generally make it large enough to satisfy near-term anticipated needs. It is alright if programs do not use all the variable space defined in an array. But we must never exceed the bounds of our arrays.

Example 6.3

Develop subprograms that will perform the following tasks on one-dimensional arrays of *n* elements.

(a) Read real values into the array.
(b) Print the values stored in the array.

```
program arrays(input,output);
type myvector = array[1..100] of real;
var x,y: myvector; ans:real;
   procedure read_array(n:integer; var a: myvector);
       var i: integer;
       begin
             for i := 1 to n do readln(a[i]);
       end;
   procedure write_array(n:integer; var c: myvector);
       var i: integer;
       begin
             writeln;
             for i:= 1 to n do writeln(c[i]:20:5);
       end;
   procedure add_vecs(n:integer; p: myvector; var q: myvector);
       (*  This procedure adds the n-dimensional vector p to the
           n-dimensional vector q  *)
       var i:integer;
       begin
           for i:= 1 to n do q[i] := p[i] + q[i];
       end;
   function get_big(n:integer;vec:myvector):real;
       (* Returns largest number in n-dimensional array *)
         var i:integer; big:real;
         begin
           big := vec[1];
           for i := 2 to n do if vec[i] > big then big := vec[i];
           get_big := big;
         end;
begin (*Start test program *)
     read_array(6,x);
     write_array(6,x);
     read_array(6,y);
     write_array(6,y);
     add_vecs(6,x,y);
     write_array(6,y);
     ans := get_big(6,y);  writeln(ans:20:5);
end.
```

Figure 6.6   A solution to Example 6.3

(c) Add the corresponding elements of a source array to a destination array.

(d) Return the largest element in the array.

Solution   Solutions and a test program are shown in Figure 6.6. Note that the array defined may contain up to 100 elements. The test program uses arrays containing only six elements.

Example 6.4

Develop procedures that perform the following tasks.

(a) Read sixteen-character names and place them in an array of names.

(b) Print the names stored in an array of names.

Solution   Solutions are given in Figures 6.7 and 6.8. The RD_NAMES procedure in Figure 6.7 reads sixteen-character names entered from a keyboard console. Each name

```
program names(input,output);
    type names = array[1..16] of char;
         class = array[1..100] of names;
      var x:class;
          procedure rd_names(m,n:integer; var nx:class);
          var i:integer; x:names;
          (** This procedure is used for entering n names from
              the console.  The names are stored in the spec-
              ified array, starting at position m.  Each name
              entered must have at least 16 characters.  **)
          begin
              if n=1 then
              writeln('  Enter 1 name.')
                    else
              writeln(' Enter ',n:3,' names');
          writeln(' Name must have at least 16 characters.');
          writeln(' Addend trailing spaces to short names.');
              writeln; writeln;
              for i := m to m + n - 1 do
                  begin
                  readln(x[1],x[2],x[3],x[4],x[5],x[6],x[7],
                     x[8],x[9],x[10],x[11],x[12],x[13],x[14],
                     x[15],x[16]);
                  nx[i]:=x;
                  end;  writeln;
          end;

          procedure pr_names(n:integer; y:class);
          (** prints first n names in array **)
          var x:names; i: integer;
          begin
              writeln;
              for i := 1 to n do
                  begin
                      x:= y[i];
                      writeln(x:25);
                  end; writeln;
          end;
begin (**** Start test program ****)
      rd_names(1,3,x);
      rd_names(4,2,x);
      pr_names(5,x);
end.
```

Figure 6.7   A solution to Example 6.4 (names are entered from console)

```
program names(input,output,myfile);
   type names = array[1..16] of char;
        class = array[1..100] of names;
      var x:class;  myfile:text;  number:integer;
         procedure read_names(var n:integer; var nx:class);
         var k,j:integer; x:names;
         (*  This procedure is used for reading n names from
             a file having a logical name of MYFILE
             into an array of names.  Long names are truncated
             to 16 characters.  Spaces are addended to short
             names. Number of names read is returned.   *)
         begin
             reset(myfile);  n:=0;
             while not eof(myfile) do
                 begin
                     j:=1;
                     while (j <=16) and not eoln(myfile) do
                         begin    read(myfile,x[j]);
                                  j:=j+1;
                         end;
                     if j<=16 then  for k:=j to 16 do
                                         x[k] :=' ';
                     readln(myfile); (* Get next line *)
                       n := n+1; nx[n]:=x;
                 end;
         end;

         procedure pr_names(n:integer; y:class);
         (** prints first n names in array **)
         var x:names; i: integer;
         begin
             writeln;
             for i := 1 to n do
                 begin
                     x:= y[i];
                     writeln(x:25);
                 end; writeln;
         end;
begin (**** Start test program ****)
     assign(myfile,'names');   (* TURBO Pascal *)
     read_names(number,x);
     pr_names(number,x);
end.
```

(a) Program

```
                    Washington,Georgie
                    Doe,Jane
                    King,Martin Luther (Jr.)
                    Chu,Ming
```

(b) Contents of file 'names'

Figure 6.8   Program and data for Review Exercise 3

entered must have at least sixteen characters. The READ_NAMES procedure shown in Figure 6.8 reads the names from a text file. Long names are truncated to sixteen characters, and trailing spaces are appended to short names.

REVIEW

1. When using arrays, why do we normally first declare a user-defined data type rather than directly declaring variables to be array types?
2. Refer to the program in Figure 6.5. Suppose we enter the data HELLO when this program is run. What is printed on each line of program output?
3. Refer to the program and data in Figure 6.8. Exactly what is printed on each line of output when the program is run using the specified data?

6.3 INTRODUCTION TO SORTING

It is easy to load data elements into an array-type structure. Elements may be numbers, names, or longer character strings such as the STUDENT_RECORDS we previously defined. More complex data types are discussed in Section 6.4.

It is common to arrange the elements stored in an array in a well-defined order. This operation, called **sorting,** is one of the most commonly performed operations in commercial computing.

Character codes for particular characters have numeric values lower than those assigned to the natural successors of the characters. Thus, inequalities such as the following can be used to compare characters or character strings:

'Jackson,Mike' > 'Jackson,Kate'

We may sort elements such as STUDENT_RECORDS according to zip code, according to GPA, or according to number of hours completed. It is very common to arrange elements alphabetically according to people's names. But concepts related to sorting do not depend on the types of elements being sorted.

Suppose we have an array of N elements. Let us compare the first element with the second. If the first is greater than the second, we exchange their positions in the array. Then we compare the second element with the third one and swap elements if necessary. We continue the process until $N - 1$ comparisons have been made. At the end of this set of operations, the *largest* element in the array must be in the Nth position.

Suppose we repeat the entire process. At the end of this second cycle, the second-largest element must be in the $(N - 1)$th position. We continue repeating the process until all elements in the array are in their proper position.

Observe that each time we pass through such a loop the largest unsorted element "bubbles up" to its proper position in the array. For this reason, this is called a **bubble sort.** A bubble sort requires a significant number of computer operations, but it is easy to develop computer code that implements this type of sort.

The following algorithm describes a procedure for a modified bubble sort: There are *N* elements stored in an array, and the elements are to be sorted in ascending order. Let *A[i]* be an element of the array. Then:

1. Set swap_count = N−1. Set SORTED = false.
2. Set i=1.
3. If SORTED = true, exit from sort algorithm.
4. Set SORTED = true.
5. If a[i] > a[i+1]   then
       (a) Swap these two elements
       (b) Set SORTED = false
6. i = i + 1
7. if i <= swap_count go back to step 5
8. swap_count = swap_count − 1;
9. Go to step 2.

Example 6.5

Develop and test a procedure that sorts an array of sixteen-character names in ascending order.

Solution   A procedure that sorts an array of names in ascending order is shown in Figure 6.9. A complete solution incorporating this procedure is given in Figure 6.10. Observe that the READ_NAMES procedure from the program in Figure 6.8 is also used. Both of these procedures may be needed in other programs. It is impractical to repeat the identical source code each time a commonly used procedure is required.

```
type names = array[1..16] of char;
     class = array[1..100] of names;

     procedure sort(n:integer;var na:class);
         var sorted:boolean; temp:names; i:integer;
         begin(* Sorts n names in ascending order *)
             n := n - 1 ; sorted := false;
             while not sorted do begin
                 sorted := true;
                 for i := 1 to n do
                     if na[i] > na[i+1] then  begin
                                         (* SWAP *)
                                         temp := na[i];
                                         na[i] := na[i+1];
                                         na[i+1] :=temp;
                                         sorted := false;
                                               end;
                     if n>1 then n:= n-1;
                                     end (* while *);
         end (* sort procedure *);
```

Figure 6.9   Procedure for a modified bubble sort of an array of sixteen-character names

```pascal
program names(input,output,myfile);
  type names = array[1..16] of char;
      class = array[1..100] of names;
   var x:class;  myfile:text;   number:integer;
   procedure sort(n:integer;var na:class);
         var sorted:boolean; temp:names; i:integer;
         begin(* Sorts n names in ascending order *)
             n := n - 1 ; sorted := false;
             while not sorted do begin
                  sorted := true;
                  for i := 1 to n do
                       if na[i] > na[i+1] then  begin
                                            (* SWAP *)
                                            temp := na[i];
                                            na[i] := na[i+1];
                                            na[i+1] :=temp;
                                            sorted := false;
                                                    end;
                       if n>1 then n:= n-1;
                                        end (* while *);
             end (* sort procedure *);
    procedure read_names(var n:integer; var nx:class);
          var k,j:integer; x:names;
          begin
             reset(myfile);   n:=0;
             while not eof(myfile) do
                  begin
                      j:=1;
                      while (j <=16) and not eoln(myfile) do
                           begin     read(myfile,x[j]);
                                        j:=j+1;
                             end;
                      if j<=16 then  for k:=j to 16 do
                                         x[k] :=' ';
                      readln(myfile); (* Get next line *)
                      n := n+1; nx[n] := x;
                  end;
          end;
    procedure pr_names(n:integer; y:class);
             (** prints first n names in array **)
             var x:names; i: integer;
             begin
               writeln;
               for i := 1 to n do
                    begin            x:= y[i];
                                     writeln(x:25);
                    end; writeln;
             end;
begin (**** Start test program ****)
    assign(myfile,'names');  (* TURBO Pascal *)
    read_names(number,x);
    pr_names(number,x);
    sort(number,x);
    pr_names(number,x);
end.
```

Figure 6.10   A solution to Example 6.5

```
program names(input,output,myfile);
   type names = array[1..16] of char;
        class = array[1..100] of names;
     var x:class;  myfile:text;  number:integer;
        procedure sort(n:integer;var na:class);
           var sorted:boolean; temp:names; i:integer;
           begin(* Sorts n names in ascending order *)
              n := n - 1 ; sorted := false;
              while not sorted do begin
                 sorted := true;
                 for i := 1 to n do
                    if na[i] > na[i+1] then  begin
                                        (* SWAP *)
                                        temp := na[i];
                                        na[i] := na[i+1];
                                        na[i+1] :=temp;
                                        sorted := false;
                                             end;
                 if n>1 then n:= n-1;
                              end (* while *);
           end (* sort procedure *);
        ($I MYSTUFF.PAS) (******** INCLUDE statement *******)
                              (* TURBO Pascal *)
begin (**** Start test program ****)
     assign(myfile,'names');  (* TURBO Pascal *)
     read_names(number,x);
     pr_names(number,x);
     sort(number,x);
     pr_names(number,x);
end.
```

Figure 6.11 Accessing procedures using INCLUDE directive

Earlier, it was suggested that commonly used subprograms be separately compiled and stored in a library of object codes accessible to all programs compiled subsequently. Unfortunately, many implementations of Pascal do not offer this capability. An alternate technique that may be available is to store procedures in a separate file and to give directives to include separate files during program compilation.

In the program in Figure 6.11, when the INCLUDE statement is encountered by the compiler, the source code stored in the file MYSTUFF.PAS is loaded and compiled. This file contains the source code for the READ_NAMES procedure.

REVIEW

1. Refer to the procedure SORT in Figure 6.10.
   (a) Why is the variable "temp" needed?
   (b) The procedure will work without the line

   if n>1 then n:=n−1;

   Why is it included?

2. In the program in Figure 6.11, the PR_NAMES procedure is invoked but not explicitly declared or defined. Where is this procedure located?
3. Modify the SORT procedure in Figure 6.11 so it sorts names in descending rather than ascending order. Test your modified procedure.

6.4 RECORDS

In Section 4.4 we created a user-defined data type called a STUDENT_RECORD, defined to be a long character string. We arbitrarily chose to store a student's name in the first sixteen character positions of this array, with other positions used to store character strings corresponding to the student's age, salary, and social security number. Thus each STUDENT_RECORD contained a "name" field, an "age" field, a "social security number" field, and an "annual salary" field.

More general **record** data types and variables may be defined and declared in Pascal, and they can be rather extensive. Furthermore, **fields** of these records may be any of the standard data types or almost any user-defined data type, and in particular may be other records.

In the program shown in Figure 6.12, a STUDENT_REC record is defined, and two variables, *a* and *b*, are declared as STUDENT_REC variables. STUDENT_REC has four fields: (1) the "name" field, a 16-character array; (2) the "gender" field, defined as a subrange of characters between "*F*" and "*M*" (only the first and last characters of this subrange are meaningful values for the gender field of a STUDENT_REC variable); (3) the "age" field, declared as a subrange of integers; and (4) the "load" field. This last is declared as a **course** type. But a course type is just another user-defined record type. Observe that one of the fields of a course-type record is another user-defined record type.

In the main program in Figure 6.12, assignments are made both to record-type variables and to various fields and subfields of record-type variables. The statements

y.hrs_earned := 12;

and

y.gpa := 3.25;

assign values to the two fields of a **past**-type variable. The command

a.load.history:= y;

assigns two values to subfields of the STUDENT_REC variable *a*. The same values

```
program records(input,output);
     type name=array[1..16] of char;
          six_names = array[1..6] of name;
          past = record (******RECORD TYPE********)
                     hrs_earned: integer; (** FIELDS **)
                     gpa: real;
               end; (* past record *)
          courses = record
                       number: 1..6;
                       course_name: six_names;
                       history: past;
               end;
          student_rec = record
                       nam: name;
                       gender: 'F'..'M';
                       age: 0..101;
                       load: courses;
               end;
     var a,b: student_rec; x:courses; y: past;
     begin
          y.hrs_earned := 12;     y.gpa:=3.25;
          a.nam := 'Smart,Becky     ';
          a.gender:='F';   a.age :=18;
          a.load.number:=3;
          a.load.course_name[1] := 'Basket Weaving  ';
          a.load.course_name[2] := 'Pig Latin       ';
          a.load.course_name[3] := 'TV Watching     ';
          a.load.history:=y;
          b:=a;
     writeln(b.nam:20,b.age:6);
     (****** The following statement performs the
         same function as the last statement.  Use
         of the WITH directive is illustrated.  ********)
     with b do
          writeln(nam:20,age:6);
     (***** Another example or using  the WITH
     directive is given below:   *******)
     with a.load.history do
                    begin
                         writeln(hrs_earned:5);
                         writeln(gpa:10:5);
                    end;
     end.
```

Figure 6.12   Record data types as variables

could be assigned to the subfields of this variable by using the following statements:

```
a.load.history.hrs_earned := 12;
a.load.history.gpa := 3.25;
```

Observe that specifying various fields and subfields of record-type variables can become quite cumbersome. The WITH statement facilitates this task, as illustrated in Figure 6.12.

Example 6.6

An INFO data type is defined by the following type statement:

```
type   str = array[1..16] of char;
       ph_num = array[1..8] of char;
       quality = 1..10;
       (*********************************)
          info = record
                    name:    str;
                    gen:     'F'..'M';
                    age:     0..110;
                    job:     str;
                    salary:  real;
                    phone:   ph_num;
                    rating:  quality;
                    gpa:     real;
          end (* record *);
```

Develop and test procedures that will do the following:

(a) Read a set of data from a text file that has a logical name MYFILE, and place the data in an array of N INFO records.

(b) Print the name, age, and gender stored in each record of an array of N INFO records.

(c) Copy each record in an array of N INFO records into a file of INFO records.
Solution A solution with a test program is shown in Figure 6.13(a)–(c). A small text file used with the test program is given in Figure 6.13(d). A larger text file that can help create a file of INFO elements is included in Appendix A.

```
program records(input,output,myfile,herfile);
type    str = array[1..16] of char;
        ph_num = array[1..8] of char;
        quality = 1..10;
        info = record
                    name:   str;
                    gen:    'F'..'M';
                    age:    0..110;
                    job:    str;
                    salary: real;
                    phone:  ph_num;
                    rating: quality;
                    gpa:    real
               end;
        black_book = array[1..100] of info;
var  myfile: text;  herfile: file of info;
        stu_recs: black_book; n:integer;
```

Figure 6.13(a) Type definitions and declarations for solution to Example 6.6

```
procedure   rd_string(var xx:str);
        var j,k: integer;
        begin
             j:=1;
             while (j<=16) and not eoln(myfile) do begin
               read(myfile,xx[j]); j:=j+1;            end;
             if j<=16 then for k:=j to 16 do xx[k]:=' ';
             readln(myfile);
        end;
procedure form_array(var nn:integer; var bb:black_book);
          var x:info;
          begin
               reset(myfile);   nn :=0;
               while not eof(myfile) do
                   begin
                     rd_string(x.name);
                     readln(myfile,x.gen);
                     readln(myfile,x.age);
                     rd_string(x.job);
                     readln(myfile,x.salary);
                     readln(myfile,x.phone[1],x.phone[2],
                                     x.phone[3],x.phone[4],
                                     x.phone[5],x.phone[6],
                                     x.phone[7],x.phone[8]);
                     readln(myfile,x.rating);
                     readln(myfile,x.gpa);
                     nn := nn + 1;
                     bb[nn]:=x;
                   end;
          end;
procedure print_data(n:integer; b:black_book);
        var i:integer;
        begin   writeln;
                for i :=1 to n do
                writeln(b[i].name,'  ',b[i].age,'   ',b[i].gen);
        end;
procedure store(n:integer; b:black_book);
        var i: integer;
        begin   rewrite(herfile);
                for i := 1 to n do write(herfile,b[i]);
                close(herfile); (** TURBO Pascal **)
        end;
```

Figure 6.13(b)   Procedures for Example 6.6

```
(******  Start test program    *******)
 begin
        assign(myfile,'mydata');   (** TURBO Pascal **)
        assign(herfile,'secretfile'); (** TURBO Pascal **)
        form_array(n,stu_recs);
        print_data(n,stu_recs);
        store(n,stu_recs);
 end.
```

Figure 6.13(c)   Test program for Example 6.6

```
Sajak,Pat
M
35
Wheel man
200000.00
454-2234
5
2.6
White,Vanna
F
29
Super star
5000000.00
555-1212
10
4.0
Jackson,Michael
M
26
Singer
3.2E18
682-9999
9
2.98
```

Figure 6.13(d)   Data for Example 6.6

REVIEW

1. Refer to the program in Figure 6.12. What will be printed when this program is run?

Note: Before you run programs developed in Review Questions 2 and 3, we suggest you build a FILE OF INFO *using the program in Figure 6.13 and the corresponding data in Appendix A.*

2. Develop and test a procedure that reads data from a FILE OF INFO and stores the data in an array of INFO records. The procedure should also return the number of records contained in the file.

3. Develop and test a procedure that arranges an array of *N* INFO records alphabetically by name.

6.5 SETS

Recall that a **set** is a collection of objects or elements. In Pascal, each element of a set must be of the same type. Not only must the type be enumerable, but in Pascal, sets generally can contain only a relatively small number of elements. The maximum size depends on the installation, but generally must be large enough to hold all standard character codes.

If set operations are unavailable in a programming language, sequences of logic operations may be used to accomplish any task performed with set operations. But set operations can significantly simplify programming tasks.

In the previous section we used a **gen** type to store information about a person's sex. A user-defined data type was declared similar to the following:

type gen = 'F'..'M';

Thus, there are eight possible values that may be assigned to any gen-type variable. But only values 'F' and 'M' are meaningful.

Suppose we have just assigned a gen-type value to x. We wish to assign this value to another variable, "gender," if it has a meaningful value. We can do this using the following program segment:

if x in ['M','F'] then gender := x
                 else writeln(' ERROR ');

In other words, if the value of the variable x is *in* the set containing the two elements 'M' and 'F', then this value will be assigned to "gender"; otherwise, an error message will be printed.

Example 6.7

The name of any Pascal variable begins with either a capital letter, a lowercase letter, or the underscore character. Develop and test a Pascal function that accepts a character value and returns the same value if it is a valid first letter for a Pascal variable name. If it is not, the function prints an error message and returns the character "?".
Solution   A solution is given in Figure 6.14.

```
program ex6_7(input,output);
    var c:char;
    function check(c:char):char;
        var x: char;
        begin
            if c in ['A'..'Z','a'..'z','_'] then
                                          x :=c
                                          else begin
                                          writeln(' ERROR! ');
                                          x := '?';
                                               end;
             check := x;
        end;
begin (*** TEST PROGRAM  ***)
        c := 'X';
        while c <> '?' do
            begin
                readln(c);
                c := check(c);
                writeln(c:25);
            end;
end.
```

Figure 6.14   A solution to Example 6.7

A set-type data structure may be defined, and set-type variables may be declared. A set-type data definition identifies all elements that may be in the particular set. A set-type variable may be assigned any subset of the defined universal set.

The general form of a set definition is

type name = set of ⟨elements⟩;

Some examples of set-type definitions, as well as variable declarations and assignments, are shown in the following program:

```
program sets;
type    grades = set of 'A'..'F';
        test_scores = set of 0..100;
        animals = set of (dog,cat,mouse,bird,fish);
var  x: grades;   y: test_scores;   z: animals;
begin
    x := ['A','C','B'];        (* A proper subset *)
    y := [];                   (* A null set *)
    y := [0..100];             (* A universal set *)
    z := [fish,cat,bird];      (* A proper subset *)
end.
```

Observe that the order in which the elements of a set are specified is not important.

Operations may be performed between set variables of the same type. For example, suppose A, B, and C are set-type variables of the same type and that each has been assigned a subset value. Then

C := A + B;	Assigns to C the union of A and B
C := A * B;	Assigns to C the intersection of A and B
C := A − B;	Assigns to C the subset containing elements in A but not in B

Relational operations may also be used to compare subsets. The following relational operations are valid:

$A = B$ is True if and only if A and B contain the same elements.

$A <> B$ is True if and only if $A = B$ is False.

$A <= B$ is True if and only if A is a subset of B.

$A >= B$ is True if and only if B is a subset of A.

The program in Figure 6.15 illustrates set operations as well as relational operators used with subsets.

REVIEW

1. Develop and test a function that accepts a character value and returns the same value if it is a letter, a numeric character, or the underscore character, or, if none of these, prints an appropriate error message and returns the dollar-sign character.

```
program sets(output);
    type animals = (dog,cat,mouse,bird,fish);
         friends = set of animals;
    var a,b,c,d,e,f,g: friends;
    procedure set_print(x:friends);
    (** Prints elements contained in subset,x  **)
    var i: animals;
    begin
         for i := dog to fish do
         if i in x then case i of
            dog: write(' dog ');
            cat: write(' cat ');
            mouse: write(' mouse ');
            bird: write(' bird ');
            fish: write(' fish ');
                        end(* case *);
         writeln;
    end;
    begin (* main *)
    a := [cat,dog,mouse];    b := [mouse,cat,dog];
    c := [];     d :=[fish,mouse,cat,bird,dog];
    e := [cat,mouse]; f :=[fish]; g :=[dog,cat];
    set_print(d);
    set_print(c);
    set_print(b);
    set_print(a + b);
    set_print(e * g);
    set_print((a * f) + (b * d));
    set_print(d - f);
    set_print(f - d);
    set_print ((a+b+c+d)-(e+f+g));
(* Illustrate use of relational operators *)
    if a = b then writeln(' true') else writeln(' false');
    if (c + a) <> b then writeln(' true')
                                    else writeln(' false');
    if (g*d) <= f then writeln(' true') else writeln(' false');
    if b >= ((a*d) + f) then writeln(' true')
                                    else writeln(' false');
    end.
```

Figure 6.15 Program illustrating set operations

2. Refer to the program in Figure 6.15. When this program is run:
   (a) What is printed each time SET_PRINT is evoked?
   (b) Which relational operations return a value of True?

EXERCISES

1. Refer to the program in Figure 6.1(a). Modify this program so the rate of pay will be increased by a factor of 1.5 for hours in excess of eight that are worked on any day. For example, if someone works twelve hours on one day, the normal rate is paid for the first eight hours and 1.5 times the normal rate is paid for the other four hours. Weekend rates for extra hours worked are also increased by this factor.

2. Develop and test a function that converts a string of base-4 characters to the corresponding integer values.

3. Develop and test a function that converts a string of hexadecimal characters to the corresponding integer values.

4. Develop a function that accepts a specified base B, where

$$2 \le B \le 10$$

The function converts a string of base-B characters to the corresponding integer values.

5. Define an array using the following **TYPE** statement:

    type cap_count = array['A'..'Z'] of integer;

    Then develop a procedure that reads all characters in a text file identified as MYFILE and returns information tabulating how many times each of the twenty-six capital letters appeared in MYFILE.

6. An n-element array of reals is frequently called a **vector**. The **magnitude of a vector** is defined as the square root of the sum of the squares of all elements in the vector. Develop a function that returns the magnitude of an n-element vector.

7. A **unit vector** of a specified vector is obtained by dividing each element of the vector by the magnitude of the vector. Develop and test a procedure that replaces a vector with the corresponding unit vector.

8. Suppose a two-dimensional array of integers is defined as follows:

    type matrix = array[1..100,1..6] of integer;

    Develop a procedure that reads and assigns numbers to an m-by-n matrix.

9. Refer to the matrix defined in Exercise 8. Develop and test a procedure that prints the numbers stored in an m-by-n matrix. Your procedure should print m lines, with n numbers on each line.

10. Suppose sixteen-character names are contained in an array of N names. Develop and test a function that accepts a user-specified name and searches the array to see if the specified name is in the array. The function returns the corresponding index if the name is found, and returns a value of zero if the name is not found.

11. Suppose an array of N names has been sorted in ascending order, or alphabetized. Formulate an algorithm that can search for a specified name. Make your algorithm more efficient than the technique in Exercise 10.

12. Refer to the algorithm in Section 6.3. Suppose this algorithm is used in a program module to sort a set of N names.
    (a) For what conditions will this algorithm require execution of the smallest number of computer commands?
    (b) For what conditions will it require execution of the largest number of computer commands?

13. Why is the WITH directive sometimes useful?

Before doing Exercises 14–20, we suggest you build a FILE OF INFO *using the program in Figure 6.13 and the corresponding data in Appendix A. Then an array of N* INFO *elements can be formed using the procedure developed in Review Question 2, Section 6.4.*

14. Develop and test a procedure that sorts an array of N INFO records according to the age specified in each INFO record.

15. Suppose an array of N INFO elements has been sorted according to age. Develop and test a procedure that prints the name, phone number, age, and gender of all people in the array who are at least N_1 years old but no older than N_2 years.

16. Modify the procedure developed in Exercise 15 so it accepts a gender specification and prints the requested information just for individuals of the requested gender.

17. Develop and test a procedure that prints the name, age, salary, and phone number of all people who work in a specified occupation. Use this procedure to find the name of the individual whose occupation is 'Cover girl

18. Develop and test a procedure that sorts an array of N INFO records according to the salary specified in the INFO records.

19. Develop and test a procedure that accepts the following arguments:
   (a) A gender specification: 'M' requests males; 'F' requests females. Any other valid character requests both.
   (b) A minimum and maximum rating specification.
   (c) A minimum and maximum salary specification.
   (d) A minimum and maximum age specification.

The procedure returns an array of INFO records that satisfy the given specifications. The procedure also returns the number of elements in this array.

20. Use the procedure developed in Exercise 19 to obtain the records of either all the number-10 males or all the number-10 females.

21. Refer to the SET_PRINT procedure in Figure 6.15. Modify this procedure so that if a null set is the argument, an appropriate message will be printed.

22. Consider the following **TYPE** definitions and variable declarations:

```
type dog = (Rover,Rex,Spot,Fido,Dottie,Hilde,Jasper,
                 Lassie,Laddie,Brutus,Snoopy,Kelly);
     dogs = set of dog;
     var big_dogs, brown_dogs,old_dogs,smart_dogs: dogs;
```

Develop a procedure that prints the names of all dogs stored in a dogs-type variable. If there are no elements in a particular variable, an appropriate message is printed.

23. In Exercise 22, suppose the following assignments are made:

```
    big_dogs := [Rover,Rex,Dottie,Hilde,Lassie,Laddie,Brutus];
  brown_dogs := [Rex,Spot,Fido,Lassie,Laddie,Brutus,Kelly];
    old_dogs := [Rex,Fido,Dottie,Hilde,Lassie,Laddie,Snoopy];
  smart_dogs := [Spot,Hilde,Lassie,Snoopy];
```

Develop program segments that will find and print the names of the following:
   (a) Big brown dogs.
   (b) Smart old dogs that are not brown.
   (c) Dogs that are either old and smart or big and brown.
   (d) Old big brown dogs that are not smart.

7

Pointers

Recall that there are two ways in which information may be passed to a Pascal subprogram: by value or by reference. When information is passed by *value*, a value of some data type is either obtained from an arithmetic expression or retrieved from the variable to which it has been assigned, and then this value is assigned to a local variable of the subprogram being invoked. When information is passed by *reference*, it must be stored in memory space assigned to the invoking routine. Furthermore, this memory space must be identified to the subprogram being invoked. The information passed to the subprogram being invoked is sometimes called a *pointer* or a *pointer value*. Recall that a pointer identifies an *address* in a computer memory. Sometimes the words *pointer* and *address* are used synonymously.

Suppose we wish to pass an array into a subprogram by reference. Since elements of an array are stored consecutively, it is only necessary to pass a pointer value that identifies the first element of the array. Although there is a single pointer value associated with each variable, it makes sense to declare **pointer variables** because different variables have different pointer values. Pointer values may then be assigned to pointer variables.

The Pascal programming language permits pointer variables, a capability that facilitates the development of a wide range of data structures for a variety of applications.

7.1 POINTERS AND DYNAMIC VARIABLES

All program variables we have discussed so far have been defined and identified at *compile* time. That is, after program compilation is completed but before the program has been run, all variables have been identified by name, and appropriate space for the variables has been allocated.

Space for local variables in subprograms is not actually allocated until the subprogram is invoked. But during compilation of these subprograms, all local variables are identified and a fixed stack size is determined so that space for each local variable is available when the subprogram is invoked.

In Pascal it is possible to create or destroy variables as the program is being run. A variable that is created or destroyed during program execution is called a **dynamic variable.** Since we never know how many variables may be created during program execution, it is impossible to declare these variables in our source code. Thus, they do not have names.

Whenever a dynamic variable is created, a pointer value is determined by the system and may be used to identify the dynamic variable. Furthermore, this value may be assigned to a pointer-type variable. The following format defines a pointer data type:

type name = ^base-type;

The base-type may be a standard Pascal data type or a user-defined data type.

There are two standard procedures associated with dynamic variables:

new(pointer_type_variable);
dispose(pointer_type_variable);

When NEW is invoked, a new variable of the specified base-type is created. No assignment is made to the variable at that time. A pointer value identifying the newly created variable is determined and assigned to the pointer-type variable.

When DISPOSE is invoked, the dynamic variable identified by the value stored in the argument variable is destroyed. The space for this variable is returned to the system and is available for new dynamic variables. Not all facilities implement the DISPOSE command. Even where available, it is generally not used when there is sufficient capacity to implement all anticipated dynamic variables.

A program introducing the use of pointers and dynamic-type variables is shown in Figure 7.1. When the first line after the word *begin* is executed, five dynamic variables are created. But after this line has been executed, it is possible to access only two of these variables. The pointer to the first one created is stored in pointer variable *a*, the pointer to the last one created is stored in variable *b*, and the other pointer values are not stored.

Dynamic variables may be accessed only through the use of pointers. Observe

```
program pointer(output);
        type four = array[1..4] of char;
             four_pt = ^four;
             ch_pt    = ^char;
             int_pt   = ^integer;
        var a,b,c:  four_pt;
            d,e,f:  ch_pt;
            g,h,i:  int_pt;
            x,y:    char;
begin
   new(a); new(b);  new(b); new(b); new(b);
   (*** Five dynamic variables are created when the above
        line is executed.  But three are not accessible!!! ***)
   c := a;(** Assigns pointer value to pointer variable **)
   (*** The following statement assigns a value to a dynamic
        variable ***)
   c^ := 'LISA';  writeln(c^);
   x := c^[3]; y:=a^[4];
   writeln(' ', x:1,y:1,'M');
   new (d); new(e);  d^ := 'd' ; e^ := 'e';
   e^ := char( ord(e^) -ord(pred(d^)) + ord('l'));
   writeln(e^);
   new (g); new(h); new(i);
   g^ :=6; h^ := g^ -2; i^ := g^ -1;
   writeln((g^ * h^) mod i^);
end.
```

Figure 7.1   Use of pointers and dynamic variables

from Figure 7.1 how a value is assigned to a dynamic variable. If a pointer to a variable is stored in a pointer variable, such as x, the following command is used:

$$x\hat{\ } := expression;$$

where the expression returns a value of the designated base-type. Also observe that dynamic variables may appear in expressions in the same ways that *named* variables appear.

Although the program in Figure 7.1 employs three different types of pointers—integer pointers, character pointers, and four-letter-word pointers—these types are seldom found in Pascal programs.

Pointers to user-defined records, however, frequently appear in Pascal programs. Furthermore, fields of user-defined records are often pointer types. These ideas are developed in the following section.

REVIEW

1. Refer to the program in Figure 7.1. When this program is run:
   (a) How many integer variables are created?
   (b) How many character variables are created?
   (c) How many four-type variables are created?

2. Refer to the program in Figure 7.1. When this program is run, four lines are printed. What is printed on each of these lines?

7.2 DATA STRUCTURES

Pointers and dynamic variables are frequently employed to implement commonly used data structures. Four such data structures are shown in Figure 7.2. In Figures 7.2(a) and (b), a rectangular box represents a user-defined record. At least one of the fields of this record contains a pointer that identifies a record of the same type. In Figures 7.2(c) and (d), the same kind of user-defined records are represented by small circles, referred to as **nodes** of the data structure.

The structure shown in Figure 7.2(a) is a **linked list.** Each record contains a pointer field, which contains a pointer value that identifies the next box. The pointer field in the last box does not identify any record. We can assign a value of *nil* to this box. In order to *enter* the linked list, the pointer value to the left box must be

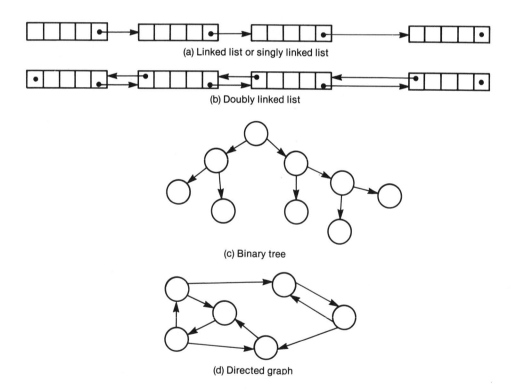

(a) Linked list or singly linked list

(b) Doubly linked list

(c) Binary tree

(d) Directed graph

Figure 7.2   Some data structures that use pointers and dynamic variables

stored in some pointer variable that is *not* part of the linked list. If this *entry* value is not stored, then nothing in the linked list is accessible.

Each record or node in a doubly linked list must contain at least two pointer fields, a left-pointer and a right-pointer. The value of the left-pointer in the first box and the value of the right-pointer in the last box are each nil.

Binary trees are popular data structures. The highest-level node is called the **root** node. Each node has two pointers. If the pointers do not have nil values, they are used to identify nodes at a lower level. A binary tree is just a special case of a directed graph, such as the one illustrated in Figure 7.2(d).

Example 7.1

A *box*-type record is to have four fields: a four-letter "name" field, an "age" field, and two pointer fields. Each of the pointer fields is for pointers to a box-type record. Develop three procedures, one for each of the following tasks:

(a) Read a set of N data records from the console, and store these data in a singly linked list.

(b) Accept a pointer value that is an entry point to a linked list of boxes, and print the name and age stored in each element.

(c) Store the elements of a linked list of box-type elements in a FILE OF BOX.

Solution   A solution is given in Figure 7.3. The test program shown carries a value of 7 into the MAKE_LIST procedure, which will make a linked list of seven box-type elements. For each element, two lines of data—a name and an age—must be entered from the console.

In the first executable line of MAKE_LIST, a dynamic box-type variable is created, and the pointer value to this variable is stored in both PTR_FIRST and p. The value assigned to PTR_FIRST will not be changed but will be returned as the entry point to the list.

During execution of the FOR loop, names and ages are read from the console and assigned to the appropriate fields of the dynamic variable. A value of nil is assigned to the $p2$ field of each dynamic variable. When the value of the index i is less than n, a new dynamic variable is created, and the pointer value to this new box is placed in the $p1$ field of the same box in which name and age data have just been entered. A value of nil is entered in the $p1$ field of the last box. Observe that the $p1$ field of each record is used to store a *forward-pointer*. For this data structure, the $p2$ field is not used.

Observe that it is very easy to implement the PRINT_LIST and STORE_LIST procedures. When the STORE_LIST procedure is invoked, the seven box-type records are stored sequentially in a file called BOXES. At the time these records are stored in the file, the pointer values stored in the first six records identify dynamic variables. However, once program execution is completed, there are no dynamic variables! In fact, none of the variables that were used are accessible. Therefore, none of the pointer values that are safely stored in the FILE OF BOXES is meaningful, except possibly the nil value. If a subsequent program is to read data from this file and place it in a linked list, the linked list must be reconstructed.

```
program link(input,output,dog);
    type four = array[1..4] of char;
    box_ptr = ^box;
        box = record
                name: four;
                age:   0..110;
                p1:     box_ptr;
                p2:     box_ptr;
            end(*record*);
    var dog: file of BOX;  entry: box_ptr;
    procedure make_list(n:integer; var ptr_first:box_ptr);
        var p,pnext:box_ptr; x:four; i:integer;
        begin
            new(ptr_first); p :=ptr_first;
            for i := 1 to n do
                begin
                    readln(x[1],x[2],x[3],x[4]);
                    readln(p^.age); p^.name:=x; p^.p2:=nil;
                    if i=n then p^.p1:=nil
                            else begin
                                    new(pnext); p^.p1:=pnext;
                                    p := pnext;
                                    end;
                end;
        end;
    procedure print_list(p:box_ptr);
        begin    writeln;
            while p<> nil do
                begin
                    writeln(p^.name,'        ',p^.age);
                    p := p^.p1;
                end;
        end;
    procedure store_list(p:box_ptr);
        begin
            rewrite(dog);
            while p<> nil do
                begin
                    write(dog,p^);
                    p := p^.p1;
                end;
            close(dog); (** TURBO Pascal **)
        end;
begin (*** Start test program ***)
        assign(dog,'boxes'); (** TURBO Pascal **)
        make_list(7,entry); (** Enter 7 sets of data **)
        print_list(entry);
        store_list(entry);
end.
```

Figure 7.3   A solution to Example 7.1

Although the printing and storing of elements of a linked list are easy procedures to implement, manipulation of data stored in a particular record can be awkward. In order to access the *k*th node, we must start with the entry pointer and procure the pointer to the subsequent node, continuing this process until we have located the pointer identifying the *k*th node. Suppose we have manipulated or adjusted the data in the *k*th node and now wish to perform operations on data in the $(k-1)$th node. We must then reenter the list using the entry pointer and proceed until we have located the pointer to the $(k - 1)$th node. This task will be facilitated greatly if our data structure is a **doubly linked list.**

In many applications, elements or nodes of a linked list are **ordered.** For example, if they are ordered by *name*, then as the list is traversed from left to right, the names would appear in alphabetical order.

Suppose a linked list is ordered. Further suppose we wish to add a node to the list. Then we need merely identify where the new node is to be placed and insert the new node into the list. This task is considerably simpler than adding a record to an alphabetized *array* of records. Algorithms for adding or deleting nodes to an ordered list are discussed in Section 7.3.

Even when a linked list is ordered, locating a particular element is still rather tedious. To locate an element in the middle of a 1024-node ordered list, we still have to walk through approximately 512 records. Use of a **binary tree** such as in Figure 7.2(c) facilitates the search for elements in an ordered structure.

The entry point to a binary tree is the *root* node. Suppose we have a binary tree ordered by name and we wish to add a new node. If the name we wish to enter is less than the name stored at the current node, we move to the left node. If it is greater, we move to the right node. We continue the process until, when we attempt to move to a lower level in the tree, there is no lower level. This happens when a nil pointer is located. Then we create a new record, insert data in the various fields of the new record, and replace the nil pointer with a pointer to the newly created record.

Let us illustrate the process of creating a binary tree. Refer again to Example 7.1 (p. 125) and the solution given in Figure 7.3 (p. 126). When this program is run, suppose the data shown in Figure 7.4 are entered from the console. After the program has been executed, seven box-type records that include those data are

Lisa
34
Lana
23
Lola
3
Mark
26
Lucy
29
Suzi
99
Bill
52

Figure 7.4   Data entered when running program in Figure 7.3

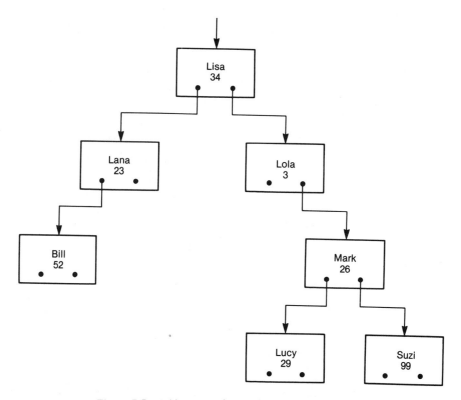

Figure 7.5   A binary tree formed from data in Figure 7.4

stored in a FILE OF BOX. Now each time a record is read from that file, it is added to a binary tree, which will have the structure shown in Figure 7.5.

Example 7.2

Develop and test a procedure that reads box-type records from a FILE OF BOX and formulates a binary tree.

Solution   A solution is given in Figure 7.6.

When working with binary trees, *recursive* subprograms are frequently employed. (See Section 9.2.)

REVIEW

1. What is a *dynamic variable*? How does this type of variable differ from the types we have previously used?

2. Suppose we have an *N*-node singly linked list of records and we wish to insert a new

```
program tree(output,cat);
    type  four = array[1..4] of char;
          box_ptr = ^box;
          box = record
                      name: four;
                      age:  0..110;
                      p1:   box_ptr;
                      p2:   box_ptr;
                 end(*record*);
    var cat:file of box; ptr, entry: box_ptr;
       procedure make_tree(var pfirst:box_ptr);
              var x:box;  p,plast:box_ptr;   left:boolean;
            begin
                new(pfirst);  p:= pfirst;  reset(cat);
                read(cat,p^);  p^.p1 := nil; p^.p2 :=nil;
                while not eof(cat) do
                  begin
                    p := pfirst;
                    read(cat,x);
                    while p <> nil do begin
                        plast := p;
                        if x.name < p^.name then begin
                                            left:=true;
                                            p:=p^.p1
                                            end
                                       else begin
                                            left:= false;
                                            p := p^.p2;
                                            end;
                                    end;
                    new (p);  p^ :=x;  p^.p1:=nil; p^.p2:=nil;
                    if left then plast^.p1 :=p
                                else plast^.p2 :=p;
                  end;
            end;
begin(*** Start test program ***)
      assign(cat,'boxes');      (** TURBO Pascal **)
      make_tree(entry);
      ptr:=entry;
      (*    Find end branches    *)
      while ptr^.p1 <> nil do ptr:=ptr^.p1;
      writeln(ptr^.name);
      ptr := entry;
      while ptr^.p2 <> nil do ptr:=ptr^.p2;
      writeln(ptr^.name);
end.
```

Figure 7.6   A solution to Example 7.2

record between the kth element and the $(k + 1)$th element, where $1 < k < N$. Formulate an algorithm for this task.

3. Suppose the file BOXES is created using the program in Figure 7.1 and the data in Figure 7.4. What two names are printed when the program shown in Figure 7.6 is run?
4. Refer to the program in Figure 7.6. Suppose the file BOXES has been created with the following data:

Anne

45

Mike

93

Dave

7

Dana

51

Tami

20

Tony

32

Davy

2

Sketch the binary tree formed when the program is run with these data.

7.3 SELECTED EXAMPLES

Formulating linked lists is relatively easy. Searching for a particular identifier in a linked list is also easy to program, but may require a relatively large amount of computer time if the list has a large number of nodes or boxes. Suppose we have a linked list of box-type elements as defined in the previous section and we wish to search the linked list for a specified name. If the name is found in one of the records, a pointer to the record is to be returned; if not, nil is to be returned. The following program segment may be used:

```
p := entry;     done := false;
while (p <> nil) and not done do
    if NAME = p^.name then done := true
        else p :=p^.p1;
```

The list is searched starting at the entry point. If the specified name is not present, the entire list must be traversed.

Searching a binary tree for a specified name is considerably more efficient. Suppose the nodes or branches of a tree are symmetrical with respect to the root node. That is, for each higher-level node (parent), there are about the same number of lower-level nodes (children) to the left of the parent as there are to the right of the parent. Now suppose we are searching a tree for a specified name. If the name is not in the root node, then we check to see if it is *less than* the name in the root node. If it is, we continue to search nodes to the left of the root node. Thus, each time we move down the tree, we eliminate approximately half of the remaining records we need to search.

Suppose a name is not present in a linked list of 1024 records. We must compare the desired name with the name in each of the records to ascertain this. Using a binary tree, only ten comparisons need to be made (Note: $2^{10} = 1024$).

Searching a binary tree is almost as easy as searching a linked list. A program segment such as the following may be used:

```
p := entry;    done := false;
while (p<>)nil) and not done do
   if NAME = p^.name then done := true
    else if NAME < p^.name then p:=p^.p1 (* GO LEFT *)
                   else p:=p^.p2 (*Go RIGHT *);
```

In order to develop meaningful programming examples, we will develop a method for creating files of meaningful records. In Figure 6.13, software for creating INFO records was developed. We will modify the structure of those records so they can be incorporated as nodes of linked lists or binary trees.

The program in Figure 7.7 can create two files of INFO-type records. Observe

```
program make_files(input,output,myfile,herfile);
(** This program is used to create 2 files of INFO elements.
    The file UNSORTED is a file of records created from data
    read from the textfile MYDATA.  The file SORTED is a
    file of the same records.  But the records are arranged
    alphabetically by name before they are stored in SORTED.
    Both pointer fields in each record have been assigned
    values of NIL.   **)
type   str = array[1..16] of char;
       ph_num = array[1..8] of char;
       quality = 1..10;
          pinfo = ^info;
          info = record
                     name:    str;
                     gen:     'F'..'M';
                     age:     0..110;
                     job:     str;
                     salary:  real;
                     phone:   ph_num;
                     rating:  quality;
                     gpa:     real;
                     p1:      pinfo ;
                     p2:      pinfo;
                 end;
             black_book = array[1..100] of info;
var  myfile: text;  herfile: file of info;
     stu_recs: black_book; n:integer;
($i fig7y.pas) (* INCLUDE STMT.  TURBO Pascal *)
($i fig7x.pas) (* INCLUDE STMT.  TURBO Pascal *)
(****** Start test program    *******)
begin
        assign(myfile,'mydata');       (** TURBO Pascal **)
        assign(herfile,'unsorted'); (** TURBO Pascal **)
        form_array(n,stu_recs);
        print_data(n,stu_recs);
        store(n,stu_recs);
        sort(n,stu_recs);
        print_data(n,stu_recs);
        assign(herfile,'sorted');
        store(n,stu_recs);
end.
```

Figure 7.7 Program that creates two files of INFO records

```
procedure  rd_string(var xx:str);
        var j,k: integer;
        begin
              j:=1;
              while (j<=16) and not eoln(myfile) do begin
                read(myfile,xx[j]); j:=j+1;            end;
              if j<=16 then for k:=j to 16 do xx[k]:=' ';
              readln(myfile);
        end;
procedure form_array(var nn:integer; var bb:black_book);
        var x:info;
        begin
              reset(myfile);   nn :=0;
              while not eof(myfile) do
                  begin
                    rd_string(x.name);
                    readln(myfile,x.gen);
                    readln(myfile,x.age);
                    rd_string(x.job);
                    readln(myfile,x.salary);
     readln(myfile,x.phone[1],x.phone[2],x.phone[3],x.phone[4],
              x.phone[5],x.phone[6],x.phone[7],x.phone[8]);
                    readln(myfile,x.rating);
                    readln(myfile,x.gpa);
                    nn := nn + 1;
                    x.p1 := nil;  x.p2 := nil;
                    bb[nn]:=x;
                  end;
        end;
procedure print_data(n:integer; b:black_book);
      var i:integer;
      begin   writeln;
              for i :=1 to n do
              writeln(b[i].name,'  ',b[i].age,'  ',b[i].gen);
      end;
procedure store(n:integer; b:black_book);
      var i: integer;
      begin   rewrite(herfile);
              for i := 1 to n do write(herfile,b[i]);
              close(herfile); (** TURBO Pascal **)
      end;
```

Figure 7.8 Procedures used with program in Figure 7.7 (file FIG7X.PAS)

that INFO-type records have been redefined to include two fields that may contain pointers to other INFO-type records. The data that are read from the text file MYFILE can be identical to the data in Section 6.4 used to construct INFO records. If relatively large files are to be constructed, the appropriate text file included in Appendix A may be used.

Procedures used to create similar files in Section 6.4 were modified to accommodate the new record structure, and these modified procedures are shown in Figure 7.8. In order to use them when we run the program in Figure 7.7, we have placed them in a file called FIG7X.PAS and used an appropriate INCLUDE statement. If your installation lacks the INCLUDE capability, the code for the procedures may be inserted in the appropriate place in the program in Figure 7.7.

```
procedure sort(n:integer;var na:black_book);
    var sorted:boolean; temp:info; i:Integer;
    begin(* Sorts n names in ascending order *)
        n := n - 1 ; sorted := false;
    while not sorted do begin
            sorted := true;
            for i := 1 to n do
        if na[i].name > na[i+1].name then  begin
                                        (* SWAP *)
                                        temp := na[i];
                                        na[i] := na[i+1];
                                        na[i+1] :=temp;
                                        sorted := false;
                                            end;
                if n>1 then n:= n-1;
                            end (* while *);
        end (* sort procedure *);
```

Figure 7.9   Sort procedure used with program in Figure 7.7 (file FIG7Y.PAS)

We often create linked lists in which the elements are ordered, frequently by name. The SORTED file created by running the program in Figure 7.7 contains a sequence of records alphabetized by name. Before we store records in this file, they are placed in an array of records, then a sort routine like the one developed in Section 6.3 is invoked. This modified procedure is shown in Figure 7.9.

The UNSORTED and SORTED files created by running the program in Figure 7.7 appear in subsequent examples, review equations, and exercises.

Example 7.3

Develop and test a procedure that creates a doubly linked list of INFO-type elements. The list is to be ordered; that is, as the list is traversed, the names appear in alphabetical order.

Solution   A procedure that reads INFO records from a FILE OF INFO is shown in Figure 7.10. To develop an *ordered* list, we must read data records in proper sequence, that is, with the name fields in alphabetical order. Thus, the SORTED file is used.

Suppose we have a linked list of elements and wish to add one or more elements to the list. If the list is not ordered, the new elements can easily be attached either to the beginning or to the end of the list. If attached to the beginning of the list, a new entry pointer value must be saved.

Suppose the list is ordered by name. Then adding a name to the list requires the new element to be placed in the proper position. For example, if the new record contains 'Jackson,Kate   ' in its name field, it may be inserted just after a box containing 'Jackson,Bo   ' but just before a box containing 'Jackson,Michael   '.

Suppose we wish to insert a new record in an ordered linked list of N records.

```
       program make_double(input,output,herfile);
type   str = array[1..16] of char;
       ph_num = array[1..8] of char;
       quality = 1..10;
          pinfo = ^info;
          info = record
                     name:    str;
                     gen:     'F'..'M';
                     age:     0..110;
                     job:     str;
                     salary:  real;
                     phone:   ph_num;
                     rating:  quality;
                     gpa:     real;
                     p1:      pinfo ;
                     p2:      pinfo;
                 end;
var  herfile: file of info;   pt,ptold,entry:pinfo;
   procedure make_double(var pfirst:pinfo);
          var p,plast:pinfo;
          begin
              reset(herfile);
              new(pfirst); p := pfirst;
              read(herfile,p^);
              p^.p1:= nil;   p^.p2:=nil;
              while not eof(herfile) do
                  begin
                      plast:=p;
                      new(p);
                      read(herfile,p^);
                      p^.p2 :=plast; (* Assign back_pointer *)
                      plast^.p1:=p;  (* Assign up_pointer *)
                      if eof(herfile) then p^.p1 := nil;
                  end;
          end;
(******  Start test program     ******)
begin
        assign(herfile,'sorted'); (** TURBO Pascal **)
        make_double(entry);
        writeln;
        pt:=entry;
        while pt <> nil do (*left-to-right*)
                        begin
                            writeln(pt^.name);
                            ptold :=pt;
                            pt:=pt^.p1;
                        end;
        writeln;
        pt:=ptold;
        while pt<> nil do (* right-to-left *)
                        begin
                            writeln(pt^.name);
                            pt:=pt^.p2;
                        end;
end.
```

Figure 7.10   A solution to Example 7.3

First we must determine where it is to be inserted. Suppose the new box is to be inserted between the kth and the $(k + 1)$th box of the ordered linked list, where

$$0 \leq k \leq N$$

(Note: If $k = 0$, the box is to be placed in front of the first box. If $k = N$, it is to be put after the last box.) Then the following algorithm may be used:
  If $k = 0$:

1. Put the pointer to the new box in the back-pointer field of the first box.
2. Put the entry pointer in the up-pointer field of the new box.
3. Assign nil to the back-pointer in the new box.
4. Replace the entry pointer with the pointer to the new box.

  If $k = N$:

1. Get the up-pointer from the $(N - 1)$th box. Put it in the back-pointer field of the new box.
2. Assign nil to the up-pointer of the new box.
3. Put the pointer to the new box in the up-pointer field of the last box.

  For $1 \leq k \leq N - 1$:

1. Put the pointer to the $(k + 1)$th box in the up-pointer field of the new box.
2. Put the pointer to the kth box in the back-pointer field of the new box.
3. Put the pointer to the new box in the up-pointer field of the kth box.
4. Put the pointer to the new box in the back-pointer field of the $(k + 1)$th box.

Similar algorithms can be formulated for inserting a new element in a singly linked list, removing an element from a singly linked list, or removing an element from a doubly linked list.

Example 7.4

Develop and test a procedure that creates a new INFO-type element, assigns values to the various fields of this new element, and then inserts this record into a linked list of INFO records ordered by name.
Solution Type definitions and variable declarations are shown in Figure 7.11(a). A procedure that performs this task is shown in Figure 7.11(b), and a test program is given in Figure 7.11(c).

```
program insert_box(input,output,herfile);
type    str = array[1..16] of char;
        ph_num = array[1..8] of char;
        quality = 1..10;
            pinfo = ^info;
            info = record
                          name :      str;
                          gen :       'F'..'M';
                          age :         0..110 ;
                          job :       str;
                          salary:     real;
                          phone:      ph_num;
                          rating:     quality;
                          gpa:        real;
                          pl:         pinfo;
                          p2:         pinfo;
                     end;
var  herfile: file of info; pt,ptold,entry:pinfo;
($i defs.pas}   (*  The procedure MAKE_DOUBLE is in DEFS.PAS *)
                (*  TURBO Pascal *)
```

Figure 7.11(a)   Type definitions and variable declarations for Example 7.4

```
procedure insert_box(var pfirst:pinfo);
            (*** This procedure creates an INFO type record,
            requests data that is stored in this record, and then
            inserts this record in an ordered (by name) doubly
            linked list identified by the pointer in the
            argument list ***)
            var  p,plast,pnew:pinfo; x:str; f:ph_num;
            begin
                new(pnew);
                writeln; writeln(' Enter name,gender,age,job,',
                        'salary,phone number,rating and GPA.');
                writeln(' Enter each item on a separate line.');
                writeln; readln(x[1],x[2],x[3],x[4],x[5],x[6],
    x[7],x[8],x[9],x[10],x[11],x[12],x[13],x[14],x[15],x[16]);
            pnew^.name:=x; readln(pnew^.gen); readln(pnew^.age);
                readln(x[1],x[2],x[3],x[4],x[5],x[6],x[7],x[8],
                x[9],x[10],x[11],x[12],x[13],x[14],x[15],x[16]);
                pnew^.job:=x; readln(p^.salary);
                readln(f[1],f[2],f[3],f[4],f[5],f[6],f[7],f[8]);
            pnew^.phone:=f; readln(pnew^.rating);readln(pnew^.gpa);
        (*** Data for new INFO record has been loaded ***)
(*** Determine where the new box should be inserted in the
        ordered list ***)
                p := pfirst;  writeln;
                while (p<>nil)and(pnew^.name > p^.name) do begin
                                                ptold:=p;
                                                p:=p^.pl;
                                                end;
```

Figure 7.11(b)   Procedure for inserting record in doubly linked list

```
        (** Check Special Cases **)
         if p = pfirst (** new box is first **)
             then    begin
                             pfirst^.p2 := pnew;
                             pnew^.p2 := nil;
                             pnew^.p1 :=pfirst;
                             pfirst:=pnew
                      end
         else if p = nil (** new box is last **)
                  then  begin
                             ptold^.p1 :=pnew;
                             pnew^.p2 := ptold;
                             pnew^.p1 :=nil
                         end
                  else begin (** inserted between 2 boxes **)
                             pnew^.p1 :=ptold^.p1;
                             pnew^.p2 :=p^.p2;
                             ptold^.p1 := pnew;
                             p^.p2 := pnew;
                         end;
    end;
```

Figure 7.11(b)   (continued)

```
 (******   Start test program     *******)
 begin
         assign(herfile,'sorted'); (** TURBO Pascal **)
         make_double(entry);
         writeln;
         insert_box(entry);
         pt:=entry;
         while pt <> nil do (*left-to-right*)
                         begin
                             writeln(pt^.name);
                             ptold :=pt;
                             pt:=pt^.p1;
                         end;
         writeln;
         pt:=ptold;
         while pt<> nil do (* right-to-left *)
                         begin
                             writeln(pt^.name);
                             pt:=pt^.p2;
                         end;
 end.
```

Figure 7.11(c)   Test program for Example 7.3

REVIEW

1. Develop and test a function that accepts a sixteen-character name and an entry pointer to a linked list of INFO records. The function searches the list. If the name is found, a pointer to the record containing the name is returned; if the name is not found, a value of nil is returned.

2. Suppose we wish to read INFO records from a file and create a binary tree. The position of the record on the tree depends on the value stored in the name field. From which of the files referred to in this section, SORTED or UNSORTED, should records be read as the tree is being formulated? Explain your answer.

3. Suppose the SORTED file was created by the program shown in Figure 7.7 using data shown in the text file in Figure 7.12. What is printed when the program in Figure 7.10 is run?

4. Formulate an algorithm for *removing* a record from a doubly linked list of N records.

```
Sajak,Pat
M
 35
Wheel man
200000.00
454-2234
 5
2.6
White,Vanna
F
 29
Super star
5000000.00
555-1212
 10
4.0
Jackson,Michael
M
 26
Singer
3.2E18
682-9999
 9
2.98
Parton,Dolly
F
 37
Cow girl
4000000.00
111-1111
 8
2.5
Jackson,Bo
M
 25
Foot (Base) player
3000000.00
222-2222
 10
2.34
Bush,George
M
 55
Who knows!
123450.00
000-0000
 4
1.07
```

Figure 7.12 Small text file used in creating SORTED and UNSORTED

EXERCISES

1. Discuss the advantages and disadvantages of using dynamic variables in Pascal programs.
2. What is a major advantage of storing ordered records in linked lists rather than in arrays?
3. Why should we never create a binary tree using a set of elements that is already ordered?
4. Suppose a procedure is employed to add a node to an ordered linked list. Why must the procedure return the value of the entry pointer?
5. Suppose a binary tree is created by the program in Figure 7.6 using the data in Figure 7.4. Develop a function that searches the tree for a specified name. If the name is found, a pointer value to the enclosing record is returned; if the name is not found, nil is returned. Test your function for both cases.
6. For the program and data in Figure 7.13, what is printed by each of the lines identified by the *QUESTION* comment?
7. For the program and data in Figure 7.14, what is printed by each of the lines identified by the *QUESTION* comment?
8. The linked lists so far discussed are called **linear** linked lists, meaning there is a *first* node and a *last* node. In a **circular** linked list, the up-pointer in the last node identifies

```
program last (output,tiger);
type       mystring = array[1..4] of char;
           pointer = ^box;
           box = record
                     name: mystring;
                     age:  1..99;
                     onepointer:    pointer;
                     otherpointer:  pointer;
                 end;
var    tiger: text;    p,p1,plast,pfirst: pointer;
procedure make_linked_list (t:pointer);
       var t1:pointer; x:mystring;
       begin
          reset(tiger);    plast:= nil;
          while not eof(tiger) do begin
                readln(tiger,x[1],x[2],x[3],x[4]);
                readln(tiger,t^.age);
                t^.name := x;
                if eof(tiger) then t^.onepointer :=nil
                else begin
                        t1:=t;
                        new(t);
                        t1^.onepointer :=t;
                        t1^.otherpointer := plast;
                        plast := t1;
                end;
                                       end;
```

Figure 7.13(a)   Program for Exercise 6

```
      end;
(***  Begin main program ***)
begin
   assign(tiger,'tiger');    (*** Turbo Pascal ***)
   new (pfirst);
   make_linked_list(pfirst);
writeln(pfirst^.name[3]);          (*** QUESTION ***)
p:=pfirst^.onepointer;
writeln(p^.name);                  (*** QUESTION ***)
p:=p^.onepointer;
writeln(p^.age);                   (*** QUESTION ***)
new (p1);   (** Create a new box **)
pfirst^.otherpointer := p1;    (**** Change one pointer ****)
make_linked_list(p1);    (** Make another LIST **)
p1:=pfirst^.otherpointer;
writeln(p1^.name);                 (*** QUESTION ***)
p1:=pfirst^.onepointer;
p1:=p1^.onepointer;
p1:=p1^.otherpointer;
writeln(p1^.age);                  (*** QUESTION ***)
p:= pfirst;
   repeat
       p:=p^.onepointer;
       p1:=p^.otherpointer;
   until p^.name = 'LORI';
writeln(p1^.name);                 (*** QUESTION ***)
writeln(p^.age);                   (*** QUESTION ***)
end.
```

Figure 7.13(a)   (continued)

the first node. In a doubly linked list, the back-pointer in the first box identifies the last box. Develop and test a procedure that builds a circular singly linked list from a file of INFO records.

9. Develop and test a procedure that builds a circular doubly linked list from a file of INFO records.

10. When traversing a linear linked list from left to right, we know the end of the list when we encounter a pointer value of nil. How do we identify the last node in a circular linked list?

11. Develop and test a procedure that accepts the value of an entry pointer to a circular singly linked list of INFO elements and prints the names and occupations of everyone on the list.

```
                        LANA
                         21
                        LISA
                         31
                        LUCY
                         27
                        LORI
                         20
                        LOLA
                          3
```

Figure 7.13(b)   Contents of file 'tiger'

```
program third(output,tiger);
type      herstring = packed array[1..4] of char;
          pointer = ^box;
          box = record
                      name: herstring;
                      uppointer: pointer;
                end;
var  tiger: text;   p,pfirst: pointer; i: integer;
procedure make_linked_list( var t: pointer);
    var t1: pointer;   x: herstring;
          begin
              reset(tiger);
              while not eof(tiger) do begin
                 readln(tiger,x[1],x[2],x[3],x[4]);
                 t^.name := x;
                 if eof(tiger) then t^.uppointer := nil
                    else begin
                           t1:= t;
                           new(t);
                           t1^.uppointer:=t;
                         end;
                                          end;
          end;
(** Begin main program **)
begin
      assign(tiger,'tiger');   (* Turbo Pascal *)
      new (pfirst);
      p:=pfirst;
      make_linked_list(p);
      writeln(p^.name);                (**** QUESTION ****)
      writeln(pfirst^.name);           (**** QUESTION ****)
      (** Now the LINEAR LINKED LIST will be changed to a structure
          called a CIRCULAR LINKED LIST **)
      p^.uppointer := pfirst;   (* Circular linked list *)
      p:= p^.uppointer;
      writeln(p^.name);                (**** QUESTION ****)
      p:= pfirst;
      for i := 1 to 513 do p := p^.uppointer;
      writeln(p^.name);                (**** QUESTION ****)
(a) end.
```

Figure 7.14(a)   Program for Exercise 7

12. Develop and test a procedure that accepts the value of an entry pointer to a circular doubly linked list of INFO elements and prints the names and occupations of everyone on the list.
13. Formulate an algorithm for inserting a box into an ordered singly linked list of boxes.
14. Formulate an algorithm for removing a box from a singly linked list of boxes.
15. Formulate an algorithm for removing a box from a doubly linked list of boxes.
16. Develop and test a procedure that creates an INFO record, assigns value to the various fields, and inserts it into an ordered singly linked list of INFO boxes.

```
LISA
LANA
LUCY
LORI
LOLA
```

Figure 7.14(b)   Contents of file 'tiger'

17. Develop and test a procedure that searches for a specified name in a singly linked list of INFO-type records. If the name is located, the enclosing record is removed from the list.
18. Do Exercise 17 for a *doubly* linked list.
19. Develop a procedure that reads INFO records from a FILE OF INFO and creates a binary tree. The position of each element on the tree depends on the value in the "salary" field of the record. Does it make any difference whether the data are read from the SORTED file or the UNSORTED file? After the tree has been formulated, develop a test program that identifies the poorest and richest person.
20. Consider a procedure that searches a large linked list of INFO records. The procedure is to identify records that satisfy certain specifications—for example, females with a GPA of at least 3.25—and return this information to the invoking program. Two ways to return the information are: (a) return an array of record elements; or (b) return an array of pointers identifying the record elements. Why is method b preferable?
21. Develop a procedure that accepts an entry pointer to a linked list of INFO records, a minimum age, a sex specification, and a minimum salary specification. The procedure searches the list and returns the number of records that satisfy the specifications as well as an array of pointers to those records. Test this procedure by locating all females in the list who are at least 70 years old and have a salary of at least $150,000.
22. Develop and test a procedure that accepts:
    (a) An entry pointer to a linked list of INFO records.
    (b) A sex specification. (Note: If any character other than 'M' or 'F' is entered, then the specification is for either male or female.
    (c) A minimum and maximum salary specification.
    (d) A minimum and maximum *quality*.
    (e) A minimum and maximum GPA.

    The procedure should return the number of records satisfying the specifications as well as an array of pointers that identify those records.
23. Use the procedure developed in Exercise 22 to identify all the number-10 individuals of a specified gender in a linked list of INFO records.

8

Some Applications

At one time, those working in engineering, mathematical science, or related occupations used computers for a relatively narrow range of applications, often to obtain numeric solutions to equations describing physical phenomena. Nowadays, computers are used for a variety of applications, not only for "number crunching" and simulation of physical phenomena, but for virtually all phases of scientific work. Some applications involve standard programming languages such as Pascal; others require general-purpose or special-purpose software packages. Engineering design, computer graphics, and the development of code for monitoring and controlling external systems are among routine applications.

Text-processing with computers may currently be more popular than the traditional number-crunching, and spreadsheet and data-base packages are employed by most computer users.

Meanwhile, engineering, mathematics, physical science, and related college curricula still emphasize traditional problems. In this chapter, certain numerical techniques common to engineering-related courses are introduced.

8.1 OPERATIONS ON TWO-DIMENSIONAL ARRAYS

A two-dimensional array of numbers is called a **matrix.** A general form for a matrix is

$$A = \begin{bmatrix} a(1,\,1) & a(1,\,2) & \cdots & a(1,\,n) \\ a(2,\,1) & a(2,\,2) & \cdots & a(2,\,n) \\ \vdots & \vdots & \vdots & \vdots \\ a(m,\,1) & a(m,\,2) & \cdots & a(m,n) \end{bmatrix}$$

which is an $m \times n$ matrix (m-by-n matrix). We say the **order** of a matrix is $m \times n$ if it has m **rows** and n **columns.**

A matrix A can also be notated in a more general way:

$$A = \{a(i,\,j)\}$$

or

$$A_{mn} = \{a(i,\,j)\}_{mn}$$

In this notation, the matrix is represented by a general element, $a(i,\,j)$, which is the number in the ith row and jth column.

The following definitions introduce matrix relationships.

Definition.   Two $m \times n$ matrices A and B are equal if and only if $a(i,\,j) = b(i,\,j)$ for all i and j

Definition.   Given two $m \times n$ matrices A and B,

$$C_{mn} = A_{mn} + B_{mn}$$

or

$$C = A + B$$

if and only if $c(i,\,j) = a(i,\,j) + b(i,\,j)$ for all i and j.

Example 8.1

For the following matrices:

$$A = \begin{bmatrix} 1 & 2 \\ 3 & 4 \\ 5 & 6 \\ 7 & 8 \end{bmatrix} \qquad B = \begin{bmatrix} 1 & 1 & 1 \\ 0 & 1 & 2 \\ 4 & 5 & 6 \end{bmatrix} \qquad C = \begin{bmatrix} 6 & 5 \\ 4 & 3 \\ 2 & 1 \\ 0 & -1 \end{bmatrix}$$

(a) Identify the order of each matrix.
(b) Identify each of the elements $a(3,\,1)$, $b(3,\,2)$, and $c(4,\,2)$.
(c) Find D, where $D = A + C$.

Solution A and C are 4×2 matrices. B is a 3×3 matrix. $a(3,\,1) = 5$, $b(3,\,2) = 5$, and $c(3,\,2) = 1$.

$$D = A + C = \begin{bmatrix} 7 & 7 \\ 7 & 7 \\ 7 & 7 \\ 7 & 7 \end{bmatrix}$$

Example 8.2

Given the following *type* definition,

$$\text{type} \quad \text{matrix} = \text{array}[1..10,1..10] \text{ of real;}$$

develop procedures that perform the following tasks:
  (a) Read values into an $m \times n$ matrix (numbers entered one per line).
  (b) Print the elements of an $m \times n$ matrix in standard matrix format.
  (c) Return the sum of two $m \times n$ matrices.

Solution   The specified procedures are shown in Figure 8.1. A test program is shown in Figure 8.2(a). When the test program is run, thirty-five numbers are entered. Two matrices printed for a selected set of input data are shown in Figure 8.2(b). Observe that immediately after data are entered, the data set is printed. This is good programming practice, especially in the debugging phase of program development.

Let us consider other properties of matrices.

Definition.   Given the two matrices A_{mp} and B_{qn}, A and B are considered **conformable** if and only if $p = q$. (Note: If matrix A is conformable with matrix B, then multiplication between A and B can be performed.)

Definition.   Given two conformable matrices A_{mp} and B_{pn},

$$C = \{c(i, j)\} = A * B$$

```
procedure rmat(m,n: integer; var zz:matrix);
    var i,j,num: integer;
    begin
      num :=m*n;    writeln(' Enter ',num:3, ' real numbers,',
                                    ' one per line.');
      (** Read numbers, one per line !! **)
      for i := 1 to m do
            for j := 1 to n do readln(zz[i,j]);
    end;
procedure pmat(m,n:integer; yy:matrix);
    var  i,j: integer; x:real;
    begin
       for i := 1 to m do begin
            for j := 1 to n do begin
                                    x:=yy[i,j];
                                    write(x:8:2);
                                  end;
              writeln;
                              end;
      end;
procedure matadd(m,n: integer; y,z:matrix; var xx: matrix);
    var i,j: integer;
    begin
       for i := 1 to m do
                for j := 1 to n do
                          xx[i,j] := y[i,j]+z[i,j];
      end;
```

Figure 8.1   Procedures for Example 8.1

```
program matrix(input,output);
type   matrix = array[1..10,1..10] of real;
var    a,b,c: matrix;
       ($i fig81.pas) (**include**) (*TURBO Pascal*)
begin(** Test program **)
       rmat(5,7,a);    writeln; writeln;
       pmat(5,7,a); (* Always echo data after entering *)
       b := a;         writeln;  writeln;
       matadd(5,7,a,b,c);
       pmat(5,7,c);
end.
```

(a) Test program that uses procedures in Figure 8.1

1.00	1.00	1.00	1.00	1.00	1.00	1.00
2.00	2.00	2.00	2.00	2.00	2.00	2.00
3.00	3.00	3.00	3.00	3.00	3.00	3.00
4.00	4.00	4.00	4.00	4.00	4.00	4.00
5.00	5.00	5.00	5.00	5.00	5.00	5.00

2.00	2.00	2.00	2.00	2.00	2.00	2.00
4.00	4.00	4.00	4.00	4.00	4.00	4.00
6.00	6.00	6.00	6.00	6.00	6.00	6.00
8.00	8.00	8.00	8.00	8.00	8.00	8.00
10.00	10.00	10.00	10.00	10.00	10.00	10.00

(b) Matrix output from test program

Figure 8.2   Solution to Example 8.1

provided that

$$c(i, j) = \sum_{k=1}^{p} a(i, k) * b(k, j) \qquad \text{for all } i \text{ and } j$$

Definition.   Given a square matrix $I_{mm} = \{i(i, j)\}_{mm}$, I is called an **identity matrix** if $i(i, j) = 1$ when $i = j$ and $i(i, j) = 0$ otherwise.

Example 8.3

Which pairs of the following matrices are conformable? Find the product of all the conformable pairs.

$$I = \begin{bmatrix} 1.0 & 0.0 & 0.0 \\ 0.0 & 1.0 & 0.0 \\ 0.0 & 0.0 & 1.0 \end{bmatrix} \qquad A = \begin{bmatrix} 1.0 & 2.0 \\ 3.0 & 4.0 \\ 5.0 & 0.0 \end{bmatrix} \qquad B = \begin{bmatrix} 1.0 & 2.0 & 3.0 \\ 0.0 & 1.0 & 2.0 \end{bmatrix}$$

$$C = \begin{bmatrix} 1.0 \\ 2.0 \\ 3.0 \end{bmatrix}$$

Solution I is conformable with A and with C. A is conformable with B. B is conformable with I, A, and C.

By the definition of matrix multiplication, the following products are obtained:

$$I * A = \begin{bmatrix} 1.0 & 2.0 \\ 3.0 & 4.0 \\ 5.0 & 0.0 \end{bmatrix} \qquad I * C = \begin{bmatrix} 1.0 \\ 2.0 \\ 3.0 \end{bmatrix} \qquad A * B = \begin{bmatrix} 1.0 & 4.0 & 7.0 \\ 3.0 & 10.0 & 17.0 \\ 5.0 & 10.0 & 15.0 \end{bmatrix}$$

$$B * I = \begin{bmatrix} 1.0 & 2.0 & 3.0 \\ 0.0 & 1.0 & 2.0 \end{bmatrix} \qquad B * A = \begin{bmatrix} 22.0 & 10.0 \\ 13.0 & 4.0 \end{bmatrix} \qquad B * C = \begin{bmatrix} 14.0 \\ 8.0 \end{bmatrix}$$

Observe that when a matrix is multiplied by an identity matrix, the following relationships hold:

$$I * X = X$$
$$Y * I = Y$$

Example 8.4

Develop procedures for the following tasks.

(a) Accept a value of N and return an $N \times N$ identity matrix.

(b) Accept values of M, N, and P, an $M \times P$ matrix A, and a $P \times N$ matrix B. Return the product of these matrices.

Solution   A solution is given in Figure 8.3. In the test program, the matrices A and

```
program matrix(input,output);
type matrix = array[1..10,1..10] of real;
var iden,a,b,c,d:  matrix;
procedure identity(n:integer; var ii:matrix);
          var i,j:integer;
          (** Returns n by n identity matrix **)
          begin
              for i := 1 to n do
                  for j := 1 to n do
                      if i=j then ii[i,j] := 1.0
                             else ii[i,j] := 0.0;
          end;
procedure matmul(m,n,p:integer; a,b:matrix; var cc:matrix);
(* returns the product of an mxp matrix and a pxn matrix *)
          var i,j,k: integer;
          begin
              for i := 1 to m do
                  for j := 1 to n do
                      begin
                          cc[i,j]:= 0.0;
                          for k := 1 to p do
                              cc[i,j] := cc[i,j] + a[i,k]*b[k,j];
                      end;
          end;
($i fig81.pas)    (* INCLUDE *) (* TURBO Pascal *)
begin   (** Start test program **)
      identity(3,iden);    (* get I *)
      rmat(3,2,a);         (* get A *)
      pmat(3,2,a);
      rmat(2,3,b);         (* get B *)
      pmat(2,3,b); writeln;writeln;
      matmul(3,2,3,iden,a,c);    (* C = I*A *)
      pmat(3,2,c); writeln; writeln;
      matmul(2,2,3,b,a,d);       (* D = B*A *)
      pmat(2,2,d);
end.
```

Figure 8.3   A solution to Example 8.4

B from Example 8.3 are entered. The products *I* ∗ *A* and *B* ∗ *A* are determined and printed.

Matrix operations such as those covered in this section have a variety of applications. More advanced concepts in matrix theory will be introduced later, but in the following section we apply already introduced concepts to the solution of simultaneous equations.

REVIEW

1. Given the following matrices,

$$A = \begin{bmatrix} 1.0 & -1.0 & 2.0 & 3.0 \\ 1.2 & 3.0 & 4.5 & 4.2 \\ 2.0 & 4.0 & 3.0 & 1.0 \end{bmatrix} \qquad B = \begin{bmatrix} 1.0 & 2.0 & 3.0 \\ 4.0 & 3.0 & 2.0 \\ 1.0 & 0.0 & -1.0 \\ -2.0 & 1.0 & 1.5 \end{bmatrix}$$

$$C = \begin{bmatrix} 4.0 & 0.0 & 1.0 \\ 3.0 & 2.5 & 1.0 \\ 2.0 & 3.0 & 4.0 \end{bmatrix}$$

find the matrix *A* ∗ *B* + *C* ∗ *C*.
2. Use the procedures developed in this section to enter the data in Review Question 1 into the specified matrices, compute the matrix *A* ∗ *B* + *C* ∗ *C*, and print the resulting 3 x 3 matrix.
3. Develop and test a procedure that accepts values of *M* and *N* and three *M* × *N* matrices. The sum of the three matrices is returned.

8.2 SOLVING EQUATIONS

In order to analyze linear systems it is frequently necessary to solve sets of equations. A set of *N* equations in *N* unknowns is said to be **independent** if there is a single or unique solution. If there are many solutions, the set of linear equations is said to be **dependent.** A set of equations that has no valid solutions is said to be **inconsistent.**

In many physical applications, the fundamental laws of nature guarantee the formulation of a set of independent linear equations, frequently referred to as **simultaneous equations.** The following set of four simultaneous equations,

$$\begin{aligned} 4W + 8X + 12Y + -12Z &= 16 \\ 2W + 4X + -8Y + -4Z &= 6 \\ 3W + 6X + 6Y + -3Z &= 12 \\ 1W + 8X + 0Y + 9Z &= -2 \end{aligned}$$

can be rewritten using matrix notation:

$$\begin{bmatrix} 4 & 8 & 12 & -12 \\ 2 & 4 & -8 & -4 \\ 3 & 6 & 6 & -3 \\ 1 & 8 & 0 & 9 \end{bmatrix} \begin{bmatrix} W \\ X \\ Y \\ Z \end{bmatrix} = \begin{bmatrix} 16 \\ 6 \\ 12 \\ -2 \end{bmatrix}$$

The 4×4 matrix is called a **matrix of coefficients.** The 4×1 matrix, or **vector,** containing W, X, Y, and Z is called a **matrix of variables.** The 4×1 matrix on the right-hand side of the equation is called a **matrix of constants.** Multiplication of the matrix of coefficients by the matrix of variables yields a 4×1 matrix. Equating the corresponding elements with those in the matrix of constants yields the same set of equations as initially expressed in standard form.

When discussing solutions of simultaneous equations, it is convenient to express them in standard form. When implementing computer solutions, on the other hand, matrix notation is convenient. Suppose we wish to multiply by K the ith equation in a set of equations. This is the same as multiplying by K both the ith row in the matrix of coefficients and the ith element in the constant vector. Similarly, adding the pth equation to the qth equation is the same as adding the pth row in the matrix of coefficients to the qth row and then adding the pth element in the vector of constants to the qth element.

We have all previously solved sets of simultaneous equations such as the one just illustrated. One standard technique is to *eliminate* the variable W in all but the first equation, then eliminate the variable X in all but the second equation, and continue this process until we reach the last equation, which will contain just the variable Z. Once we know the value of Z, we can go back and find the values of the other variables.

Let us illustrate this technique with the same set of four equations in four unknowns. Assume the coefficient of W in the first equation is *not* 0. Then multiply the first equation by the reciprocal of the coefficient of W. This leaves the following set of equations:

$$1W + 2X + \quad 3Y + -3Z = \quad 4$$
$$2W + 4X + -8Y + -4Z = \quad 6$$
$$3W + 6X + \quad 6Y + -3Z = 12$$
$$1W + 8X + \quad 0Y + \quad 9Z = -2$$

To eliminate W in all but the first equation, we:

(a) Add -2 times the first equation to the second equation.
(b) Add -3 times the first equation to the third equation.
(c) Add -1 times the first equation to the fourth equation.

This leaves the following set of equations:

$$
\begin{aligned}
1W + 2X + \quad 3Y + -3Z &= \quad 4 \\
0W + 0X + -14Y + \quad 2Z &= -2 \\
0W + 0X + \quad -3Y + \quad 6Z &= \quad 0 \\
0W + 6X + \quad -3Y + \ 12Z &= -6
\end{aligned}
$$

The next step is to eliminate X from the third and fourth equations. To do this in the same way we eliminated W from the second, third, and fourth equations, we first multiply the second equation by the reciprocal of the coefficient of X. But this *cannot* be done, since the coefficient of X in the second equation is zero. This shows that we first must check to see if the coefficient of X is zero. If not, then we can multiply the second equation by the reciprocal of the coefficient. If this coefficient *is* zero, then we may *exchange* this equation with one of the remaining equations. After all, the order in which we write the equations does not matter.

Suppose we swap the second equation with the third. After this swap, the coefficient of X is still zero. Thus, we should never swap the position of two equations unless it causes the zero-valued coefficient to be replaced with one that is not zero. If none of the remaining equations permits such a swap, then the set of equations is either dependent or inconsistent, and a unique solution cannot be obtained.

In our set of equations, we can exchange the second equation with the fourth equation, a swap that yields the following set of equations:

$$
\begin{aligned}
1W + 2X + \quad 3Y + -3Z &= \quad 4 \\
0W + 6X + \quad -3Y + \ 12Z &= -6 \\
0W + PX + \quad -3Y + \quad 6Z &= \quad 0 \\
0W + QX + -14Y + \quad 2Z &= -2
\end{aligned}
$$

where $P = 0$ and $Q = 0$.

Next we multiply the second equation by the reciprocal of 6. Then, in order to eliminate X from the remaining equations, we add $-P$ times the second equation to the third equation. Likewise, we add $-Q$ times the second equation to the fourth equation. This yields

$$
\begin{aligned}
1W + 2X + \quad 3Y + -3Z &= \quad 4 \\
0W + 1X + -.5Y + \quad 2Z &= -1 \\
0W + 0X + \quad -3Y + \quad 6Z &= \quad 0 \\
0W + 0X + -14Y + \quad 2Z &= -2
\end{aligned}
$$

Since the coefficient of Y in the third equation is not zero, we multiply the third equation by the reciprocal of the coefficient of Y, then add $-(-14)$ times the third equation to the fourth equation, yielding

$$
\begin{aligned}
1W + 2X + \quad 3Y + \ -3Z &= \quad 4 \\
0W + 1X + -.5Y + \quad 2Z &= -1 \\
0W + 0X + \quad 1Y + \ -2Z &= \quad 0 \\
0W + 0X + \quad 0Y + -26Z &= -2
\end{aligned}
$$

Finally, we check to see if the coefficient of Z in the fourth equation is zero. Since it is not, we multiply the fourth equation by the reciprocal of this coefficient, and the fourth equation becomes

$$0W + 0X + 0Y + 1Z = \frac{-2}{-26}$$

or

$$Z = \frac{2}{26}$$

Thus, we have found the value of one of the unknowns using the elimination method.

Let us review the procedure. First we check the coefficient of the first variable in the first equation. If it is not zero, we multiply the first equation by its reciprocal, then eliminate the first variable from the other equations by adding an appropriate constant times the first equation to each of the other equations. Next we check the coefficient of the second variable in the second equation to see if it is zero. If not, we multiply the second row by its reciprocal and then eliminate the second variable in the subsequent equations. The process is continued until the last equation yields the value of the last variable.

Suppose, however, that we are about to multiply the ith equation by the reciprocal of the coefficient of the ith variable and find that the coefficient *is* zero. We then try to exchange this equation with one of the remaining equations that does not have a zero coefficient in the corresponding position. If such an exchange is possible, the process continues. If not, the set of simultaneous equations has no unique solution.

It is relatively easy to program the subtasks required to solve simultaneous equations. But there is one possible pitfall. If we wish to check the ith coefficient of the ith equation to see if it is zero, we might consider using a Pascal command such as

if coefficient = 0.0 then try_to_swap_two_equations;

or

if coefficient <> 0.0 then multiply_by_reciprocal;

Although these Pascal statements are certainly logical, such statements should *not* be used. Recall that the coefficients are *real* numbers, or *floating points*. As discussed in Section 1.2, most floating point values cannot be represented exactly, only approximately, and this is true in any number system. For example, in the expression

$$X = \frac{2.0}{3.0} - 2.0* \frac{1.0}{3.0}$$

x clearly should have a value of zero. Now suppose we approximate each of the quotients as well as possible with five-digit real numbers. Then

$$\frac{2.0}{3.0} \cong .66667$$

and

$$\frac{1.0}{3.0} \cong .33333$$

If we substitute these "best" approximations in the above equation, then

$$x = .66667 - 2.0 * .33333 = .66667 - .66666 = .00001$$

which is not zero. Now, if we are comparing x with a set of numbers whose magnitudes are between 1 and 10, then x is relatively small, perhaps insignificant. On the other hand, if we compare x with numbers having magnitudes between .0000000001 and .00000000001, then the value of x is relatively large.

We should *never* use the relational operators "=" or "<>" when trying to identify specific values of real numbers. Instead of statement segments such as

if x = 0.0 then . . .

we should use

if abs(x) < EPSILON then . . .

where EPSILON is a small positive constant.

Likewise, instead of using

if x <> 0.0 then . . .

we should substitute a statement such as

if abs(x) > EPSILON then . . .

Since EPSILON is to be a small positive number, how *small* is *small?* A good working rule is: If the magnitudes of typical nonzero coefficients are within an order of magnitude, then the value of EPSILON should be four or five times smaller than that order of magnitude. For example, suppose all nonzero coefficients in a matrix of coefficients have magnitudes between 1 and 10. Then values of EPSILON between 1.0E-4 and 1.0E-5 are good approximations. On the other hand, if all nonzero coefficients have magnitudes in the order of 1.0E10, then we would consider 1.0E05 to be a small value of EPSILON.

If a matrix of coefficients has some values with very large magnitudes and other nonzero coefficients with very small magnitudes, the matrix is said to be **ill-conditioned.** No computer techniques guarantee good solutions to systems of equations having ill-conditioned matrices. Systems of simultaneous equations that describe real physical systems are generally *not* ill-conditioned.

Example 8.5

Develop procedures to perform the following tasks.

(a) Exchange two rows in an $n \times n$ matrix. The corresponding elements in a vector should also be exchanged.

(b) Assuming the ith coefficient in the ith equation of a set of n simultaneous equations is approximately zero, swap the ith row of the matrix of coefficients with a subsequent row and the ith element of a vector of constants with the corresponding subsequent element if and only if the swap yields a nonzero coefficient in the ith row and column. If an exchange *cannot* be made, this information is returned from the procedure.

(c) Request n real numbers to be entered, and assign these numbers to the first n elements of a vector.

(d) Multiply the kth row of an $n \times n$ matrix as well as the kth element of a vector by a specified real number.

(e) Add a constant times the pth row of an $n \times n$ matrix to the qth row. Also add the constant times the pth element of a vector to the qth element.

Solution   Procedures for the specified tasks are shown in Figure 8.4.

Example 8.6

Develop and test a procedure that accepts a value n, an $n \times n$ matrix of coefficients, and a vector of n constants. The data describe a set of n simultaneous equations. The procedure returns the value of one of the unknowns, the last one, if the set of equations has a unique solution. A boolean value is returned to indicate whether or not a unique solution exists.

Solution   A solution with a test program is given in Figure 8.5. The procedures RMAT and PMAT are included in FIG81.PAS. The procedures shown in Figure 8.4 are stored in a file called FIG84.PAS.

The procedure FIND_ROOT in Figure 8.5 finds the value of only one of the unknowns, the last one, if a unique solution exists. Now consider the four equations in four unknowns discussed earlier in this section. We wrote the W variable and its coefficients in the first column and the Z variable and its coefficients in the fourth column. If we exchange the first column with the fourth column, the equations are still the same. But application of the same elimination technique now yields the value of W rather than the value of Z. Thus, we can find the value of any of the unknowns using FIND_ROOT if we first exchange the appropriate column with the last column of the matrix of coefficients.

Example 8.7

Develop a procedure that will solve n equations in n unknowns if a unique solution exists. Test this procedure for the following sets of equations:

(a) $X + Y = 5$
$\quad\quad X - Y = -3$

```
procedure row_swap(p,q,n:integer; var aa:matrix; var xx:vector);
(** Exchanges rows p and q of an nxn matrix,aa.  Also exchanges
    elements p and q in vector, xx **)
    var temp:real; j: integer;
      begin
        for j:=1 to n do                    begin
                        temp :=aa[p,j];
                        aa[p,j] := aa[q,j];
                        aa[q,j] := temp;         end;
            temp:=xx[p]; xx[p]:=xx[q]; xx[q] :=temp;
        end (*row_swap*);
procedure check(j,n:integer; var  aaa:matrix; var xxx:vector;
                                          var ff: boolean);
(** This procedure is entered if the coefficient aaa[j,j] in a
    set of n linear equations has a value of 0.0.  The procedure
    exchanges the equation with a subsequent equation if and
    only if after the exchange is made, the new value of aaa[j,j]
    will NOT be zero.  If the exchange cannot be made, the set of
    equations does not have a unique solution, and a value,
    ff = FALSE is returned!  **)
    var k:integer;
      begin
        ff := false;  k := j +1;
        while (k <= n) and not ff do
            if abs(aaa[k,j]) > EPSILON then begin
                                      ff := true;
                                      row_swap(j,k,n,aaa,xxx)
                                         end
                              else k:=k+1;
      end;
procedure rvec(n:integer; var vvvv:vector);
(*  reads constants into a vector *)
    var i: integer;
    begin    writeln(' Enter ',n:2, ' constants, one per line.');
             writeln; for i := 1 to n do readln(vvvv[i]);
             writeln;
    end;
procedure multx(k,n:integer; x:real; var az:matrix;
                                      var xz:vector);
(** Multiplies kth equation in set of n equations by a
    constant, x **)
    var j:  integer;
        begin  xz[k] := x*xz[k];
               for j:= 1 to n do az[k,j] := x * az[k,j];
        end;
procedure addeq(p,q,n:integer; x:real; var aaz:matrix;
                                      var xxz:vector);
(*  Adds x times pth equation to qth equation in a set
    of n simultaneous equations *)
    var j:integer;
      begin
            xxz[q] := xxz[q] + x*xxz[p];
            for j := 1 to n do
                    aaz[q,j] := aaz[q,j] + x*aaz[p,j];
      end;
```

Figure 8.4   Solution to Example 8.5

```
program find_root(input,output);
type  matrix = array[1..10,1..10] of real;
      vector = array[1..10] of real;
 const EPSILON = 1.0E-5;
 var  i,n:integer; answer:real; ok:boolean;
                   a:matrix; x: vector;
 {$i fig81.pas} (* INCLUDE *) (* TURBO Pascal *)
 {$i fig84.pas} (* TURBO Pascal *)
 procedure find_root(n:integer; a:matrix; x:vector;
                     var root: real; var flag: boolean);
 (* If flag returned is TRUE, one root from a system of
    n simultaneous equations is returned.  If flag is
    FALSE, system of equations is either dependent or
    inconsistent *)
    var i,j: integer;
    begin
       flag := true;  i := 1;
       while flag and (i<=n) do
          begin
             if abs(a[i,i]) < EPSILON then check(i,n,a,x,flag);
             if flag then
                begin
                   multx(i,n,1.0/a[i,i],a,x);
                   if i<> n then for j:= i+1 to n do
                      addeq(i,j,n,-a[j,i],a,x);
                end;
             i := i + 1;
          end;
       root := x[n];
    end;
 begin(** Start test program *)
    n :=2;
    rmat(n,n,a); writeln; pmat(n,n,a); writeln;
    rvec(n,x); writeln;
    for i:=1 to n do writeln(x[i]:20:4); writeln;
    find_root(n,a,x,answer,ok);
    if ok then writeln(answer:10:3) else writeln(' BAD');
 end.
```

Figure 8.5   Solution to Example 8.6

(b) $X - 2Y + 0.5Z = 4$
       $X - \ \ Y + \ \ 2Z = 0$
       $2X - 4Y + \ \ \ \ Z = -2$

(c) $14W + 3X + 0Y + \ \ Z = \ \ 5$
       $3W - 2X + \ \ Y + 2Z = -2$
       $-10W + \ \ X + 3Y - \ \ Z = \ \ 1$
       $7W + 2X + 4Y + 2Z = \ \ 4$

(d) $10V + 2W - \ \ X + 0Y + \ \ Z = 16$
       $-5V - 3W - \ \ X + 5Y - 2Z = -4$
       $V + \ \ W + \ \ X + \ \ Y - \ \ Z = \ \ 5$
       $8V + 2W + 3X + 0Y - 2Z = 11$
       $2V + \ \ W + \ \ X - \ \ Y + 0Z = \ \ 3$

Solution   The procedure SOLVE_SIM shown in Figure 8.6 can be used to solve a set of n simultaneous equations. Observe that this procedure invokes FIND_ROOT, which is now stored in a file called FIG5a.PAS. Another procedure used by SOLVE_SIM, called

```
program solve(input,output);
type  matrix = array[1..10,1..10] of real;
      vector = array[1..10] of real;
 const EPSILON = 1.0E-5;
 var  n:integer; answer:vector; ok:boolean;
                    a:matrix; x: vector;
 ($i fig81.pas) (* INCLUDE *) (* TURBO Pascal *)
 ($i fig84.pas) (* TURBO Pascal *)
 ($i fig85a.pas) (* TURBO Pascal *)
 procedure pvec(n:integer; v:vector);
 (*  Prints the n numbers in a vector *)
     var i:integer;
     begin
             writeln;
             for i:= 1 to n do writeln(v[i]:20:2);
             writeln;
        end;
 procedure swap_cols(p,q,n: integer; var mm:matrix);
 (*  Exchanges columns p and q in an n by n matrix *)
     var i:integer; x:real;
     begin
         for i := 1 to n do begin
                                 x:=mm[i,p];
                                 mm[i,p]:= mm[i,q];
                                 mm[i,q]:=x;
                             end;
     end;
 procedure solve_sim(n:integer; a:matrix; v:vector;
                       var ans:vector; var success:boolean);
 (* Solves a set of n independent simultaneous equations.
    If set is dependent or inconsistent, a value of
    success = FALSE is returned.   *)
    const EPSILON = 1.0E-5;
    var i: integer;
             begin
                 i:= 1;  success :=true;
                 while success and (i<=n) do
                     begin
                         swap_cols(i,n,n,a);
                         find_root(n,a,v,ans[i],success);
                         swap_cols(i,n,n,a); (* "Unswap" *)
                         i:=i+1;
                     end;
         end;
 begin (*  Start test program *)
     for n := 2 to 5 do
         begin
             rmat(n,n,a); writeln; pmat(n,n,a); writeln;
             rvec(n,x); writeln; pvec(n,x); writeln;
             solve_sim(n,a,x,answer,ok);
             if ok then pvec(n,answer) else
                 writeln(' Set of equations is not independent.');
         end;
 end.
```

Figure 8.6   Solution to Example 8.7 (Solving *n* equations in *n* unknowns)

SWAP_COLS, is also shown in Figure 8.6. The given test program will accommodate the four sets of equations specified in this example. When data for these four sets of equations are entered, solutions to two of the systems will be returned and printed: One set of equations is inconsistent; another set is consistent but not independent.

REVIEW

1. Refer to the program in Figure 8.5. What number will be printed when the following data are entered as the program is run?

1.0
2.0
1.0
−2.0

5.0
−3.0

2. Use the procedure SOLVE_SIM to find the solutions to the equations shown in Example 8.7. Which two sets of equations are not independent? What are the values of the unknowns in the other two equations?
3. Suppose the nonzero coefficients and constants in a set of simultaneous equations all have magnitudes in the neighborhood of 10^5. Select an appropriate value of EPSILON. Using this value and the procedure SOLVE_SIM, solve the following sets of equations. (Note: Only one of these sets is independent.)

   (a) $53000.0X + 120000.0Y = 220000.0$
          $159000.0X + 360000.0Y = 660000.0$

   (b) $.65E5X + 1.32E5Y + .76E6Z = 1.0E5$
          $1.2E5X + 2.0E5Y + .86E6Z = 2.2E5$
          $.55E5X + .68E5Y + .1E6Z = 1.2E5$

   (c) $2.5E5W + 4.0E5X + 2.0E5Y + 7.0E5Z = 4.0E5$
          $2.0E5W + 1.0E5X − 2.0E5Y + 3.0E5Z = −2.0E5$
          $−1.0E5W + .3E6X + 3.0E5Y − 1.0E6Z = 1.0E5$
          $1.0E5W + 0.0X + .3E6Y + .14E7Z = .5E6$

8.3 OPERATIONS ON COMPLEX NUMBERS

Complex numbers appear in a variety of applications in engineering and science. Recall that a complex number C may be expressed as

$$C = A + Bi$$

where A and B are real numbers and i is the square root of -1. In engineering applications, a complex number is generally expressed in a slightly different form,

$$C = A + jB$$

where j is the square root of -1. The real number A is called the *real* part of the complex number. The real number B is called the *imaginary*, or the j, part of the complex number. This is called the **rectangular** representation of a complex number.

Frequently, a complex number is defined as an *ordered pair* of real numbers, a definition that implies that the second number in the pair is multiplied by j.

Specific complex numbers may be represented as points on the **complex plane.** Consider the following two complex numbers:

$$X = 3 + j4$$

$$Y = -2 + j(-2) = -2 - j2$$

Representation of these numbers as points on the complex plane is given in Figure 8.7. Observe that the point X may be represented in classical rectangular form or simply as the ordered pair of real numbers (3.0, 4.0). Y is similarly represented.

An alternate way to represent a complex number is to specify a **distance** from the origin at a specified angle. This is the **polar** representation of a complex number. Observe that the distance may be computed with the Pythagorean Theorem. Also observe that the tangent of the angle θ is the imaginary part of the complex number divided by the real part. Thus,

$$\text{angle} = \theta = \arctan\left(\frac{B}{A}\right)$$

where B is the imaginary part and A is the real part of the complex number.

The numbers X and Y represented in polar form are approximately

$$X = 5\angle 53.2°$$

$$Y = 2.82\angle -135°$$

Let us consider the four standard arithmetic operations: addition, subtraction, multiplication, and division. Let

$$P = A + jB$$

$$Q = C + jD$$

Then:

Addition:	$P + Q = (A + C) + j(B + D)$
Subtraction:	$P - Q = (A - C) + j(B - D)$
Multiplication:	$P * Q = (A + jB) * (C + jD) = A * C + jA * D + jB * C + j * j * B * D$

But $j * j = -1$. Therefore,

$$P * Q = (A * C - B * D) + j(A * D + B * C)$$

Before illustrating division, we must present a definition.

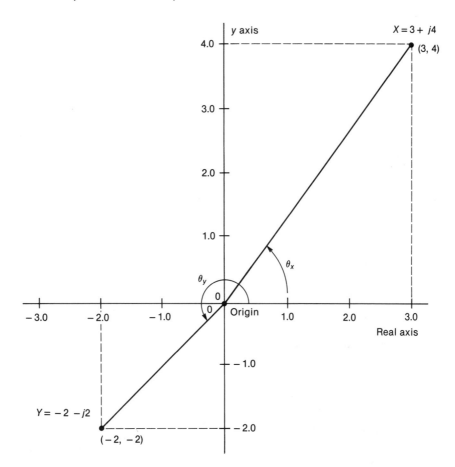

Figure 8.7   Representing complex numbers as points on the complex plane

Definition.   Given a complex number $C = A + jB$, the **conjugate** of C is the complex number $A - jB$.

Division: $\dfrac{P}{Q} = \dfrac{A + jB}{C + jD}$

Multiply the top and bottom of this expression by the conjugate of Q. Then

$$\frac{P}{Q} = \frac{A * C + B * D}{C * C + D * D} + \frac{j(B * C - A * D)}{C * C + D * D}$$

The Pascal programming language generally does not provide facilities for performing operations on complex numbers. But it is easy to develop a set of user-defined functions and procedures to manipulate complex quantities. Since a complex number is an ordered pair of real numbers, we can define a complex data type with the following statement:

type   complex = array[1..2] of real;

Then when developing functions, we interpret the first element of the array as the real part and the second element as the imaginary part of a complex number. Unfortunately, Pascal functions cannot return a structured data type, such as an array. Therefore, we must use a procedure if we wish a subprogram to return a complex quantity.

Extensive computations on complex quantities can be performed with a relatively small set of functions and procedures. In Figure 8.8, a set of user-defined subprograms

Function	Comment
1. creal(a:complex):real;	Returns real part of a complex number
2. cimag(a:complex):real;	Returns imaginary part of a complex number
3. cabs(a:complex): real;	Returns magnitude of a complex number
4. cang(a:complex): real;	Returns angle (in degrees) of a complex number

Procedure	Comment
5. cread(var cc:complex);	Accepts two real numbers from console and assigns them to a complex variable
6. cwrite(a:complex);	Prints complex value
7. cconj(a:complex;var cc:complex);	Returns complex conjugate
8. cadd(a,b:complex;var cc:complex);	Returns complex sum
9. csub(a,b:complex;var cc:complex);	Returns $a - b$
10. cmul(a,b:complex;var cc:complex);	Returns complex product
11. cdiv(a,b:complex;var cc:complex);	Returns a/b
12. ccosh(a:complex;var cc:complex);	Returns complex hyperbolic cosine
13. csinh(a:complex;var cc:complex);	Returns complex hyperbolic sine
14. ccomplex(r,i:real;var cc:complex);	Converts two real numbers to a complex number
15. cpolar(mag,ang:real;var cc:complex);	Converts a magnitude and an angle (in degrees) to the corresponding complex number

Figure 8.8   Some user-defined subprograms for performing operations on complex numbers

is described. Once written, these subprograms should be stored in either a library file or an INCLUDE file so they are readily available when needed.

Example 8.8

Develop and test the following Pascal subprograms, which are defined in Figure 8.8:

(a) cread   (b) cwrite   (c) cimag

(d) cabs   (e) cadd   (f) cdiv

Solution   The subprograms are shown in Figure 8.9. After each subprogram is developed, we will assume it is placed in an INCLUDE file called CSUBS.PAS. A test program using these subprograms is shown in Figure 8.10.

Suppose we wish to represent a complex number in polar form. We have already developed a function that returns the magnitude of a complex number.

```
procedure cread(var cc:complex);
   (** The user is prompted with "cpx:".  Then two character
       stings representing real numbers are to be entered on
       the same line.  DO NOT ENTER a "j" !! **)
   begin
         write(' cpx:    ');  readln(cc[1],cc[2]);
   end;
procedure cwrite(a:complex);
   (** Prints a complex number.  **)
   begin
         writeln(a[1]:12:2,'   +   j ', a[2]:12:2);
   end;
function  cimag(a:complex):real;
   (** Returns imaginary part of complex number **)
   begin
          cimag := a[2];
   end;
function cabs(a:complex):real;
   (** Returns magnitude of a complex number **)
   var x:real;
   begin
          x := sqrt(a[1]*a[1] + a[2]*a[2]);
          cabs :=x;
   end;
procedure cadd(a,b:complex; var cc: complex);
   (** Returns sum of two complex numbers **)
   begin
          cc[1]:= a[1] + b[1];  cc[2] := a[2] + b[2];
   end;
procedure cdiv(a,b:complex; var cc: complex);
   (** Returns complex quotient, a/b **)
   var x:real;
   begin
          x := b[1]*b[1] + b[2]*b[2];
          cc[1] := (a[1]*b[1] + a[2]*b[2])/x;
          cc[2] := (a[2]*b[1] - a[1]*b[2])/x;
   end;
```

Figure 8.9 Subprograms for Example 8.8

```
program test(input,output);
    type complex = array[1..2] of real;
    var cx,cy,cz:  complex;    x,y,z:   real;
    ($i csubs.pas) (** INCLUDE **) (** TURBO Pascal **)
    begin (** Start test program **)
        cread(cx);(** Enter:     8.0   -6.0 **)
        cwrite(cx);
        cread (cy); (** Enter: -5.0    10.0 **)
        cwrite(cy);
        x:=cimag(cx);  y:=cabs(cx);
        writeln(x:10:2,y:10:2);
        cadd(cx,cy,cz);
        cwrite(cz);
        cadd(cy,cy,cz);
        cdiv(cz,cx,cz);
        cwrite(cz);
    end.
```

Figure 8.10   Test program for Example 8.8

Observe from Figure 8.7 that the angle is obtained by taking the arctangent of the imaginary part over the real part. But also observe that the angle may be in one of four quadrants. Most ATAN functions require just a single argument; thus, they can return angles only in the principal quadrants, the first and fourth.

Example 8.9

Develop each of the following subprograms.

(a) An arctangent function that accepts two arguments, y and x, and returns the arctangent of y/x in the proper quadrant. If x is approximately 0, and the magnitude of y is significantly larger than the magnitude of x, then an angle with magnitude 90° will be returned. If both x and y are approximately 0, a message is printed indicating an indeterminate form.

(b) A procedure CCOMPLEX that converts two real numbers to the corresponding complex number.

(c) A function CANG that returns the angle (in degrees) of a complex number.
Solution   The subprograms, shown in Figure 8.11, are also appended to the file CSUBS.PAS. A test program is shown in Figure 8.12.

The function ATAN2 in Figure 8.11 returns arctangent(y/x) in the proper quadrant. The development of this function is straightforward when neither y nor x has a value of 0.0. Since real numbers cannot be represented exactly, and since roundoff errors may accrue, we consider a number to be 0.0 if its absolute value is less than EPS. In this program, EPS is selected to be 1.0E-20. If x has a nominal value of 0.0, the function returns a value of either $\pi/2$ or $-\pi/2$, depending on whether y is positive or negative. If y is also 0.0, then the quotient y/x is an indeterminate form. If x is considered to be 0.0, we consider y to be 0.0 if its absolute value is less than 100 * EPS.

When developing the function ATAN2, certain approximations were made. Although approximations are never perfect, they are considered good if they yield acceptable answers for the types of problems we plan to work.

```
function creal(a:complex):real;
    begin
          creal := a[1];
    end;
function atan2(y,x:real): real;
    const  EPS = 1.0E-20;
           PI = 3.14159265;
    var z: real;
    begin
      if abs(x) < EPS then  (** x is approximately 0.0 **)
                            if abs(y) < (100.0*EPS ) then
    (** x & y are both 0.0 **)   writeln(' Indeterminate form',
                              '.  0.0 is returned.')
                                                              else
                        BEGIN
                        z:= PI/2.0; (* 90 degrees *)
                        if y < 0.0 then z:= -z
                        END
                else z := arctan(abs(y)/abs(x));
    (** Find angle if y = 0.0 **)
      if(abs(y)<EPS)and(abs(x)>EPS) then if x>0.0 then z:=0.0
                                             else z:=PI;
    (** Now find quadrant **)  (** neither x nor y are 0.0 **)
      if (abs(x) > EPS) and (abs(y) > EPS)  then     BEGIN
      if (x < 0.0) and (y > 0.0) then (** second quadrant **)
                                z := PI -z;
      if (x < 0.0) and (y < 0.0) then (** third quadrant **)
                                z := PI + z;
      if (x > 0.0) and (y < 0.0) then (** fourth quadrant **)
                                z := -z;
                                                     END;
atan2:=z;
    end;

procedure ccomplex(r,i: real; var cc:complex);
  (** Converts a pair of real numbers to a complex number **)
    begin
        cc[1] := r; cc[2] :=i;
    end;

function cang(a:complex): real;
  (** Returns angle ( degrees)  of a complex number **)
    var x:real;
    begin
        x := atan2(cimag(a),creal(a)) * 180.0/3.14159265;
        cang := x;
    end;
```

Figure 8.11 Subprograms for Example 8.9

Example 8.10

Develop and test a procedure that returns the complex hyperbolic cosine of a complex argument.

Solution The following identities are useful if we wish to evaluate either CCOSH or CSINH:

$$ccosh(A + jB) = \cosh(A) * \cos(B) + j \sinh(A) * \sin(B)$$

$$csinh(A + jB) = \sinh(A) * \cos(B) + j \cosh(A) * \sin(B)$$

```
program test(input,output);
     type complex = array[1..2] of real;
     var a:complex; x: real;
     ($i csubs.pas) (** INCLUDE**) (** TURBO Pascal **)
     begin
          ccomplex(4.0,3.0,a);
          x:=cang(a);   writeln(x:10:2);
          ccomplex(-4.0,3.0,a);
          x:=cang(a);   writeln(x:10:2);
          ccomplex(-4.0,-3.0,a);
          x:=cang(a);   writeln(x:10:2);
          ccomplex(4.0,-3.0,a);
          x:=cang(a);   writeln(x:10:2);
          ccomplex(2.0,0.0,a);
          x:=cang(a);   writeln(x:10:2);
          ccomplex(-1.0,0.0,a);
          x:=cang(a);   writeln(x:10:2);
          ccomplex(0.0,0.0,a);
          x:=cang(a);   writeln(x:10:2);
          ccomplex(0.0,4.0,a);
          x:=cang(a);   writeln(x:10:2);
          ccomplex(0.0,-2.1234,a);
          x:=cang(a);   writeln(x:10:2);
     end.
```

Figure 8.12   Test program for Example 8.9

A solution and a test program are shown in Figure 8.13. The function CCOSH should also be appended to the file CSUBS.PAS.

REVIEW

1. Refer to the program in Figure 8.10. When this program is run, the data identified in the comment statements are entered. After these data are echoed, three lines are printed. What is printed on each of the three lines?
2. Refer to the program in Figure 8.12. When this program is run, *ten* (not nine) lines are printed. What is printed on each line?
3. Refer to the procedure CPOLAR identified in Figure 8.8. Develop and test this procedure.

8.4 SELECTED EXAMPLES

The material covered in this chapter has numerous applications in engineering and the applied sciences. We will illustrate two examples in this section.

The following function is the ratio of two polynomials:

$$T(S) = \frac{2S^3 + 12S^2 + 8S + 6.5}{S^4 + 7S^3 + 6.5S^2 + 4S + 1}$$

```
program hyper(output);
  type complex = array[1..2] of real;
  var x: complex;
  {$i csubs.pas} (**INCLUDE **) (** TURBO Pascal **)
  procedure ccosh(a:complex;var cc:complex);
   (** Returns hyperbolic cosine of complex argument **)
   var cosh,sinh:real;
   begin
        cosh := 0.5*(exp(a[1]) + exp(-a[1]));
        sinh := 0.5*(exp(a[1]) - exp(-a[1]));
        cc[1] := cosh*cos(a[2]);
        cc[2] := sinh*sin(a[2]);
   end;
begin  (** Start test program **)
      ccomplex(0.0,0.0,x);
      ccosh(x,x);
      cwrite(x);
      ccomplex(0.0695865,0.495134,x);
      ccosh(x,x);
      cwrite(x);
end.
```

Figure 8.13   Solution to Example 8.10

Functions of this form are called **transfer functions** of linear systems. They can model a wide variety of systems. The variable S is in general a complex variable. But if we wish to obtain a **frequency response** of the system being modeled, we let

$$S = j\omega,$$

where $j\omega$ is a *pure* imaginary number. In physical systems, ω corresponds to frequency expressed in radians per second. For almost any value of frequency, the transfer function is a complex number.

Example 8.11

For the transfer function $T(S)$ displayed above, develop a program that computes the magnitude and angle of the transfer function for $s = j\omega$, as ω is varied from 0 to 10 radians per second in increments of 1 radian per second.

Solution   When $S = j\omega$, even powers of the variable are real numbers, and odd powers are pure imaginary numbers. For specified values of ω, both the numerator and the denominator of the transfer function may be expressed as complex numbers. A solution that uses subprograms developed in this chapter is shown in Figure 8.14.

Numerous problems in engineering and the sciences require the solution of sets of simultaneous equations. Consider Figure 8.15, which is an electrical circuit diagram. (The identical model could be used to represent a hydraulic circuit.) The circular elements represent **voltage sources.** The other elements in the network are **resistors.** There are five **meshes** in the network. (A *mesh* is a closed loop that does not enclose any other closed loop.) There are five mesh currents in this network, labeled i_1, i_2, i_3, i_4, and i_5. In a typical problem, the values of the voltage sources

```
program transfer_function(output);
    type complex = array[1..2] of real;
    var top,bottom,t: complex;   mag,ang,w:  real;
    ($i csubs.pas) (**INCLUDE **) (** TURBO Pascal **)
    begin
        w := 0.0 ;  writeln;
        while w <= 10.0 do
        begin
        ccomplex(-12.0*w*w +6.5,-2.0*w*w*w +8.0*w,top);
        ccomplex(w*w*w*w-6.5*w*w+1.0,-7.0*w*w*w+4*w,bottom);
        cdiv(top,bottom,t);
        mag:=cabs(t); ang :=cang(t);
        writeln(w:10:1,mag:12:2,ang:12:2);
        w:= w+1.0;
        end;
    end.
```

Figure 8.14   Solution to Example 8.11

and resistances are known or specified. The values of mesh currents must be computed. For the network in Figure 8.15 the values of mesh currents may be computed from the following set of equations:

$$r_{11}i_1 + r_{12}i_2 + r_{13}i_3 + r_{14}i_4 + r_{15}i_5 = v_1$$
$$r_{21}i_1 + r_{22}i_2 + r_{23}i_3 + r_{24}i_4 + r_{25}i_5 = v_2$$
$$r_{31}i_1 + r_{32}i_2 + r_{33}i_3 + r_{34}i_4 + r_{35}i_5 = v_3$$
$$r_{41}i_1 + r_{42}i_2 + r_{43}i_3 + r_{44}i_4 + r_{45}i_5 = v_4$$
$$r_{51}i_1 + r_{52}i_2 + r_{53}i_3 + r_{54}i_4 + r_{55}i_5 = v_5$$

The 5-by-5 matrix $R = \{r_{ij}\}$ is the matrix of coefficients, and the five-element vector $v = \{v_j\}$ is the vector of constants. If the values of these elements are known, the equations can be solved using the techniques and Pascal procedures developed in Section 8.2.

The values of the coefficients and constants can be obtained with the following rules. Refer to Figure 8.15.

1. The voltage v_j is the algebraic sum of the voltage sources around the jth loop or mesh. If the arrow associated with a voltage source is in the same direction as the corresponding loop current, the value of the source is added to the sum. If the two arrows point in opposite directions, the value of the voltage source is subtracted from the sum. For example, for the mesh identified by the mesh current i_1 in Figure 8.15, the constant v_1 is

$$v_1 = 12 - 6 - 3 + 1.5 = 4.5$$

2. Values in the matrix of coefficients are: (a) If $i = j$, then $r_{ij} = r_{ii} =$ the sum of all the resistance values around the ith loop; (b) if $i \langle \rangle j$, then $r_{ij} = -1$ times the value of resistance that is common to both mesh i and mesh j. Of course,

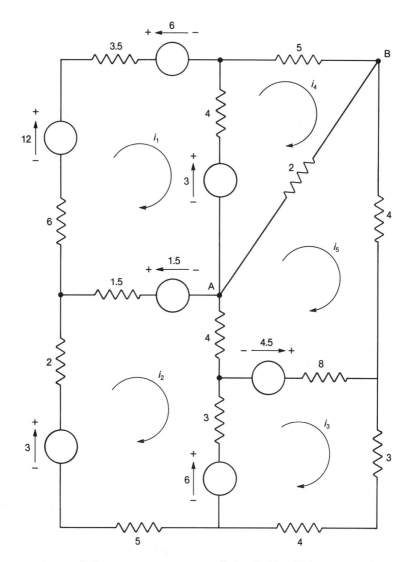

Figure 8.15   Circuit diagram representing a linear system

if there is no common resistor, the value is 0.0. For example, for mesh 1 in Figure 8.15), $r_{11} = 15.0$, $r_{14} = -4.0$, and $r_{15} = 0.0$.

Example 8.12

Refer to Figure 8.15. Find the mesh currents.
Solution   The matrix of coefficients is

$$R = \begin{bmatrix} 15.0 & -1.5 & 0.0 & -4.0 & 0.0 \\ -1.5 & 15.5 & -3.0 & 0.0 & -4.0 \\ 0.0 & -3.0 & 18.0 & 0.0 & -8.0 \\ -4.0 & 0.0 & 0.0 & 11.0 & -2.0 \\ 0.0 & -4.0 & -8.0 & -2.0 & 18.0 \end{bmatrix}$$

The vector of constants is

$$V = \begin{bmatrix} 4.5 \\ -4.5 \\ 10.5 \\ 3.0 \\ -4.5 \end{bmatrix}$$

The program in Figure 8.6 may be used to obtain the five mesh currents. One change should be made to the test program in Figure 8.6. The statement

for n := 2 to 5 do

should be replaced by the statement

n := 5

In some engineering applications, values of voltage sources and "resistors," such as shown in Figure 8.15, are complex numbers rather than real numbers. To solve these equations, a procedure similar to SOLVE_SIM in Figure 8.6 can be developed. The only difference is that operations are performed on complex rather than real numbers.

REVIEW

1. Refer to the program in Figure 8.14. When this program is run, eleven lines of output will be printed. What numbers are printed on the first line of output? What numbers are printed on the last line of output?
2. Refer to the circuit diagram in Figure 8.15. Find the five mesh currents.
3. Refer to Figure 8.15. If the resistor connected between points A and B (value of 2) is removed from the circuit, only four meshes will remain. Find the matrix of coefficients and the vector of constants. Then find the four mesh currents.

EXERCISES

1. Develop a function that returns the largest number in an m-by-n matrix.
2. Develop a procedure that returns the smallest "nonzero" number in an m-by-n matrix.
3. The **transpose** of an m-by-n matrix is an n-by-m matrix containing the same numbers, except the element in the ith row and jth column of the matrix is located in the jth row

and ith column of its transpose. Develop a procedure that accepts a matrix by value and returns its transpose; that is, the procedure has the following defining statement:

procedure transpose(m,n:integer; a:matrix; var bb:matrix);

Test this procedure in such a way that it replaces a matrix with its transpose.

4. Write and test a procedure that returns the difference of two $m \times n$ matrices.
5. Develop and test the following procedure:

rmatfile(m,n:integer; var aa:matrix)

which reads real numbers, one per line, from a text file identified as MYFILE, and assigns these numbers to the elements of an m-by-n matrix. Assume the text file has already been opened.

6. Develop a procedure

conmult(k:real; m,n:integer; var aa: matrix)

that multiplies every element of an m-by-n matrix by the constant k.

7. Develop a procedure that raises a k-by-k matrix to the nth power, where n is a nonnegative integer. Note: if $n = 0$, the k-by-k identity matrix is returned.

Use the following matrices for Exercises 8, 9, and 10:

$$A = \begin{bmatrix} 1.0 & 3.2 & 4.3 & -2.0 \\ 2.5 & -6.0 & -1.0 & -3.0 \\ 0.0 & 3.2 & 4.0 & 0.0 \\ 1.0 & 2.0 & 0.0 & 2.0 \end{bmatrix} \qquad B = \begin{bmatrix} 2.0 & 0.0 \\ 1.0 & -3.0 \\ -2.0 & 1.5 \\ 0.0 & 3.6 \end{bmatrix}$$

$$C = \begin{bmatrix} 4.0 & -1.0 & 2.0 & 3.5 \\ 0.0 & 2.0 & -3.0 & 1.0 \end{bmatrix}$$

8. Write a program that finds and prints $A + B * C$.
9. Write a program that finds and prints $A - 4.0 * B * C$. Note: Multiplying a matrix by a constant is defined as multiplying each element in the matrix by the constant.
10. Write a program that finds and prints A raised to the sixth power.
11. Develop and test a procedure that exchanges two specified columns in an m-by-n matrix.
12. Develop and test a procedure

addcol(p,q,m,n:integer; k:real; var aa:matrix)

that adds k times the pth column to the qth column of an m-by-n matrix.

13. One of the following sets of equations is independent. Use the procedure SOLVE_SIM to identify the set of independent equations and to find the six unknowns.

$$\begin{aligned}
\text{(a)} \qquad A + B + 3C + 2D + E + 3F &= 1 \\
-A - 2B + 1.5C + 2E - F &= 0 \\
2A + 3.5B + C - D - 3E + 2F &= -1 \\
A + 3B + 3C + 4D + E + F &= 5 \\
-1.5A - 1.5B + 3D + E + F &= 3.3 \\
0.5A + 2B - 2.5C - 4F &= 1.7
\end{aligned}$$

$$
\begin{array}{rrrrrrr}
\textbf{(b)} \quad - & A + & B + & C + & D + & E + & F = & 0 \\
 & 2A + & B + & & 2D + & E + & F = & -1 \\
 & -A + & B + & C + & D + & E - & 2F = & -3 \\
 & A + & & & D + & & F = & 1 \\
 & & B + & C - & D + & 2E + & F = & 3 \\
 & A - & B + & C - & D + & E - & F = & -4
\end{array}
$$

14. Develop and test the following procedures, which are described in Figure 8.8.
    (a) csub   **(b)** cmul   **(c)** cconj

    Append these procedures to an INCLUDE file or to a library of complex subprograms.
15. Develop and test the CSINH procedure described in Figure 8.8.
16. Develop a procedure that returns the square root of a complex number. Note: To find a square root of a complex number: (a) Convert the number to polar form; (b) take the square root of the magnitude; (c) divide the angle by 2; then (d) convert back to rectangular form.
17. Develop and test a procedure that raises a complex number to the nth power, where n is an integer. Note: To raise a complex number to the nth power: (a) If $n = 0$, then return $1.0 + j0.0$; (b) if $n > 0$, then raise the magnitude to the nth power and multiply the angle by n; or (c) if $n < 0$, then raise the reciprocal of the complex number to the $-n$th power.
18. Develop a procedure

    cexp(a:complex; var cc: complex)

    that raises the transcendental number e to a complex power. Recall from the laws of exponents that

    $$\exp(A + jB) = \exp(A) * \exp(jB)$$

    The factor $\exp(A)$ is a real number. The factor $\exp(jB)$ is complex and may be obtained from the following relationship, referred to as **Euler's Law:**

    $$\exp(jB) = \cos(B) + j\sin(B)$$

19. For the transfer function

    $$T(S) = \frac{s(S^3 + 12S^2 + 16S + 4)}{S^5 + 4S^4 + 9S^3 + 2S^2 + S + 1}$$

    let $S = j2 * PI * f$, where $PI = 3.1415 \ldots$. Then f is frequency, in Hertz (cycles per second). Develop a program that computes and prints the magnitude and angle of the transfer function for different frequencies as f is varied from 0 to 20 Hz in increments of 1 Hz.
20. For each circuit diagram in Figure 8.16:
    (a) Find the matrix of coefficients and the matrix of constants.
    (b) Use procedures developed in this section to find the mesh currents.
21. Develop and test procedures similar to the following procedures (which were developed in Figure 8.4):
    (a) check   **(b)** rvec   **(c)** multx   **(d)** addeq

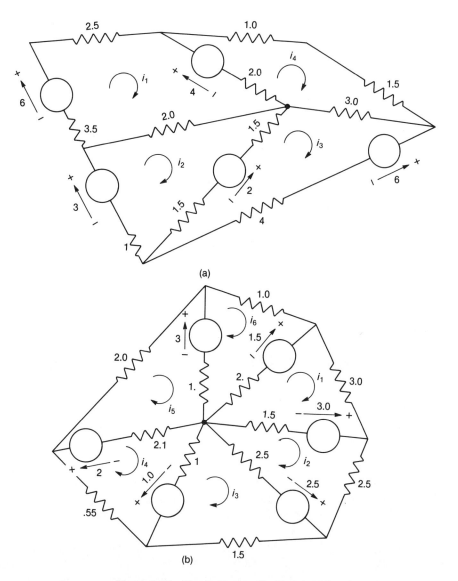

Figure 8.16 Circuit diagrams for Exercise 20

However, the new procedures should be able to perform their tasks on matrices whose elements are *complex* numbers rather than real numbers.

22. Develop a procedure that returns one root in a set of N simultaneous equations. Elements of both the matrix of coefficients and the matrix of constants are complex numbers.

23. Develop a procedure that returns values of the n unknowns in a set of n independent equations in which the coefficients and constants are complex.

9

Subprograms: Advanced Topics

Pascal is a **block-structured** programming language. The *main program* is considered a block, as are each function and procedure. In a sense, each block is independent of all other blocks, although certain variables from other blocks may be accessible. In this chapter, we identify the scope of Pascal variables.

Pascal functions and procedures were introduced in Chapter 3 and have been illustrated in numerous examples. Recall that each subprogram may include a set of local variables—that is, variables may be defined within the subprogram block. In addition, arguments may be carried into a subprogram by value, meaning the value of an argument is transmitted to a local variable. In this latter case, the local variable is defined within the call list of the subprogram declaration statement.

Transmitting arguments by value enables subprograms to function recursively; that is, a subprogram may invoke itself, as was illustrated in Section 3.2. At first, novice programmers may view recursive techniques as complicated and confusing. Yet their primary advantage is to ease programming! In this chapter we show how recursive techniques can perform programming tasks that would be quite difficult otherwise.

9.1 SCOPE OF VARIABLES

In previous examples in which we developed functions and procedures, these programming blocks were declared and defined within a main program block. Sometimes, main program variables were invoked by subprograms defined within the main program. In particular, variables associated with file names were defined within the main program and used within subprograms.

In previous examples, any variable declared in the main program was accessible to subprograms as long as the subprogram did not declare the same variable name. However, local variables defined in the subprograms could not be used by the main program or by other subprograms.

Procedures and functions may be declared and defined within any programming block. This means they may be declared within other procedures or functions. In Figure 9.1, the main program block is called DOG. The subprograms, or subblocks,

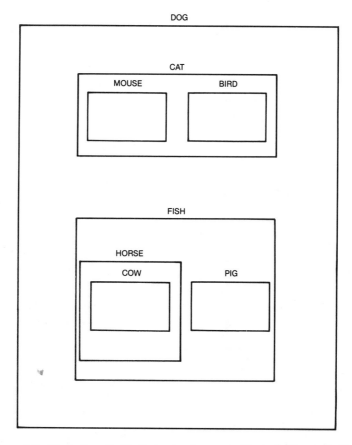

Figure 9.1   Illustration of a block-structured program. The lexical level of a block is the number of blocks enclosing it.

defined within DOG are CAT and FISH. Two subblocks are defined within each of those blocks. Note that the block called COW is a subblock of HORSE, which is a subblock of FISH.

The **lexical level** of a block in a block-structured language is the number of other blocks that enclose it. Thus, DOG has a lexical level of 0; CAT and FISH have lexical level 1; MOUSE, BIRD, HORSE, and PIG have lexical level 2; and COW has a lexical level of 3. Generally, level 0 is considered the highest. And lexical level i is greater than lexical level j if $j > i$.

A block of lexical level k may have access to its own variables and to some variables of lexical level $k - 1, k - 2, \ldots 0$. In particular, a block has access to its own variables and to the variables of all blocks enclosing it. However, if the same variable name is used by more than one of the enclosing blocks, the block has access to only the variable in the innermost block in which it is defined.

In a block-structured language, access to subprograms is similar to access to variables. A subprogram is accessible to the block enclosing it. Therefore, all subprograms of lexical level 1 are accessible at lexical level 0, meaning they are accessible to *all* blocks. Furthermore, all *system* subprograms are declared and defined at lexical level 1.

It is clear in Figure 9.1 that while both CAT and FISH can be invoked by DOG, subprograms MOUSE, BIRD, HORSE, COW, and PIG cannot. From the rules of access just stated, it appears that MOUSE may invoke itself, BIRD, CAT, or FISH. But there is one additional rule in Pascal: A subprogram may be invoked only if it has been declared previously. Thus, from a lexical viewpoint, MOUSE can *always* invoke CAT or MOUSE, but it can invoke BIRD and FISH only if they have previously been declared. From a practical viewpoint, recursive calls should be made only to subprograms designed to handle recursive calls.

Example 9.1

Develop a program that has a block structure identical to that shown in Figure 9.1. If the statements in the subprogram COW are then to be modified, which variables may be accessed by COW and which subprograms may be invoked by COW?

Solution A solution is given in Figure 9.2. If we wish to modify statements in the function COW, we would have access to: local variables b and e, which are declared in COW; variables c and d, which are declared in HORSE; and variable a, which is declared in FISH. The user-defined subprograms that may be invoked by COW are HORSE, FISH, CAT, and COW. Of course, COW should not invoke itself, since it is not developed in a way that can be used recursively.

REVIEW

1. Two lines of output are printed when the program in Figure 9.2 is run. What numbers are printed on each line?
2. Suppose the statements in the subprogram PIG in Figure 9.2 are to be modified.

```
program dog(output);
     var a,b:  integer;
 (*** CAT BLOCK ******************************************)
     procedure cat(var xx: integer);
        var b,c:  integer;
               function mouse(x:integer): integer;
                    var c,d:  integer;
                      begin
                          d:= x + 1;
                          mouse := d;
                      end;
                  procedure bird;
                      var d,e:integer;
                      begin
                            a := 5;
                      end;
         begin
             xx := xx -2;
             xx := mouse(xx);
             bird;
         end;
 (*** END CAT BLOCK.  Start FISH BLOCK *******************)
     procedure fish(var ff:integer);
          var a,c,d:integer;
             procedure horse;
                 var b,c,d:integer;
                       function cow(b:integer):integer;
                          var e:integer;
                          begin
                              e:= b div 2;
                              a:= 8;
                              cow :=e;
                          end;
                 begin
                     b:=cow(4);
                 end;
             procedure pig;
                 begin
                     writeln(' oink');
                 end;
         begin
             horse;
             ff:=a;
         end;
 (***    END FISH BLOCK *********************************)
 begin (** Main program **)
      b:=3;
      cat(b);
      writeln(a:10,b:10);
      fish(b);
      writeln(a:10,b:10);
 end.
```

Figure 9.2   Solution to Example 9.1

(a) Which variables may be accessed by PIG?

(b) Which subprograms may be invoked by PIG?

3. Modify the structure of the program in Figure 9.2 so while it keeps the same lexical structure as in Figure 9.1, the procedure PIG can be invoked from statements in the function COW.

9.2 USING RECURSIVE TECHNIQUES

A recursive subprogram is one that can invoke itself. Recursion was introduced, with simple examples, in Section 3.2. Let us review this concept.

Consider a recursive function that computes the factorial of some small positive integer N. The simplest way to do this is to multiply N by the factorial of $N - 1$. But to get the factorial of $N - 1$, the recursive function merely invokes itself with an argument of $N - 1$. Of course, if a function continues to invoke itself for any argument entered, the program goes into an infinite loop. In a recursive factorial function, there must be at least one argument value for which the function will not invoke itself but will just return a value. For example, if the argument carried in is 1, a value of 1 may be returned.

It is easy to write a recursive function that computes the factorial of a positive integer. (The techniques were discussed thoroughly in Section 3.2.) Unfortunately, it is even easier to develop a **nonrecursive** technique to perform the same task. And nonrecursive techniques are certainly less mind boggling, especially to the novice!

There are a number of problems that are relatively easy to solve using recursive techniques but quite difficult to solve otherwise. For example, in Figure 7.6, a procedure called MAKE_TREE is employed to place box-type records in a data structure called a *binary tree*. The position of a box in this data structure depends on the alphabetical ordering of the various name fields. Figure 9.3 presents a diagram of a typical binary tree ordered by the name field. Of course, a tree may contain hundreds or even thousands of elements.

Suppose we wish to print names of all people listed in the tree. Since the tree is *ordered*, it makes sense to print the names in alphabetical order. First we must carry the value of the root pointer into the procedure. Then the following sequence of statements may be performed:

TREE_PRINT: If the pointer value is nil, then return from the procedure. Otherwise:

1. Invoke TREE_PRINT. Carry in the current left-pointer.
2. Print the name identified by the current pointer. (Note: To get to this step, a value of nil must have been the argument carried into TREE_PRINT the last time TREE_PRINT was invoked.
3. Invoke TREE_PRINT. Carry in the current right-pointer.
4. Return from the procedure.

Example 9.2

Develop and test a procedure that prints in alphabetical order the names in a tree of box-type records that is ordered by name.
Solution   A solution is given in Figure 9.4. The procedure MAKE_TREE shown in Figure 7.6 is in the INCLUDE file called FIG76.PAS.

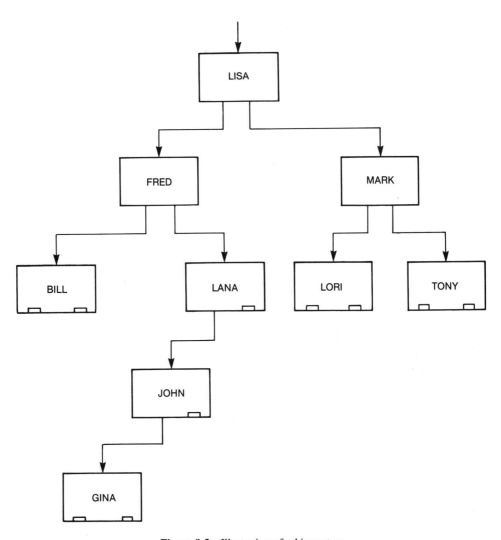

Figure 9.3   Illustration of a binary tree

The procedure PRINT_TREE in Figure 9.4 is quite concise. It contains just three executable statements, and two of these invoke itself. We will use a simple example to illustrate how this procedure functions.

In Figure 9.5, a three-node binary tree is illustrated and the procedure PRINT_TREE is shown. Program flow when this procedure is invoked is:

0. PRINT_TREE is invoked from an external block. The LISA-pointer is carried into the procedure.

```
program tree(output,cat);
   type  four = array[1..4] of char;
         box_ptr = ^box;
         box = record
                    name: four;
                    age:  0..110;
                    p1:   box_ptr;
                    p2:   box_ptr;
                end(*record*);
   var cat:file of box;  entry: box_ptr;
   ($i fig76.pas) (* INCLUDE *) (* TURBO Pascal *)
   procedure print_tree(p:box_ptr);
   (**** Prints names in a binary tree  ****)
      begin
         if p <> nil then
                    begin
                       print_tree(p^.p1);    (***   X   ***)
                       writeln('   ',p^.name); (*LINE_AFTER_X*)
                       print_tree(p^.p2);    (***   Y   ***)
                    end;                       (*LINE_AFTER_Y*)
      end;
begin(*** Start test program ***)
    assign(cat,'boxes');     (** TURBO Pascal **)
    make_tree(entry); writeln;
    print_tree(entry);
end.
```

Figure 9.4 A solution to Example 9.2

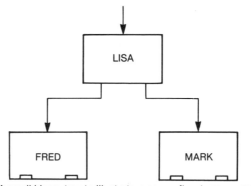

(a) A small binary tree to illustrate program flow in PRINT_TREE

```
procedure print_tree(p:box_ptr);
(**** Prints names in a binary tree  ****)
   begin
      if p <> nil then
                 begin
                    print_tree(p^.p1);    (***   X   ***)
                    writeln('   ',p^.name); (*LINE_AFTER_X*)
                    print_tree(p^.p2);    (***   Y   ***)
                 end;                       (*LINE_AFTER_Y*)
   end;
```

(b) Recursive function PRINT_TREE

Figure 9.5 Use of PRINT_TREE with a small tree

1. PRINT_TREE is invoked at point X with the FRED-pointer.

   2. PRINT_TREE is invoked at point X with the nil left-pointer.

3. Return to LINE_AFTER_X. Print FRED.

   4. PRINT_TREE is invoked from point Y with the nil right-pointer.

5. Return to LINE_AFTER_Y. But this is end of procedure, therefore:

6. Return to LINE_AFTER_X. Print LISA.

   7. PRINT_TREE is invoked from Y with the MARK-pointer.

   8. PRINT_TREE is invoked from X with the nil left-pointer.

9. Return to LINE_AFTER_X. Print MARK.

   10. PRINT_TREE is invoked from Y with the nil right-pointer.

11. Return to LINE_AFTER_Y. End of procedure, therefore:

12. Return to LINE_AFTER_Y. End of procedure, therefore:

13. Return to invoking program.

Observe that PRINT_TREE is invoked seven times in order to print the three names on the tree in Figure 9.5(a). Although the recursive procedure is quite short, following the flow of the procedure is somewhat tedious.

It is relatively easy to develop recursive procedures if problem statements are expressed in a recursive manner. The following concept is of great use in scientific problem solving.

A *determinant* is a unique number associated with an $n \times n$ matrix. The value of a determinant is a sum of various products of elements of the matrix. Since addition and multiplication are both associative and commutative, there are a number of different ways to define this sum of products. We shall use the following definition.

Definition.   Given an $n \times n$ matrix, $A = \{a_{ij}\}$, the **determinant** of A, is:

$$\text{DET}(A) = \sum_{j=1}^{n} a_{1j} * \text{COF}(a_{1j})$$

where $\text{COF}(a_{1j})$ is the cofactor of the element in the first row and jth column. (*Cofactor* is defined next.)

Definition.   The **cofactor** of an element a_{ij} in an $n \times n$ matrix is

$$\text{COF}(a_{ij}) = (-1)^{i+j} * \text{MINOR}(a_{ij})$$

Definition.   The **minor** of an element a_{ij} in an $n \times n$ matrix is the determinant of the $(n - 1) \times (n - 1)$ submatrix obtained by deleting the ith row and the jth column.

We have defined determinant in terms of a sum involving *cofactors*. We have defined cofactors using *minors*. We have defined a minor to be a *determinant*. The reasoning appears to be circular. However, a minor is defined as a determinant of a *smaller* matrix, an $(n - 1) \times (n - 1)$ matrix. The following definition completes our **recursive definition.**

Definition.   The determinant of a 1×1 matrix is the element in the matrix.

Example 9.3

Use the above recursive definition to find the determinant of the following matrix:

$$A = \begin{bmatrix} 2 & 3 & 4 \\ 5 & 6 & 7 \\ 8 & 9 & 0 \end{bmatrix}$$

Solution

$$\text{DET}(A) \triangleq \begin{vmatrix} 2 & 3 & 4 \\ 5 & 6 & 7 \\ 8 & 9 & 0 \end{vmatrix}$$

$$= 2 * 1 * \begin{vmatrix} 6 & 7 \\ 9 & 0 \end{vmatrix} + 3 * (-1) * \begin{vmatrix} 5 & 7 \\ 8 & 0 \end{vmatrix} + 4 * 1 * \begin{vmatrix} 5 & 6 \\ 8 & 9 \end{vmatrix}$$

But

$$\begin{vmatrix} 6 & 7 \\ 9 & 0 \end{vmatrix} = 6 * 1 * |0| + 7 * (-1) * |9|$$

and

$$\begin{vmatrix} 5 & 7 \\ 8 & 0 \end{vmatrix} = 5 * 1 * |0| + 7 * (-1) * |8|$$

and

$$\begin{vmatrix} 5 & 6 \\ 8 & 9 \end{vmatrix} = 5 * 1 * |9| + 6 * (-1) * |8|$$

The determinant of each 1×1 matrix is the element itself. Therefore, by collecting all terms, we see that $\text{DET}(A) = 30$.

Note in the solution to Example 9.3 the parallel lines surrounding each matrix. They indicate the determinant of that particular matrix. We can think of this notation as invoking a function that returns the value of the determinant. The function is invoked once from an external block. The argument is a 3×3 matrix. Before a value is returned, the function invokes itself nine more times. First it invokes itself to find the determinant

$$\begin{vmatrix} 6 & 7 \\ 9 & 0 \end{vmatrix}$$

Before it can return a value of this determinant, the function must invoke itself twice more. The first time, it invokes itself to find $|0|$. It returns a value of 0, and then invokes itself to find $|9|$. It returns 9, computes the determinant of the first 2×2 matrix, and returns this value. Next, the same function must find the determinant

$$\begin{vmatrix} 5 & 7 \\ 8 & 0 \end{vmatrix}$$

The process continues until the determinant of the 3×3 matrix is returned to the invoking statement in an external block.

Example 9.4

Develop a function that returns the determinant of an $n \times n$ matrix.

Solution   A solution is shown in Figure 9.6. The procedure DELETE1J is used to delete the first row and jth column of an $n \times n$ matrix. The function DET is used to compute the determinant. In order to compute the cofactor of a_{11}, the first row and first column of the matrix must be deleted. But to get subsequent cofactors, the original matrix is still needed. Therefore, the original matrix is stored in the local variable "temp" before the computation loop is entered.

The test program in Figure 9.6 uses the procedures RMAT and PMAT, which are stored in the file FIG81.PAS and accessed using an INCLUDE statement.

```
program determinant(input,output);
    type matrix = array[1..10,1..10] of real;
    var m:matrix; x:real;
    ($i fig81.pas) (**INCLUDE**)   (** TURBO Pascal **)
    procedure delete1j(j,n:integer; var mm:matrix);
    (** Deletes first row and jth column from an nxn matrix **)
        var p,q:integer;
        begin
            for p := 1 to n-1 do
                    for q:= 1 to n do mm[p,q]:=mm[p+1,q];
            for p := 1 to n-1 do
                    for q:= j to n-1 do mm[p,q]:=mm[p,q+1];
        end;
    function det(n:integer; mm:matrix):real;
        (** Returns determinant of an nxn matrix **)
        var y,sum,sign : real;   j : integer; temp: matrix;
        begin
            if n = 1 then sum := mm[1,1]   else
              begin
                temp := mm; (** save array as TEMP **)
                for j := 1 to n do
                    begin
                        mm := temp;
                        if j = 1 then sum := 0.0;
                        y := mm[1,j];
                        if odd(j) then sign := 1.0 else sign := -1.0;
                        deletelj(j,n,mm);
                        sum := sum + y*sign*det(n-1,mm);
                    end;
              end;
            det := sum;
        end;
    (*** Start test program ***)
    begin
        rmat(3,3,m);   pmat(3,3,m);   writeln;
        x:=det(3,m);   writeln(x:10:2);      (* 3x3 matrix *)
        rmat(4,4,m);   pmat(4,4,m);   writeln;
        x:=det(4,m);   writeln(x:10:2);
    end.
```

Figure 9.6   Solution to Example 9.4

REVIEW

1. Refer to the procedure PRINT_TREE in Figure 9.4 and to the binary tree in Figure 9.3. If PRINT_TREE is invoked from an external block, how many times will PRINT_TREE invoke itself before returning to the external block?
2. Develop and test a procedure that prints the names in a tree of box-type elements in *backwards* alphabetical order.
3. Use the recursive definition of a determinant to compute the determinant of the following 4 × 4 matrix.

$$
A = \begin{bmatrix}
2.0 & -3.0 & 0.0 & 5.0 \\
-1.0 & 2.0 & 4.0 & -3.0 \\
2.0 & -1.0 & 3.0 & 4.0 \\
5.0 & 4.0 & 2.0 & -2.0
\end{bmatrix}
$$

Then use the function DET and a program similar to the one in Figure 9.6 to check your answer.
4. How many times must DET invoke itself to compute the determinant of a 4 × 4 matrix?

9.3 SELECTED EXAMPLES

Recall that all information stored in computer memory may be represented as sequences of the binary characters 0 and 1. If we wish to print the value of an integer, we first must convert the value of the integer to a corresponding sequence of character codes, then the character codes are printed. Virtually all high-level programming languages provide system subprograms for performing this task. For example, if an integer value has been assigned to the integer variable n, then the Pascal subprogram WRITELN(n) converts this number to a set of character codes and prints the characters corresponding to the integer value.

Sometimes the system subprograms do not satisfy a user's needs. In some scientific applications, it is much more convenient to represent numbers in some base other than base-10. For example, to print the value of a nonnegative integer using base-8, or *octal*, representation, the following algorithm can be employed. (Note: We will assume that the value of the integer can be represented in ten or fewer octal characters.)

Let NUMBER be the integer to be printed. Then:

0. Set all values in an array of ten characters to ' ', or the space character.
1. Set $j = 10$.
2. Divide NUMBER by 8. Let Q be the quotient and R be the remainder.
3. Convert R to a character code and store in position j of the character array.
4. NUMBER = Q.
5. $j = j - 1$

6. If NUMBER $<>$ 0, then go to step 2.

7. Print the array of characters.

Note that the first character to be determined is the last character printed. Also note that regardless of the value of the number, ten character codes are printed. Of course, if the number is small, most of the characters printed will be spaces.

It is convenient to use a recursive subprogram to perform this task.

Example 9.5

Develop a recursive procedure that prints the value of a nonnegative integer using base-8 representation.

Solution   The procedure and a test program are shown in Figure 9.7. Observe that this procedure prints the minimum number of characters required to represent the argument value. Also observe that the procedure may easily be modified to print values in other number systems between base-2 and base-10.

Determinants, which were defined in Section 9.2, are used in a wide variety of engineering and scientific applications. One such application involves determining the value of one of the unknowns in a set of n equations in n unknowns, a procedure called **Cramer's Rule.**

Given a set of n equations in n unknowns, let us represent the equations, as previously, with an $n \times n$ matrix of coefficients and an n-element vector of constants. Then, by Cramer's Rule,

$$\text{Value of } j\text{th unknown} = \frac{\text{DET}(cnew)}{\text{DET}(c)}$$

where c is the $n \times n$ matrix of coefficients and $cnew$ is an $n \times n$ matrix that is a modified matrix of coefficients. In particular, all columns of $cnew$ are the same as those in the matrix of coefficients except the jth column, which has been replaced with the vector of constants.

```
program octal(input,output);
    procedure print_num(num:integer);
    (** Prints value of num using base-8 **)
      var  rem,quot,i: integer;  c:char;
      begin
        quot := num div 8;  if quot <> 0 then print_num(quot);
        rem := num mod 8;
        i := rem + ord('0'); (* Get ord of character *)
        c := chr(i);  write(c:1);
      end;
begin(** Start test program **)
    writeln; print_num(20);  writeln;
             print_num(4095); writeln;
             print_num(21345); writeln;
end.
```

Figure 9.7   Solution to Example 9.5

Example 9.6

Use Cramer's Rule to find the value of Y in the following set of equations:

$$3.5W - 2X + 2Y - 4Z = -10.5$$
$$2W + 3X - 6Y + 3Z = 2$$
$$W + X + Y - Z = 2$$
$$W - 2Y + Z = -1$$

Solution   The matrix of coefficients is

$$C = \begin{bmatrix} 3.5 & -2 & 2 & -4 \\ 2 & 3 & -6 & 3 \\ 1 & 1 & 1 & -1 \\ 1 & 0 & -2 & 1 \end{bmatrix}$$

The modified matrix of coefficients is

$$CNEW = \begin{bmatrix} 3.5 & -2 & -10.5 & -4 \\ 2 & 3 & 2 & 3 \\ 1 & 1 & 2 & -1 \\ 1 & 0 & -1 & 1 \end{bmatrix}$$

Therefore,

$$Y = \frac{DET(CNEW)}{DET(C)} = 3$$

Example 9.7

Develop a procedure that uses Cramer's Rule to solve a set of n simultaneous equations.
Solution   The procedure SOLVE is shown in Figure 9.8. If the determinant of the matrix of coefficients is 0, the set of equations is not independent. Since floating point values are not expressed exactly, the value to be used for 0 must be approximated.

When using this method to solve a set of simultaneous equations, the coefficients should not have excessively large (or small) values. For example, if each coefficient in a set of four equations has a value in the range of 1.0E20, the product of four terms used in finding the determinant will have a value in the range of 1.0E80. Such values exceed the maximum limits for floating points on most systems. This problem can be avoided by normalizing the equations before solving them.

REVIEW

1. Refer to the program in Figure 9.7. What three numbers are printed when this program is run?
2. Develop and test a procedure (or procedures) that prints the value of a nonnegative integer in each of the following:
   (a) The binary number system.
   (b) The base-10 number system.

```
program cramer(input,output);
     type matrix = array[1..10,1..10] of real;
          vector = array[1..10] of real;
     const EPSILON = 0.00001;
     var a:matrix;  b,c:vector; independent: boolean;
     {$i fig81.pas} (* TURBO Pascal *)
     {$i vec.pas} (* TURBO Pascal *)
          (* Contains RVEC and PVEC *)
     {$i det.pas}  (* TURBO Pascal *)
     procedure cnew(j,n:integer; v:vector; var cc: matrix);
     (*  Replaces jth column in an nxn matrix of coefficients
         with a vector of constants *)
        var i: integer;
           begin
              for i := 1 to n do cc[i,j] := v[i];
           end;
     procedure solve(n:integer; m:matrix; v:vector;
                           var ans:vector;var  flag:boolean);
           var i:integer; x:real; top:matrix;
           begin
              x := det(n,m); flag:=true;
              if abs(x) < EPSILON then flag:= false
              else
                 for i := 1 to n do
                    begin
                       top:=m;
                       cnew(i,n,v,top);
                       ans[i]:=det(n,top)/x;
                    end;
           end;
begin (** Start test program **)
     rmat(4,4,a); writeln; pmat(4,4,a); writeln;
     rvec(4,b); writeln;pvec(4,b); writeln;
     solve(4,a,b,c,independent);
     if independent then pvec(4,c) else
        writeln(' Set of equations is not independent! ');
end.
```

Figure 9.8   Solution to Example 9.7

3. Develop and test a function that uses Cramer's Rule and returns just one specified root in a set of *n* independent equations.

9.4 MATRIX TECHNIQUES

Several matrix operations were introduced in Chapter 8. Matrix addition and multiplication operations were defined, and properties of the *identity* matrix were introduced. In Section 8.2 sets of equations were written in matrix notation. Then a technique was developed for solving a set of *n* equations in *n* unknowns. In Section 9.3, Cramer's Rule helped us solve a set of *n* simultaneous equations.

Matrix techniques are frequently used to solve sets of simultaneous equations. Before illustrating this, a few definitions are required.

Definition.   Given an $m \times n$ matrix $A = (a_{ij})$, the **transpose** of this matrix is an $n \times m$ matrix $C = (c_{ij})$, where $c_{ij} = a_{ji}$ for all i and j.

Definition.   An $n \times n$ matrix A is **singular** if and only if

$$\text{DET}(A) = 0$$

Definition.   Given a nonsingular $n \times n$ matrix A, there exists a matrix A^{-1}, called the **inverse** of A, that has the following property:

$$AA^{-1} = A^{-1}A = I$$

where I is the $n \times n$ identity matrix.

Definition.   Given an $n \times n$ matrix A, the **matrix of cofactors** of A is the $n \times n$ matrix $C = (c_{ij})$, where c_{ij} is the cofactor of the element in the ith row and jth column of matrix A.

Definition.   Given an $n \times n$ matrix A, ADJ(A), called the **adjoint** of A, is the transpose of the matrix of cofactors of A.

It is easy to find the inverse of a matrix. It can be shown that if A is a nonsingular $n \times n$ matrix, then the inverse of A can be obtained from the following relationship:

$$A^{-1} = \frac{\text{ADJ}(A)}{\text{DET}(A)}$$

Note that dividing a matrix by a constant is the same as dividing each element of the matrix by that constant.

Now consider the following set of n equations in n unknowns.

$$a_{11}x_1 + a_{12}x_2 \ldots + a_{1n}x_n = c_1$$
$$a_{21}x_1 + a_{22}x_2 \ldots + a_{2n}x_n = c_2$$
$$\vdots \qquad \vdots \qquad\qquad \vdots \qquad \vdots$$
$$a_{n1}x_1 + a_{n2}x_2 \ldots + a_{nn}x_n = c_n$$

Expressed in matrix form, this is

$$AX = C$$

where A is the matrix of coefficients, C is the vector of constants, and

$$X = \begin{bmatrix} x_1 \\ x_2 \\ \vdots \\ x_n \end{bmatrix}$$

is the vector of unknowns. The solution of this set of equations is obtained by multiplying both sides of the equation by A^{-1}.

Thus,

$$X = A^{-1}C$$

Example 9.8

Develop and test a procedure that returns the inverse of an $n \times n$ matrix.
Solution A solution is given in Figure 9.9. The value of EPS in the procedure
INVERSE is selected for matrices in which the "typical" nonzero element has a magnitude
somewhere between 0.1 and 10.0. For matrices whose "typical" nonzero element
has a much larger or a much smaller magnitude, the value of EPS must be modified.
A more general procedure may be developed in which the value of EPS is carried
into the procedure as part of the argument list.

```
program inverse(input,output);
    type matrix= array[1..10,1..10] of real;
    var m,inv,ans:matrix; x:real; test:boolean;
    ($i matmul.pas) (**INCLUDE**) (**Turbo Pascal**)
    ($i fig81.pas) (**INCLUDE**) (** TURBO Pascal **)
    ($i mat1.pas)  (**INCLUDE**) (** TURBO Pascal **)
(*  mat1.pas contains the function DET and the
                procedure DELETEIJ *)

procedure inverse(n:integer; var flag: boolean; m:matrix; var mi:matrix)
   (* returns inverse of an nxn matrix. Flag is set true if inverse
      exists, and false if matrix is singular. *)
      const EPS = 0.00001;
      var i,j,s: integer; x: real;   temp: matrix;
      begin
            flag := true;
            x := det(n,m);
            if (abs(x) < EPS) then flag := false
                else
                        for i := 1 to n do
                          for j := 1 to n do
                            begin
                                temp := m;
                                deleteij(i,j,n,temp);
                                if not odd(i+j) then s:=1 else s:=-1;
                                mi[j,i] := s*det(n-1,temp)/x;
                            end;
      end;

(** Start test program **)
begin
    rmat(3,3,m);  pmat(3,3,m);     writeln;
    inverse(3,test,m,inv);
    if not test then
        writeln(' Matrix is singular.  There is no inverse.')
            else
                begin
                    pmat(3,3,inv);    writeln;
                    matmul(3,3,3,m,inv,ans);
                    pmat(3,3,ans);
                end;
end.
```

Figure 9.9   Solution to Example 9.8

REVIEW

1. The procedure INVERSE in Figure 9.9 invokes a procedure cailed DELETEIJ that deletes the ith row and jth column of an $n \times n$ matrix. Develop the procedure to perform this task.
2. Find the inverse of each of the following matrices.

(a) $\begin{bmatrix} 1.0 & 2.0 \\ 2.0 & 3.0 \end{bmatrix}$ (b) $\begin{bmatrix} 4.0 & 0.0 & 0.5 \\ 2.0 & 4.0 & 0.0 \\ 0.0 & 8.0 & 2.0 \end{bmatrix}$

3. For the program in Figure 9.9, what will be printed when data corresponding to each of the following matrices are entered?

(a) $\begin{bmatrix} 2.0 & 1.0 & 3.0 \\ 3.0 & 2.0 & 1.0 \\ 5.0 & 3.0 & 4.0 \end{bmatrix}$ (b) $\begin{bmatrix} 0.2 & 0.1 & -0.05 \\ -0.1 & 0.2 & 0.025 \\ 0.4 & -0.8 & 0.4 \end{bmatrix}$

EXERCISES

1. What is the lexical level of each block in Figure 9.10?
2. In Figure 9.10, which block's variables may be used by (a) RED?   (b) YELLOW?
3. For Figure 9.10, assuming subprograms have been previously declared, which subprograms may be invoked by (a) PINK?   (b) STRIPED?
4. Which variables in the program in Figure 9.11 are accessible to (a) lori?   (b) lola?
5. Which subprograms in the program in Figure 9.11 may be invoked by (a) luke?   (b) lois?
6. Develop a recursive function that accepts a real number corresponding to one of the natural numbers and returns its factorial, expressed as a real number. What is the advantage of using reals rather than integers in this function?
7. Develop a simple way of determining how many times a recursive procedure is invoked during execution of a program.
8. Refer to the program in Figure 9.4. Modify this program in each of the following manners:
   (a) Declare an additional integer variable in the main program block.
   (b) Increment this variable in the first executable statement of PRINT_TREE.
   (c) Print the value of the variable just before the end of the program. What information does this value yield?
9. Refer to Figure 9.5(a). Suppose one additional box is added to this binary tree and the left-pointer in the FRED box points to a box containing BILL.
   (a) Identify in detail the program flow of PRINT_TREE when it is printing the name fields in this binary tree.
   (b) How many times does PRINT_TREE invoke itself when printing the names in this binary tree?
10. Refer to the function DET in the program in Figure 9.6. If DET is invoked to find the determinant of a 5×5 matrix, how many times will DET invoke itself before returning to an external block?

11. An alternate definition of the determinant of an $n \times n$ matrix is

$$\sum_{i=1}^{n} a_{i1} \, \text{COF}(a_{i1})$$

Use this definition to develop a function that returns the determinant of an $n \times n$ matrix.

12. The procedure PRINT_NUM in Figure 9.7 prints the value of a nonnegative integer in the octal number system. Modify this procedure so it accepts two integer values, *num* and

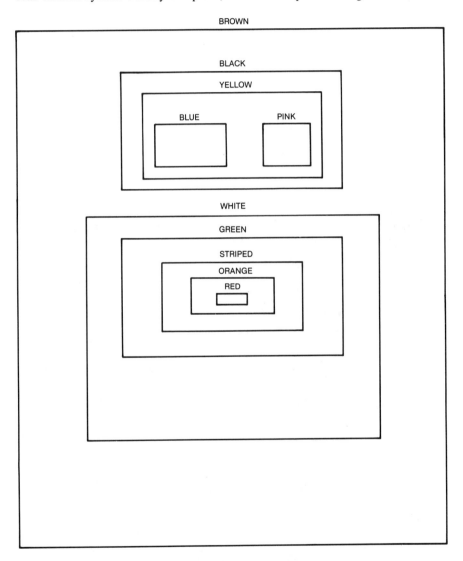

Figure 9.10   Block-structured program for Exercises 1, 2, and 3

```
program lisa(input,output);
   var a,b,c: integer;
   procedure lana(a,d: integer);
         var c,f:integer;
         procedure lupi(b:integer);
            var a,c: integer;
            function lori(g:integer):integer;
               var b,h: integer;
               function luke(p:integer): integer;
                  var c:integer;
                  begin (* luke *)
                     writeln;
                     (** Some luke statements **)
                  end;   (* luke *)
                  procedure lola(d,g:integer);
                     var b,p: integer;
                     begin  (* lola *)
                        writeln;
                        (** Some lola statements **)
                     end;    (* lola *)
                  begin    (* lori * )
                     writeln;
                     (** Some lori statements **)
                  end;      (* lori *)
            begin           (* lupi *)
               writeln;
               (** Some lupi statements **)
            end;            (* lupi *)
      begin                 (* lana *)
         writeln;
         (** Some lana statements **)
      end (* lana *);
   procedure lois(b:integer);
      begin (* lois *)
         writeln;
         (** Some lois statements **)
      end;   (* lois *)
begin (* lisa *)
   writeln;
   (** Some lisa statements **)
end (* lisa *).
```

Figure 9.11   Program for Exercises 4 and 5

b (*num* is still a nonnegative integer). The argument *b* must be in the subrange between 2 and 10. The function prints the value of *num* in the base-*b* number-system.

13. Develop a recursive procedure that prints the value of a nonnegative integer as a hexadecimal number.
14. Modify the procedure developed in Exercise 12 so it prints the value of any integer.
15. Modify the procedure developed in Exercise 13 so it prints the value of any integer.
16. What modifications should be made to the following two sets of equations before we use a computer implementation of Cramer's Rule to find the unknowns?

(a) $2.0E20V + 1.0E20W + 1.0E20X - 1.0E20Y + 0.0E20Z = 3.0$
$8.0E20V + 2.0E20W + 3.0E20X + 0.0E20Y - 2.0E20Z = 11.0$
$2.0E20V + 2.0E20W + 2.0E20X + 2.0E20Y - 2.0E20Z = 10.0$
$5.0E20V + 3.0E20W + 1.0E20X - 5.0E20Y + 2.0E20Z = 4.0$
$5.0E20V + 1.0E20W - 0.5E20X + 0.0E20Y + 0.5E20Z = 8.0$

(b) $2.0E\text{-}22X - 4.0E\text{-}22Y + 1.0E\text{-}22Z = -2.0E\text{-}22$
$2.0E\text{-}22X - 2.0E\text{-}22Y + 4.0E\text{-}22Z =\ \ \ 0.0$
$1.0E\text{-}22X - 2.0E\text{-}22Y + 0.5E\text{-}22Z =\ \ \ 4.0E\text{-}22$

17. Use the procedure SOLVE shown in Figure 9.8 to find the unknowns in the sets of equations in Exercise 16.

18. Develop a procedure that accepts character inputs from a file called MYFILE. This procedure uses a global integer variable (one defined at lexical level 0). The value of the global variable is to be initialized to 0 before the procedure is entered for the first time. The procedure is to accept character inputs from MYFILE until one of the following three characters is encountered:

$$\text{`(`}\qquad\text{`)`}\qquad\text{`;`}$$

The following tasks should be performed when one of these three characters is read:
(a) If '(' is read, then:
   (1) The value in the global variable is incremented.
   (2) The procedure invokes itself.
(b) If ')' is read, then:
   (1) The value in the global variable is decremented.
   (2) If the value assigned to the global variable is less than 0, then:
      (i) The value in the global variable should be set to 0.
      (ii) An appropriate error message should be printed, such as "EXCESSIVE RIGHT PARENTHESES."
   (3) Program control passes to the end of the procedure.
(c) If ';' is read, then:
   (1) The value assigned to the global variable is checked. If this value is greater than 0, then:
      (i) A value of 0 is assigned to the global variable.
      (ii) An appropriate error message is printed.
   (2) Program control exits from this block back to the invoking block.
Test this procedure for the following three sets of input data:
(a) $2 + (3 * 6 - 2 * (4 - 3 * (8 - 6)))$;
(b) $dog/(3 * sqrt(16)$;
(c) $x + (y + 2))$;

19. Refer to Exercise 20 in Chapter 8. Use the matrix techniques from Section 9.4 to find the mesh currents.

10

From Pascal to FORTRAN

Niklaus Wirth and his colleagues intended Pascal to be a good "first" programming language, a general-purpose language that could help novices learn programming concepts. It appears their objective has been realized. But Pascal is not the only popular high-level language.

For decades, engineers and others have used FORTRAN (FORmula TRANslation) for solving scientific problems, and there is already an immense reservoir of useful software written in the language. Most experienced engineers have studied FORTRAN. Furthermore, it is a standardized language, with most of its modern implementations rigidly adhering to the standards of FORTRAN 77.

There are a number of drawbacks to FORTRAN, however. A FORTRAN compiler is a rather large piece of software. At one time, most FORTRAN programs were run on large, centrally located main-frame computers. Now much software is developed on personal computers. Although FORTRAN is available for use on small personal computers, developing FORTRAN programs on these instruments is often inconvenient and time consuming. Furthermore, as an older language, FORTRAN does not support recursive techniques or ease the implementation of a number of common data structures.

But regardless of its limitations, most engineering students will still need to use FORTRAN. Fortunately, once basic programming concepts such as those discussed in the previous chapters have been mastered, learning FORTRAN is quite easy. This chapter provides the material needed to develop programs in FORTRAN.

10.1 INTRODUCTION TO FORTRAN

Although Pascal and FORTRAN have many similarities (for example, the general concepts related to problem solving are the same), there are also a number of differences. For instance, observe the following in the FORTRAN program in Figure 10.1.

1. Comments are single lines. A *c* or an asterisk in column 1 indicates that the rest of the line is a comment statement.

2. Declaration statements are not essential to a FORTRAN program.

3. A *statement terminator* is an End-of-line or a Newline mark. There can be no more than one executable statement per line. There are just two executable statements in this program, PRINT* and STOP. The STOP statement causes control to revert to the operating system.

4. Executable statements in FORTRAN cannot start before column 7. Thus, when developing a FORTRAN program using a line editor or a word processor, at least six spaces must precede each executable statement. (At one time, FORTRAN programs were punched on IBM cards, and no executable statement could precede column 7 of the card. This restriction has carried over to modern implementations.) Unlike Pascal, FORTRAN is not format-free.

5. The END statement merely informs the compiler where the program block ends.

The program in Figure 10.2(a) illustrates FORTRAN variables and assignments. Observe that in FORTRAN the equals sign is the assignment operator and *not* a relational operator. Also note in Figure 10.2(a) the variable ''bird'' is explicitly declared as a character*1 variable type, which is identical to a ''char'' variable in Pascal. Note the following:

1. The PRINT* statement, which is considered an unformatted print statement, has three arguments here: (1) a character string consisting of just a single space; (2) the value stored in the variable ''bird''; and (3) a nontrivial character string.

```
*  Comment!  Asterisk or a 'c' must  be in column 1!
c  Executable  statements start in Column 7 or to the
c     right of column 7!
      print*, ' My first FORTRAN  program!'
      stop
      end
```
Figure 10.1   A FORTRAN program

```
*  FORTRAN: Variables  and assignments
        character*1 bird
        bird = 'X'
        print*, ' ',bird,' is assigned  to bird.'
        dog = 1.0
        cat = 2.0
        mouse  = 3
        write(6,99) dog,cat,mouse
99      format(//,'      ',f6.1,f6.1,i6,///)
        stop
        end
```

(a) Program

X is assigned to bird.

       1.0   2.0   3

(b) Output

Figure 10.2 Program, and its output, illustrating the use of FORTRAN variables

2. The variables "dog," "cat," and "mouse" are not explicitly declared. When variables are not explicitly declared, those beginning with the letters i, j, k, l, m, or n are integer variables; all others are real variables.

3. Rules for naming variables are almost the same as in Pascal, with two differences: (1) FORTRAN variables generally may contain no more than six characters; and (2) the underscore symbol should *not* appear as part of a variable name.

4. The WRITE statement in this example illustrates formatted output. The first number in the argument, a 6, is a *logical unit number*, analogous to a logical file name in Pascal. Most systems permit logical unit numbers between 0 and 19. Unit number 6 is generally the default number for console output, corresponding to the logical file name OUTPUT in Pascal.

5. The second number in the argument list of WRITE is a *statement number*, which must lie somewhere in columns 1 to 5. Any number between 1 and 99999 may be used. This particular statement number identifies a FORMAT statement, which may be located anywhere in the program.

6. The format statement indicates how, from among a wide variety of allowable formats, the variables in the argument list of the WRITE statement are to be printed. In this format statement, there are two slashes, each causing a new line to be printed. Next, a string of several spaces is printed. Then the values of the variables "dog," "cat," and "mouse" are printed in the specified formats. An f6.1 format specifies six positions, or columns, for the output, one of them to the right of the decimal point. The i6 format specifies a field width of six. The integer value assigned to "mouse" will be printed within this field, right-justified. Figure 10.2(b) lists the printed output.

```
* $$$$$$$$$$$$$$$$$$$$$$$$$$$$$$
      dog  = 7.0/2
      print*,dog
      cat = 7/2
      print*,cat
      mouse = dog
      print*,mouse
* $$$$$$$$$$$$$$$$$$$$$$$$$$$$$$
      stop
      end
```

Figure 10.3   Example of mixing integers and reals

The five arithmetic operators in FORTRAN are

$$+ \quad - \quad * \quad / \quad **$$

which stand for addition, subtraction, multiplication, division, and exponentiation, respectively. All operations are valid for either integer or real operands. If an operation involves both a real and an integer operand, the integer value is first converted to the corresponding real before the operation is performed. Exponentiation has the highest priority. Multiplication and division have the next highest priority. As in Pascal, operations within inner parentheses are performed first.

If a real value is assigned to an integer variable, the value is first truncated and then converted to the appropriate integer. Integer values may be assigned to real variables. An internal conversion of data types takes place before the assignment is made. Operations involving mixed modes, reals and integers, are illustrated in Figure 10.3.

Looping operations in FORTRAN are similar to those in Pascal. In Figure 10.4, the first loop starts with the statement

do 123 i = 1,10

which initiates a loop and assigns 1 to integer variable *i*. All statements up to and including statement 123 are executed; then *i* is incremented and control reverts to the beginning of the loop. Control exits from the loop when the value assigned to variable *i exceeds* the upper limit, which is 10 in this case. The CONTINUE statement in statement 123 performs no useful function other than terminating the DO loop.

The second loop in Figure 10.4 is also a DO loop. In this case, the value assigned to integer variable *i* is incremented by 10 rather than 1, so the statements in this loop are executed five times.

FORTRAN 77 does not support a WHILE statement. However, the IF . . . THEN . . . ENDIF statement in Figure 10.4 can be used to implement the same type of structure. Following the IF statement is a condition that evaluates to either True or False. The statements preceding ENDIF are executed only if the condition is True. The GO TO statement just prior to the ENDIF directive sends control back to the beginning of the loop.

```
cccccccccccccccc LOOPING cccccccccccccccccc
          do 123 i = 1,10
                  print*, ' Merry Christmas '
                  print*, ' and Happy New Year ! '
      123         continue
      **************************************************
          do 98 i = 1,50,10
      98          print*, ' Long live Wayne Gretzky!!'
      **************************************************
          i = 1
          x = 2
      1           if (i .le. 8) then
                  y = x**i
                  write(6,999) i,y
                  i = i+1
                  go to 1
                  endif
      999         format (/,10x,i6,10x,f10.0)
      **************************************************
                  stop
                  end
```

Figure 10.4 Implementing looping operations in FORTRAN

FORTRAN also provides an IF . . . THEN . . . ELSE statement that works in the same way as the corresponding Pascal statement. In Figure 10.4, to implement an IF . . . THEN . . . ELSE statement, replace the word ENDIF with ELSE, follow this with a set of statements to be executed only if the condition is False, and terminate this series of statements with an ENDIF directive.

The *condition* in an IF statement generally involves relational operators, which in FORTRAN are essentially the same as in Pascal, except for the syntax:

Pascal:	=	<	>	<=	>=	<>
FORTRAN:	.eq.	.lt.	.gt.	.le.	.ge.	.ne.

In addition, logic operations may be performed on the boolean values that result from these relational operators. The Pascal logic operators AND, OR, and NOT are also available in FORTRAN, but the syntax is .AND., .OR., and .NOT.

Example 10.1

An investor deposits $1000 into a money market fund on the first day of each year, beginning in 1990. The fund pays an annual interest of 9.65%, computed on the last day of each year and deposited back into the fund. Develop a FORTRAN program that computes and prints annual interest and total balance at the end of each year from 1990 to 2010.

Solution   This is the same problem as in Example 2.2. A Pascal solution is given in Figure 2.5. A very similar FORTRAN program appears in Figure 10.5. Observe that the variables in this program are explicitly declared. Since we want "year" to be an integer variable, it is necessary to declare it as an integer. Likewise, "int" must be declared a real. It is unnecessary to explicitly declare "ydep," "rate," or "total"; it is done here to improve the program's readability.

```
*    Solution to Example 10.1
             integer year
             real ydep,rate,int,total
             rate = .0965
             year = 1990
             total = 0.
             ydep = 1000.
    25       format(//)
             write(6,25)
* Skip  2 lines
             print*, '    YEAR           INTEREST
         & ,'TOTAL'
* The "&"  in column 6 above indicates continuing the previous line!
*   the following statement causes one  line to be skipped
             print*,' '
******    Initialization is done.  Start loop.  ******
    9999     if (year .le.2010) then
                  total = total  + ydep
                  int = total *rate
                  total = total + int
                  write (6,99) year,int,total
    99            format(i8,f17.2,f17.2)
                  year =  year + 1
                  go to 9999
             else
                  write(6,25)
             endif
             end
```

Figure 10.5   Solution to Example 10.1

All FORTRAN commands must be written between columns 7 and 72. Commands too long to fit in this space may be extended to the following line, as illustrated by the first PRINT* command in Figure 10.5. To extend a line, a character such as an ampersand is written in column 6 of the *following* line, and the previous line is then extended to the right of this character.

REVIEW

1. Refer to the program in Figure 10.3. What is printed when this program is run?
2. Refer to the program in Figure 10.4, in particular, the loop between statements 1 and 999.
   (a) What numbers are printed during execution of this loop?
   (b) Run this program, then explain what the purpose is of the expression $10x$ in the FORMAT statement (number 999).
3. Develop and run a FORTRAN program that prints values of N, the square root of N, the cube root of N, N-squared, and N-cubed for all odd values of N between 0 and 100. (Note: Use the exponentiation operator to get the square roots and cube roots.)

10.2 FORTRAN SUBPROGRAMS

There are two types of FORTRAN subprograms: **functions** and **subroutines.** A function returns a single value. Of the relatively large number of *intrinsic* FORTRAN functions, some can be used with a variety of argument data types, others are rarely employed now but are supported because they once worked with older versions of FORTRAN. Common standard FORTRAN functions are shown in Figure 10.6. Some of them may be used in a more general manner than described there.

In addition to the standard functions, *user-defined* functions and subroutines are employed, and are essential for the systematic development of programs. FORTRAN functions and subroutines are similar to Pascal functions and procedures. In fact, some operating systems facilitate the use of FORTRAN subprograms in Pascal programs, and vice versa. Example 10.2 illustrates how to develop FORTRAN subprograms.

Example 10.2

Develop subprograms to perform each of the following tasks:
(a) Accept four reals and return their average.
(b) Accept three reals and return their average.
(c) Accept five integers and return their average.
(d) Accept four reals and return the largest and smallest.

Function name	Type of argument	Type returned by function	Comment
SQRT(X)	integer or real	real	Square root
ABS(X)	integer or real	real	Absolute value
EXP(X)	integer or real	real	Raises e to a power
LOG(X)	real	real	Log to base-e
ALOG10(X)	real	real	Log to base-10
MOD(X, Y)	integer, int	integer	Remainder from X/Y
MAX(W, X, . . .)	integer or real	integer or real	Returns maximum value
MIN(W, X, . . .)	integer or real	integer or real	Returns minimum value
SIN(X)	real	real	Sine(X) (radians)
COS(X)	real	real	Cos(X) (radians)
TAN(X)	real	real	Tan(X) (radians)
ASIN(X)	real	real	Arcsine(X) (radians)
ACOS(X)	real	real	Arccosine(X) (radians)
ATAN(X)	real	real	Atan(X) (principal quadrant)
ATAN2(Y, X)	real, real	real	Atan(Y/X) (any quadrant)
SINH(X)	real	real	Hyperbolic sine
COSH(X)	real	real	Hyperbolic cosine
TANH(X)	real	real	Hyperbolic tangent

Figure 10.6   Some standard FORTRAN functions

```
              ave3(x,y,z) = (x+y+z)/3.0
              integer ave5
              a = 4.0
              b = -1.0
              c = 21.0
              x  = ave3(a,b,c)
              print*, x
        ******************************************
              d = 16.0
              x = ave4(a,b,c,d)
              print*,x
        ******************************************
              k =   ave5(4,-16,5,8,66)
              print*,k
        ******************************************
9999          call biglit(a,b,c,d,xbig,xlit)
              print*, xbig,xlit
        ******************************************
              stop
              end
        **********************************************************
        **********************************************************
              function ave4(p,q,r,s)
                 x = p+q+r
                 ave4 = (x  + s)/4.
                 return
              end
        **********************************************************
        **********************************************************
              integer function ave5(k1,k2,k3,k4,k5)
                 ave5 = (k1+k2+k3+k4+k5)/5
                 return
              end
        **********************************************************
        **********************************************************
              subroutine biglit(x1,x2,x3,x4,big,small)
        * $$$$$ Finds largest and smallest of 4 real numbers   $$$$
                 big  = max(x1,x2,x3,x4)
                 small = min(x1,x2,x3,x4)
                 return
              end
```

Figure 10.7   Program illustrating user-defined subprograms

Solution   A solution is shown in Figure 10.7. Since three of the subprograms return just a single value, these three are defined as functions. Observe that the function AVE4 is not defined until *after* it has been invoked in the main program. (In FORTRAN, it is common to define user-defined subprogram blocks *after* the main program. Often these subprograms are stored in different files from the one containing the main program.)

The FORTRAN function AVE4 in Figure 10.7 appears to be much like a Pascal function. In Pascal, of course, the function name is always explicitly declared. The function name AVE4 is a *real* because it is implicitly declared in the same manner as other FORTRAN variables. The variable x in the second line of this function is a *local* variable; that is, it is defined only while program control is within the function. The command RETURN causes program control to revert back to the invoking block. In this example, RETURN appears at the end of the function. In general, however, the command may be used anywhere in the function and as often as necessary.

If the value to be returned by a FORTRAN function can be expressed by a single arithmetic statement, the function can be written in **arithmetic statement form** and defined at the beginning of the program, as, for example, the function AVE3 at the beginning of the program in Figure 10.7.

Function names may be explicitly declared. Since the function AVE5 in Figure 10.7 returns an integer, it is necessary to declare the function as an *integer* function. AVE5 must also be declared in blocks that invoke the function.

FORTRAN subroutines are similar to Pascal procedures. Subroutines are called or invoked using the CALL statement, as illustrated in statement 9999 in Figure 10.7. In the subroutine BIGLIT, observe the two intrinsic FORTRAN functions. Also note that the argument list contains six variable names and none of them begin with *i*, *j*, *k*, *l*, *m*, or *n*, meaning they are associated with real variables. Variable names within the argument list may be explicitly declared within a subprogram. If explicit declaration is required, this is done at the beginning of a subprogram. Similarly, local variables may be declared at the beginning of a subprogram.

There is one major difference between FORTRAN and Pascal subprograms. In Pascal, arguments may be carried into subprograms either by value or by reference. In FORTRAN, arguments are *always* carried into subprograms by reference, which means that the variables or formal parameters in the call list of the defined subprogram are *not* local variables but are merely locally defined identifiers for variables that are defined elsewhere. It also means that any *changes* made to values assigned to names in the argument list are returned to the corresponding variables in the block in which the subprogram is invoked.

The statement that invokes AVE5 in Figure 10.7 is

$$k = ave5 \ (4,-16,5,8,66)$$

which certainly appears to be carrying or transmitting five values into the function AVE5. But values cannot be transmitted in FORTRAN. It would be nice if such statements were illegal. But older implementations of FORTRAN support such statements, and it is desirable that FORTRAN 77 be compatible with older versions.

When statements such as the above are encountered, they are frequently implemented by a compiler in a manner similar to the following (we consider just the first value in the argument list):

(1) A value 4 is assigned to a variable called "4."
(Note: 4 would be an illegal name for a user-defined variable.)
(2) A pointer to the variable "4" is carried into the subprogram. That is, the variable is carried into the subprogram by reference.

```
          x   = dumb(2)
          call stupid(2)
          stop
          end
********************************
          function dumb(n)
                    n = n-1
                    dumb = n
                    return
          end
********************************
          subroutine stupid(m)
                    print*,m
                    return
          end
```

Figure 10.8 Arguments are carried into subprograms by reference. Caution is required when it appears arguments are being transmitted by value

If any changes are made in values assigned to the corresponding parameter in the subprogram, they are made to the value assigned to the variable "4." Thus, after such an assignment is made, a value of 4 may no longer be stored in this variable.

One number is printed when the program in Figure 10.8 is run. In most installations, the number will be a 1. Even experienced programmers are sometimes surprised that a 2 is *not* printed. Remember, variables in FORTRAN are carried into subprograms by reference. When we write statements that appear to be carrying values into subprograms by value, we must be cautious.

REVIEW

1. Develop and test each of the following functions: CUBE(X) (returns the cube of a real argument); CUBRT(X) (returns the real cube root of a real argument); CUBRTI(I) (returns the real cube root of an integer argument); and EXP2(I) (raises the integer 2 to the Ith power and returns the resulting integer. (Note: I is a nonnegative integer.)
2. Develop a subroutine that accepts the three coefficients of a quadratic equation. If the roots are not real, the subroutine prints an appropriate message and returns a value of 0.0 for each of the roots; if the roots are real, the values of the roots are returned.
3. Develop a function that accepts arguments A and B and returns values of the following equation:

$$\text{chmag} = \text{sqrt}((\cosh(A) * \cos(B))^2 + (\sinh(A) * \sin(B))^2)$$

Test your function for the following two cases:
(a) $A = 0.0$ and $B = 0.0$ (answer: 1.0)
(b) $A = .048$ and $B = .465$ (answer: .895)

10.3 INPUT AND OUTPUT

FORTRAN has many capabilities for entering and storing or printing data. We will cover some of these, in particular, those most useful for solving engineering problems.

We have already introduced statements for unformatted output:

```
print*, variable list
write(6,*) variable list
```

The number 6 is the default unit number for console output. But these statements may be used with other valid unit numbers. Recall that a unit number is analogous to a logical file name. That is, a unit number is valid syntax for representing some true file name as defined by an operating system.

There are similar statements for input from the user's console keyboard:

```
read*, variable list
read(5,*) variable list
```

Unit number 5 is the default unit number for console keyboard input. The elements read from a data list are separated using commas or new lines. Each time a READ statement is encountered, data input starts with a new line. The program in

```
*    Program illustrating unformatted input and output
      real L1,L2,L3
      read*,L1,L2,L3,w1,w2,w3
      write(6,*) '         AREA1          AREA2          AREA3'
      print*,' '
      A1 = L1*w1
      A2 = L2*w2
      A3 = L3*w3
      print*,'      ',A1,A2,A3
      write(6,*) ' '
      print*, ' $$$$$$$$$$$$$$$$$$$$$$$$$$$$$$$$$$$$$$$$$$$$$$$$$$$$ '
      print*,' '
      read(5,*) x
      read(5,*) y,z
      a = x + y +  z
      print*, x,' plus ',y, ' plus ',z,' equals ',a,' .'
      stop
      end
```

(a) Program illustrating input/output commands

```
1.0,2.0,3.0,4.0
5.0, 6.0, 7.0
2.5,3.5, 4.5
5.5,6.5,7.5
```

(b) Data

Figure 10.9   Use of unformatted input/output commands

Figure 10.9(a) illustrates unformatted, or **list-directed,** input and output. Input data for this program are shown in Figure 10.9(b). Observe that not all of the input data are read during program execution. In particular, the numbers 7.0, 3.5, 4.5, and 7.5 are never read.

Formatted output, already introduced, involves a FORMAT statement that identifies the manner in which the output is to be printed. A list of common symbols for formatted output is given in Figure 10.10.

Symbols that identify the format of a number assigned to a variable are also used with formatted input, in particular, the symbols related to f, i, a, e, and g formats shown in Figure 10.10. The program in Figure 10.11(a) uses all of the symbols defined in Figure 10.10. Data for this program are given in Figure 10.11(b); program output is shown in Figure 10.11(c). Some notes about formatted input and output follow.

1. In i (integer) format, numbers are right-justified. For instance, if the number 35 is printed in i6 format, four spaces are printed before the characters 3 and 5 are printed. If the number 35 is to be read using i6 format, four blanks must be entered before the 3 and 5 are entered.

Symbol	Name	Purpose
/	slash	Skips a line.
x	space	Prints a space.
Nx		Prints N spaces.
'STRING'	literal	Prints STRING.
fw.d	floating point	w spaces, d to the right of the decimal.
Nfw.d		N of the above.
iw	integer	w spaces, right-justified.
Niw		N of the above.
a	alphameric	Prints entire character string.
aw		If w < string length, prints the first w characters; if w > string length, prints the string in w spaces, right-justified.
Na or Naw		N of the above.
ew.d	exponential	Prints in exponential format, w spaces, d to the right of the decimal. (Note: w ≥ d + 7)
New.d		N of the above.
gw.d	g format	Same as f format if the number fits in the specified width. Otherwise, the number is expressed in e format. (Note: w ≥ d + 7)
Ngw.d		N of the above.
tn	tab	Next output starts at column n.

Figure 10.10   Common specifications for formatted output

```
        character*1 c
        character*16 name,name1,name2
        read(5,99) i,j,k
99      format (2i6,i7)
*   integer data must be RIGHT JUSTIFIED!!
        write(6,98)  i,j,k
98      format (//,20x,3i8)
        read(5,97) pie,avacad
97      format(f12.8,e16.8)
        write(6,97) pie,avacad
***  Warning:  It does not matter how many characters are entered.
***            The PRECISION of a floating point depends only on the
***            number of bits in the  mantissa or significand of the
***            floating point   representation!!!
        write (6,96) pie,avacad
96      format(1x, 'G-FORMAT',t30,2g12.4)
        read(5,95) c
        read(5,95) name
        read(5,95) name1
        read(5,95) name2
95      format(a)
        write(6,94) c,name,name1,name2
94      format(//,t5,a3,3a18)
        write(6,93)
93      format(' 2345678901234567890123456789012345678901234567890')
        stop
        end
```

(a) Program

```
                         1       2        3
                    3.14156265        6.02e23
                    $
                    Lisa
                    Mouse,Mickey Oswald
                    Walters,Barbara
```

(b) Input data

```
                         1       2        3
    3.14156270   .60200002E+24
    G-FORMAT                        3.142       .6020E+24


        $ Lisa              Mouse,Mickey Osw  Walters,Barbara
    2345678901234567890123456789012345678901234567890
```

(c) Program Output

Figure 10.11 Formatted input and output

2. With f, e, or g format for input, the exact format can be, and generally is, overridden by entering a dot or decimal point as part of the number. For example, to read a single floating point value of 3.14 in f20.10 format, the number string 3.14 may be entered anywhere within the first twenty columns.

3. Character strings are entered and printed using a (alphameric) format. In Figure 10.11, the variables c, "name," "name1," and "name2" are all character string variables. Variable c may be assigned a string of one character. Variables "name," "name1," and "name2" may be assigned strings of sixteen characters. In format a, the entire string is read or printed. However, format a4 for a string of sixteen characters in an output statement causes only the first four characters of the string to be printed. If an a20 format is specified for a variable that stores sixteen characters, the sixteen characters are usually printed right-justified in a field of size 20.

4. When writing FORTRAN programs, it is good practice *never* to place any character other than a blank in column 1 of formatted output. This is because programs used to be entered on punched IBM cards and output printed on large line printers, whose spacing is controlled by column 1 of formatted output (for example, a 1 makes the line printer advance a page). Therefore, we should use a format statement such as

                    99   format(' Help')

instead of

                    99   format('Help')

So far the only input/output operations we have considered are data transfers to and from user consoles. Frequently, data are read from or entered into *files*, in which case a few additional FORTRAN commands are required. The form of the command required to open a file is

           OPEN(UNIT=number, FILE='filename', STATUS='statdef')

The number assigned to UNIT is usually between 0 and 29, with 5 and 6 generally reserved for console input and output. Other numbers may be reserved on some systems. To read from or write to a file, READ and WRITE commands using the assigned unit number are employed.

The string 'filename' is the true name of the file. The string 'statdef' may be either 'old' or 'new' depending on whether the file already exists or is being created during program execution. If 'statdef' is 'scratch,' then the file is a temporary one for use during program execution but is deleted just prior to program termination.

Files opened during execution of a FORTRAN program are automatically closed when program execution terminates. To close a file prior to program execution, one may use the command

                    CLOSE(UNIT=number)

which closes the file and frees the unit number previously assigned to that file by the OPEN statement.

When we desire to read information from a file more than once during program execution, we can use the command

REWIND(unit=number)

which resets the file pointer back to the beginning of the file.

With Pascal, we frequently read data until "end-of-file," using the Pascal function EOF(filename). Similar tasks may be performed in FORTRAN.

We have used the formatted READ statement

READ(unit-number,statement-number) argument list

for example,

READ (5,99) x,y,z

A more general READ statement is:

READ (unit-number,statement-number, END=another-statement-num)

For example, the statement

888   READ(10,99,end=20)x,y,z

causes data to be read from unit 10 in the format specified by the format statement at statement 99. The data are assigned to variables x, y, and z. Generally, a READ statement of this type is part of a loop. For instance, if the next statement is

GO TO 888

then, when there are no more data to be read (perhaps "end-of-file" is encountered), program control transfers to the statement number assigned to END in the read statement's argument list. This is illustrated in Example 10.3.

Example 10.3

Refer to the INFO-type record defined in Example 6.6, which consists of eight fields. INFO-type records were constructed from data stored in text files. Short text files containing data are shown in Figures 6.13(d) and 7.12. A longer text file containing INFO-type data is included in Appendix A. A sample of text file data defining an INFO-type record is:

Sajak,Pat
M
   35
Wheel man
20000.00
454-2234
   5
2.6

Develop Fortran subroutines to perform each of the following tasks:

(a) Read all records from a text file of INFO-type data, and return the number of males and the number of females whose records are stored in the file.

(b) Read a file of INFO-type elements. Find the names of all individuals of a specified gender, and write those names in a new file.

(c) Print all the names in a file of names. (Note: Each name is stored in a character∗16 variable.)

Then write a main program that reads a file of INFO elements and creates a file of names. If the number of males in the INFO file is greater than the number of females, a file containing the names of all males is created; otherwise, a file containing the names of all females is created.

Solution   The subroutines are shown in Figure 10.12. Observe that all lines of the file are read as character strings. If we wish to know an individual's age, we can read the corresponding line in i3 format. To learn an individual's "quality," the corresponding line is read in i2 format. For values of "salary" or "gpa," a format of g20.10 is satisfactory.

The main program is shown in Figure 10.13. The file containing the main program and the file containing the subroutines can be compiled at the same time.

REVIEW

1. Refer to the program and data in Figure 10.9. What is printed in the two lines of numerical output produced when the program is run?
2. Refer to the subroutine MKFILE in Figure 10.12. Modify this subroutine so the valid values of "gen" are M, F, and B. If the B specification is carried into the routine, names of *all* persons in the file are stored in the file identified as unit number 11.
3. Develop and test a subroutine that reads a text file of INFO-type records and prints the names of all people at least 21 years old but no older than 59.

10.4 STRUCTURED DATA TYPES

Unlike Pascal, FORTRAN does *not* support record-type variables, pointers, or dynamic data types. But similar to PASCAL, arrays of variables in FORTRAN must be declared, and space must be reserved for array elements. In FORTRAN, both one-dimensional arrays and multidimensional arrays (up to seven dimensions) can appear.

The program in Figure 10.14 illustrates the declaration and use of arrays. The DIMENSION statement in the first line declares and reserves space for 230 real variables. From the perspective of a programmer, an array is a set of contiguous variables associated with computer memory. There are ten elements in vector A. There are 120 real variables in the four-dimensional array B, and 100 real variables in the matrix c.

Although DIMENSION statements are found frequently in FORTRAN, they are

```
***************      Subroutines *************************
        subroutine getcnt(iguy,igirl)
*** Returns the number of Males and the number of Females in
***   a TEXTFILE of INFO type records ***
        character*16 x
        character*1  c
99      format(a)
98      format(a1)
            rewind(unit=10)
            iguy = 0
            igirl = 0
97          read(10,99,end=13) x
            read(10,98) c
            if (c .eq. 'M') then
                iguy = iguy +1
            endif
            if (c .eq. 'F') then
                igirl = igirl + 1
            endif
            do 96 i = 1,6
96          read(10,99) x
            go to  97
13          return
            end
***********************************************************
        subroutine mkfile(gen)
***   Reads names from a TEXTFILE of INFO type elements.
***   Writes names of specified gender into  another file
        character*16  x
        character*1   c,gen
        rewind(unit=10)
99      format(a16)
98      format(a1)
97      read(10,99,end=13) x
        read(10,98)  c
        if (c .eq.gen) then
            write(11,99) x
        endif
        do 96 i=1,6
96      read(10,99) x
        go to 97
13      return
        end
***********************************************************
        subroutine ptfile
*** Prints all names in a file of 16-letter  names ***
        character*16 name
99      format (a16)
98      format(20x,a)
        print*, ' '
        rewind(unit=10)
97      read(10,99,end=96) name
        write(6,98) name
        go  to 97
96      return
        end
```

Figure 10.12 Subroutines for Example 10.3

```
**** Solution to Example 10.12 ***
        integer boys,girls
        character*1  sex
        open(unit=10, file='mydata',status='old')
        call getcnt(boys,girls)
        if (boys .gt. girls) then
                sex = 'M'
        else
                sex = 'F'
        endif
        open(unit=11,file  = 'namefile',status = 'new')
        call mkfile(sex)
        close(unit=10)
        close(unit=11)
        open(unit=10,file='namefile',status='old')
        call ptfile
        stop
        end
```

Figure 10.13 Main program for Example 10.3

never really needed, for TYPE declaration statements may be used to declare arrays. This is illustrated in line 2 of the program in Figure 10.14. D is a real vector containing twelve elements, and IX is a 10×10 matrix of real elements. P and Q are each five-element vectors. The elements in vector Q are identified as $Q(-2)$, $Q(-1)$, $Q(0)$, $Q(1)$, and $Q(2)$.

In lines 3 and 4, X is declared as an array of twenty integers, and *name* is declared as an array of twenty character*16 variables. Each character*16 variable is an array of sixteen characters.

In the first DO loop in Figure 10.14, ten integers are read into the first ten elements of array X. In the next DO loop, the first ten numbers stored in this array are printed. Then a subroutine is invoked with the command.

call rmat(2, 3, C)

which transfers control to RMAT. The third argument in the argument list, which may be properly referred to as an *array pointer*, identifies the array $C(10, 10)$. In the subroutine RMAT, this array pointer is called A. The declaration statement in RMAT,

real A(10,10)

identifies A as an array pointer. It does not reserve any space, since A is the same as the array pointer called C in the invoking statement. Observe that A is dimensioned in the subroutine in exactly the same way as C is dimensioned in the main program! Until we have more knowledge about arrays, this practice should be followed. That is,

Multidimensional arrays in a subprogram should be declared in the same way the corresponding array is declared in the invoking program.

```
           dimension a(10),b(2,4,3,5),c(10,10)
           real d(12),ix(10,10),p(0:4),q(-2:2)
           integer x(20)
           character*16 name(20)
9999       format(//)
           do 99 i = 1,10
99         read*,x(i)
           write(6,9999)
           do 98 i=1,10
98         write(6,80) x(i)
80         format (i50)
           call rmat(2,3,c)
           write(6,9999)
           call pmat(2,3,c)
           write(6,9999)
           call getnam(6,name)
           do 90 i=1,6
90         write(6,70) name(i)
70         format(30x,a)
           stop
           end
***********************************************************
           subroutine  rmat(m,n,a)
***   Reads an m x n  matrix ***
***  enter  each number on separate line **
           real a(10,10)
           do 99 i=1,m
                do 99 j=1,n
99         read(5,98) a(i,j)
98         format (g20.10)
           return
           end
***********************************************************
           subroutine pmat(m,n,a)
***  Prints an m x n matrix
           real a(10,1)
           do 99  i=1,m
99         write(6,98)(a(i,j), j=1,n)
98         format(10g10.4)
           return
           end
***********************************************************
           subroutine getnam(n,a)
***  puts n names in array of  names ***
           character*16 a(1),b(100)
           do 99 i=1,n
99         read (5,97) b(i)
97         format(a)
*** names are first stored in LOCAL variables. ****
*** This is done for illustrative purposes !! ****
           do 95 i=1,n
95         a(i) = b(i)
           return
           end
```

Figure 10.14   Program illustrating arrays in FORTRAN

Observe that the subroutine RMAT reads elements of an $m \times n$ matrix, with each element entered on a separate line. The subroutine PMAT prints the elements of an $m \times n$ matrix, in matrix form, using an *implied* DO loop, as seen in statement 99 of subroutine PMAT.

Observe in subroutine PMAT that we are relaxing the rule just stated, for matrix A is dimensioned by the statement

real A(10,1)

whereas the corresponding array in the invoking program is dimensioned as a 10 $\times$ 10 matrix. When carrying a two-dimensional array pointer into a subroutine in FORTRAN, it is only necessary that the first dimension, called the **ROW DIMEN-SION,** be the same in the subprogram as in the invoking program. Shortly we will see why.

Note the subroutine GETNAM in Figure 10.14. It reads an array of N names and returns them to the invoking program. Observe that the character*16 array pointer, A, is dimensioned with the statement

character*16 A(1),B(100)

It is necessary to dimension A as an array because this is the only way to identify A as an array pointer. In a one-dimensional array, however, it makes *no* difference what number dimensions A, since no space is reserved in the subroutine. Observe that B is also dimensioned in the subprogram. Since B is not in the subprogram's argument list, this portion of the implicit dimension statement defines and creates 100 local character*16 variables. Of course, when control exits from the subprogram, these variables and their assigned values are lost.

Sample data for the program in Figure 10.14 appear in Figure 10.15(a). Output for these data are shown in Figure 10.15(b).

The elements of one-dimensional arrays may be considered as stored in contiguous memory locations. In multidimensional arrays, elements are also stored in contiguous locations. For example, the 2-dimensional array

DIMENSION A(4,6)

Two-dimensional arrays in FORTRAN are generally stored *column-wise*. That is, the first column is stored first, then the second column, and so on. See Figure 10.16. In general, the element $A(i, j)$ is the same as the one in position k, where

$$k = i + (j - 1) * \text{ROW\_DIMENSION}$$

For instance, in Figure 10.16, for the case in which $i = 2$ and $j = 4$, the position of $a(2, 4)$ is k, where $k = 2 + (4 - 1) * 4 = 14$.

In Figure 10.17, we see that arrays dimensioned as 1-dimensional in the main program are specified as two-dimensional in the subroutine. In particular, array x

```
20
2222
123
34
-2
1
2
3
4
905
1.0
2.0
3.0
4.0
5.0
6.0
Lassie Dog
Bugs Bunny
Snoopy
Bambi Deer
Dumbo the Elephant
Freddy Fish
```

(a) Input data

```
20
2222
123
34
-2
1
2
3
4
905
```

```
1.000     2.000     3.000
4.000     5.000     6.000
```

```
Lassie Dog
Bugs Bunny
Snoopy
Bambi Deer
Dumbo the Elepha
Freddy Fish
```

Figure 10.15 Sample input and output
for the program in Figure 10.14

(b) Program output

is dimensioned as a 4 × 7 array in SUBR. Therefore, the element $x(3, 5)$ is the one in position $3 + (5 - 1) * 4 = 19$ of array A. Thus, the first number printed in the subroutine is the one stored in position 19, which is 19.0.

When using a subprogram with different sets of two-dimensional arrays, it is impractical to dimension arrays in the call list with the same row dimension as in the invoking routines. So the value of the row dimension is frequently included as part of the argument list, and the subprograms identify elements of two-dimensional arrays by their position in the array.

Example 10.4

Develop subroutines for the following matrix operations. The subroutines should work for input arrays that are dimensioned differently.

(a) Reading an $m \times n$ matrix.
(b) Printing an $m \times n$ matrix.
(c) Finding the sum of two $m \times n$ matrices.

Array pointer	Element	Position in array	Element	Position in array
A →	A(1, 1)	1	A(1, 4)	13
	A(2, 1)	2	A(2, 4)	14
	A(3, 1)	3	A(3, 4)	15
	A(4, 1)	4	A(4, 4)	16
	A(1, 2)	5	A(1, 5)	17
	A(2, 2)	6	A(2, 5)	18
	A(3, 2)	7	A(3, 5)	19
	A(4, 2)	8	A(4, 5)	20
	A(1, 3)	9	A(1, 6)	21
	A(2, 3)	10	A(2, 6)	22
	A(3, 3)	11	A(3, 6)	23
	A(4, 3)	12	A(4, 6)	24

Figure 10.16   Order in which the elements of a 4×6 array are stored in a FORTRAN program

```
      dimension a(100),b(100),c(100)
      do  99 i =1,100
      b(i)=i
      c(i)=i
99    a(i) = i
      call subr(a,b,c)
      stop
      end
*******************************
      subroutine subr(x,y,z)
      real x(4,7),y(10,8),z(7,12)
      print*, x(3,5),y(3,5),z(3,5)
      return
      end
```

Figure 10.17   Program illustrating the effect of row dimension

```
***** Use of GENERAL MATRIX SUBROUTINES   *******
** ROW DIMENSION must be carried into routine **
           real a(5,7), b(8,3), c(11,5)
           call matrd(3,3,a,5)
           call matpnt(3,3,a,5)
           call matrd(3,3,b,8)
           call matpnt(3,3,b,8)
           call matadd(3,3,a,b,c,5,8,11)
           call matpnt(3,3,c,11)
           stop
           end
**  SUBROUTINES!   Require ROW DIMENSION **
        subroutine matrd(m,n,x,rowdim)
           real x(1)
           integer rowdim
           k = m*n
           write(6,99) k
99         format(/,' Enter ',i4,' real numbers, one per  line',/)
           do 98   i = 1,m
              do 98 j   = 1,n
              k = i + (j-1)*rowdim
98         read(5,97) x(k)
97         format(g20.10)
           return
           end
        subroutine matpnt(m,n,x,rowdim)
           real x(1)
           integer rowdim
           print*,' '
           do 99 i=1,m
99         write(6,98)  (x(i+(j-1)*rowdim),j=1,n)
98         format(10g12.3)
           return
           end
        subroutine matadd(m,n,x,y,z,rdimx,rdimy,rdimz)
           real x(1),y(1),z(1)
           integer rdimx,rdimy,rdimz
           do 99 i=1,m
           do 99 j=1,n
           k1=i + (j-1)*rdimx
           k2=i + (j-1)*rdimy
           k3=i + (j-1)*rdimz
99         z(k3) = x(k1) + y(k2)
           return
           end
```

Figure 10.18   Solution to Example 10.4

Solution   It is necessary to include the row dimension of the corresponding matrix as part of the argument list. Since three matrices are included in the argument list in the subroutine that finds a matrix sum, the row dimension of each of these matrices must be included in the argument list. A solution and a test program are shown in Figure 10.18.

We have used character*N variables in several examples. These variables are similar to arrays of CHAR in Pascal. However, FORTRAN provides more facilities for manipulating character strings. For example, in the declarations and assignments

```
character*4    a,b
character*12   c
a = 'Old'
b = '  dog'
```

the first executable statement assigns values of *O*, *l*, *d*, and space to the elements of *a*. The next statement assigns values of space, *d*, *o*, and *g* to the four elements of *b*. FORTRAN has a **concatenation** operator, //, that joins or combines strings. This operator appears twice in the following statement to join three strings:

$$c = a \, // \, \text{'bird'} \, // \, b$$

after which the value assigned to *c* is

'Old bird dog'

FORTRAN can also access substrings of character*n variables. For example, the statement

$$c(1:2) = c(5:6)$$

assigns *b* and *i* to the first two elements of *c*, and the statement

$$c(3:3) = \text{'g'}$$

assigns a value to just the third element, after which the value assigned to *c* is

'big bird dog'

Other examples related to character strings are shown in the program in Figure 10.19(a); corresponding output is in Figure 10.19(b).

One reason FORTRAN is so popular for solving scientific problems is that it provides COMPLEX as a standard data type. That is, variables may be declared as complex, assignments made to these variables, and the standard arithmetic operations performed on complex quantities or expressions. Furthermore, a set of intrinsic functions is available. Standard FORTRAN functions that operate on complex quantities are shown in Figure 10.20.

Complex quantities are stored in rectangular form in FORTRAN. That is, both the real and the imaginary parts of a number are assigned to a complex variable. Operations on complex quantities and the use of complex functions are illustrated in Example 10.5.

Example 10.5

The equation for the voltage along a transmission line is

$$V = VR * \cosh(\gamma * x) + IR * ZC * \sinh(\gamma * x)$$

```
          character*4 a,b,c
          character*20  e
          character*16 p,q,r,s
          a = 'Dec'
          b='25'
          c='1990'
          e= a//b//c
          e(18:20) = '!!!'
          write(6,99) e
    99    format(/,10x,a)
          p = 'G.W. CARVER'
          q = 'GINA LOLA'
          r = '3-BASE HIT'
          s = 'CAVE MOUSE'
          e = 'JANE ADAMS'
          e(4:6) = q(3:5)
          e(7:7) = p(3:3)
          e(8:10) = r(8:10)
          e(11:17) = s(10:16)
          e(1:1) = p(9:9)
          write(6,99)  e
          stop
          end
```

(a) Program illustrating string operations

```
Dec 25   1990      !!!

VANNA WHITE
```

(b) Program output

Figure 10.19   String manipulation in FORTRAN

Function name	Type of argument	Type returned by function	Comment
CSQRT(X)	complex	complex	Complex square root of complex argument
CABS(X)	complex	real	Magnitude of complex number
CEXP(X)	complex	complex	Transcendental number e raised to a complex power
CLOG(X)	complex	complex	Log to base-e
CSIN(X)	complex	complex	Complex sine
CCOS(X)	complex	complex	Complex cosine
CMPLX(A, B)	real, real	complex	Returns $A + Bi$
CONJ(X)	complex	complex	Returns conjugate
REAL(X)	complex	real	Returns real part of X
AIMAG(X)	complex	real	Returns imaginary part of X

Figure 10.20   Intrinsic FORTRAN functions for operations on complex numbers

```
**** Transmission line program *******
        complex v,vr,ir,gamma,zc,arg
        complex ccosh,csinh
        vr = (127000.,0.0)
************        ^^^^^^ COMPLEX CONSTANT
        ir = cmplx(104.94,-50.82)
*******        ^^^  use of CMPLX function
        zc =  (390.98,-48.1)
        gamma = cmplx(2.558e-4,2.0776e-3)
        write(6,100)
100     format(//,10x,'DISTANCE',10x,'VOLTAGE MAGNITUDE',/);
        do 99 i = 25,400,25
            x = i
            arg = gamma*x
            v = vr*ccosh(arg) + ir*zc*csinh(arg)
            ans = cabs(v)
99          write(6,98) x,ans
98      format(5x,2g20.10)
        stop
        end
************* Define functions ********
        complex function ccosh(x)
        complex x
            ccosh=(cexp(x)+cexp(-x))/2.
        return
        end
        complex  function csinh(x)
        complex x
            csinh = (cexp(x)-cexp(-x))/2.
        return
        end
```

Figure 10.21   Solution to Example 10.5

where *VR* is a complex number representing voltage at the end of the line; *IR* is ɑ complex number representing electrical current at the end of the line; *ZC* and γ are complex numbers that describe the line; and *x* is length, measured from the end of the line, in miles. In a given line,

$$VR = 127000.0 + 0.0i$$
$$IR = 104.94 - 50.82i$$
$$\gamma = 2.558\text{E-}4 + 2.0776\text{E-}3 \ i$$
$$ZC = 390.98 - 48.1i$$

Write a program that computes and prints the magnitude of the voltage at twenty-five-mile intervals along a 400-mile line.
Solution   A solution is shown in Figure 10.21.

REVIEW

1. For how many real variables is space reserved by each of the following declaration statements?
   (a) Real $i(5, 7)$, $j(2, 3, 4, 5)$, $x(-10:2)$
   (b) Complex $a(10, 10)$

2. Refer to the program in Figure 10.17. What numbers are printed when this program is run?

3. Suppose names are stored in an array of character∗16 elements. Develop and test a subroutine that sorts these names in alphabetical order.

4. Develop and test a FORTRAN function that returns the angle of a complex number, expressed in degrees.

10.5 MISCELLANY

Several of the capabilities of FORTRAN that make it useful for solving scientific problems are introduced in this section.

CASE-like Commands

FORTRAN has no CASE statement, but it has two commands that are somewhat similar to the CASE statement in Pascal. The *arithmetic* IF statement has the form

if (arithmetic expression) num1, num2, num3

where num1, num2, and num3 are statement numbers. After this statement is executed, execution proceeds from statement num1, num2, or num3, depending on whether the value of the arithmetic expression is negative, zero, or positive. For example, once the statement

if $(j - 2)$ 10, 20, 30

is executed, the program resumes at statement 10, 20, or 30, depending on whether $(j - 2)$ is negative, zero, or positive.

The *computed* GO TO statement has the form

go to (N1,N2,N3, . . . Nk) integer_expression

If the integer expression yields a value i, where $1 \le i \le k$, then program control branches to statement Ni. Otherwise, program control passes to the statement following the computed GO TO statement. For example, if $j = 5$, then the following statement will cause program control to branch to statement 257:

go to (200,100,150,81,257,98) j

Common Blocks

A **common block** is a set of variables that may be shared by different independent modules in a FORTRAN program. Variables accessed from a common block are identified by their position in the block. The declaration statements

```
*************************** main program
      common a,b,c,d(5)
      common /tiger/ x(4),y,z,i(2)
      common /dog/  p,q,r,s

      . . . . . . . . . . . . .
      end
      subroutine subl
          common /tiger/ y(6),n(2)
          common /dog/ a,b,c(2)

          . . . . . . . . . . . .
      end
      subroutine sub2
          common x(4),y(4)
          common /tiger/a,b,c,d(3),k,k1

          . . . . . . . . . .
      end
***************************
```

contain three common blocks: an unnamed block, a block called *tiger*, and a block called *dog*. The unnamed block contains eight real variables and is shared by the main program and sub2. *Tiger* contains six reals and two integers and is shared by the main program, sub1, and sub2. *Dog* contains four reals that can be accessed by either the main program or by sub1. Observe that the variables in a common block may be referenced by different names in different modules. For example, in the common block *tiger*, the variable called y in the main program is called $y(5)$ in sub1 and $d(2)$ in sub2.

Common blocks are especially helpful when a large number of variables must be accessible to different independent modules.

Initialization of Variables

Variables may be assigned values at compile time, that is, *before* a program is actually run, using one or more DATA statements following the variable declaration statements. A DATA statement has the form

$$\text{data variable\_list /value\_list/}$$

For example, the statement

$$\text{data a,b,c(3),d /1.0,2.0,2.0,2.0,3.0,4.0/}$$

initially makes the following assignments:

$$a = 1.0, \qquad b = 2.0, \qquad c(1) = 2.0, \qquad c(2) = 2.0, \qquad c(3) = 3.0, \qquad d = 4.0$$

The same data statement may be written as

$$\text{data a,b,c(3), d /1.0,3*2.0,3.0,4.0/}$$

```
      common a,b,d(5)
      common /tiger/ x(4),y,z,i(2)
      common /dog/ p,q,r,s
      real bird(4)
      integer cat(10)
****  INITIALIALIZE SOME OF THE VARIABLES
      data  mouse,bird,cat /5,2*2.0,2*7.0,4*6,6*8/
      n = 4
      if (n-4) 20,50,37
37    stop
20    stop
50    print*,' Illustration of ARITHMETIC IF statement'
      go to (37,20,50,37,88,37,20) n+i
88    print*,' Illustration of COMPUTED GO TO statement'
**** Print some of the initialized variables
      print*, mouse,bird(1),bird(4),cat(4),cat(5)
      call sub1
      call sub2(n,cat,rat)
      stop
      end
**************** SUBROUTINES ****************
      subroutine sub1
        common /tiger/ y(6),n(2)
        common /dog/ a,b,c(2)
        print*, y(3),n(1),b,c(2)
        return
      end
      subroutine sub2(i,j1,j2)
        common x(4),y(4)
        common /tiger/a,b,c,d(3),k,k1
        dimension j1(1),j2(1)
        print*, j1(i)
        print*, x(2),y(2),k,d(2)
        return
      end
*********** COMMON BLOCK INITIALIZATION **********
      block data
        common a(8)
        common /tiger/ b(6),i,j
        common /dog/ c(4)
        data i,j /7,8/
        data a,b,c /3*1.0,3*2.0,3*3.0,2*4.0,4*5.0,3*6.0/
      end
```

(a) Program

```
Illustration of ARITHMETIC IF statement
Illustration of COMPUTED GO TO statement
5   2.00000000   7.00000000   6  8
 4.00000000   7   6.00000000    6.00000000
6
 1.00000000    2.00000000   7   5.00000000
```

(b) Program output

Figure 10.22 Program illustrating arithmetic IF, computed GO TO, common blocks, and initialization of variables

Variables in a common block should be initialized using an independent **block data** module. This and other concepts discussed in this section are illustrated in Figure 10.22.

Logical Variables and Values

Logical variables in FORTRAN are very similar to boolean variables in Pascal. Only one of two different values may be assigned to logical variables, .true. or .false. For instance:

```
logical x,y,flag
x = .true.
y = .false.
flag = x
```

Logical values may also be read or written, in which case only a t or an f is read or printed. The LN format is used in reading or writing logical values, where N is a positive integer.

The .AND., .OR., or .NOT. operations may be used with logical expressions. Two logical expressions may be compared with either the .EQV. or the .NEQV. relationship to determine whether or not they are equivalent.

Double-Precision Variables

Double precision is a standard FORTRAN data type. Recall that the number of bits in the significand field of a real number determines the precision of the number. Double-precision numbers have significands that are at least *twice* as large as those of real numbers. Double-precision variables are declared as follows:

```
DOUBLE PRECISION   x,y,z
```

The standard FORTRAN functions that may be used with double-precision operands include DSQRT, DABS, DEXP, DLOG, DLOG10, DSIN, DCOS, DTAN, DATAN, DATAN2, DSINH, DCOSH, and DTANH. User-defined functions that return double-precision values must be explicitly declared as double precision.

Parameter Definitions

The **parameter** definition statement in FORTRAN is like the CONST statement in Pascal; its form is

```
PARAMETER (NAME1=expression1, NAME2=expression2, . . .)
```

The expressions may contain variables already defined in a DATA statement, for example,

```
data x,y,halfdz /1.0,2.0,6.0/
parameter (PI=3.14159, AVAGAD=6.02E23, DOZEN=2*halfdz)
```

Parameter definitions can improve the readability and maintainability of a program. Capital letters are common.

IMPLICIT **Statement**

Unless overridden by explicit declarations, variables beginning with the letter i, j, k, l, m, or n are *implicitly* declared as integers. Other variables are implicitly declared to be reals. The IMPLICIT statement, which allows this implicit definition to be overridden, must be placed before any explicit declaration statements. The statement

```
implicit integer(a-z)
```

causes all variables to be implicitly declared as integer variables. With the statements

```
implicit complex(a-c),double precision (d-g), logical(h)
character*20 cstrgn
```

variables beginning with letters a to c are complex, except for the variable ''cstrng.'' Similarly, variables beginning with letters d to g are double precision, and those starting with h are logical. Of course, these implicit declarations may be overridden by subsequent explicit declarations.

EQUIVALENCE **Statement**

A variable name is associated with data storage space in computer memory. The EQUIVALENCE statement permits different variable names to share the identical storage space. In the statements

```
real x,b(20), c(30),d(5,4),e(25)
equivalence (x,b(3),c(8)), (e(5), d(4,2))
```

the EQUIVALENCE statement indicates that x, $b(3)$, and $c(8)$ are to share the same variable space, which means that any value assigned to the variable x is also assigned to $b(3)$ and $c(8)$. But it also follows that $b(4)$ shares the same space as $c(9)$, $b(5)$ shares the same space as $c(10)$, and so on.

In the second field of the above EQUIVALENCE statement, a value assigned to $e(5)$ is also assigned to $d(4, 2)$. Likewise, $e(6)$ is the same as $d(5, 2)$, and $e(7)$ is the same as $d(1, 3)$.

The program in Figure 10.23 illustrates the use of the EQUIVALENCE, IMPLICIT, logical, double-precision, and parameter directives.

```
            implicit double precision(d),logical(f)
            parameter (PI=3.4159,AVAGAD=6.02E23,DOZEN=2.0*halfdz)
***         Constants should not be used in FORMAT statements
            character*40 a
            character*10 x
            integer p(30),q(20),r(6,8)
            equivalence (k7,p(20),q(10)), (a(11:11),x(1:1)), (p(4),r(2,2))
            data halfdz /6.0/
              z1=1.0/3.0
              dx = 1.0D00
**************** ^^^^ Double precision constant!
            dy = 3.0D00
            d1 = dx/dy
            z2 = DOZEN
            write(6,99) z1,d1,z2
99          format(f25.18,d25.18,f8.1)
            flag1 = .true.
            flag2 = .false.
            flag3 = (z1 .le. DOZEN) .and. (.not. flag2)
            if ((flag1 .eqv. flag2) .or. (flag2 .neqv. flag3)) then
                print*,'    dog'
            else
                print*, ' cat'
            endif
            write (6,13) flag1,flag2,flag3
13          format(3L20)
            k7  = AVAGAD * PI
            do 999  i = 1,30
999           p(i) = i
            a = 'abcdefghijklmnopqrstuvwxyz'
            print*, k7,q(15),x,r(3,3)
            stop
            end
```

(a) Program

```
     .333333343267440800    .3333333333333331E+00      12.0
    dog
                    T                      F                    T
20    25 klmnopqrst 11
```

(b) Program output

Figure 10.23 Program illustrating the use of IMPLICIT, PARAMETER, LOGICAL, DOUBLE PRECISION, and EQUIVALENCE

REVIEW

1. Refer to the program in Figure 10.22. What would the output be if the last data statement in the block data segment were changed to the following?

data a,b,c /6*3.0,6*4.0,6*5.0/

2. What would the output be of the program in Figure 10.23 if the EQUIVALENCE statement were modified to the following?

    equivalence (k7,p(8),q(2)) , (a(5:5), x (2:2)) , (p(1),r(6,1))

3. Consider a text file of character*50 data, the fields of whose data words are as defined in Example 4.4. Data for creating this file are shown in Figure 4.11(b). A larger data set is given in Appendix A. Develop a program module that reads each of these fifty-character records and prints the name, gender, and age of each individual. Use the EQUIVA-LENCE capability to simplify this task.

EXERCISES

1. Identify the types of variables available in FORTRAN.
2. Write a FORTRAN program that prints $\sin(x)$, $\cos(x)$, and $\tan(x)$ for values of x between $0°$ and $89°$ in increments of $1°$.
3. Develop a FORTRAN function that accepts an integer N and an array pointer A and returns the average of the N real numbers in array A.
4. Develop a FORTRAN function that accepts an integer N and an array pointer A and returns the standard deviation of the N real numbers in array A.
5. Develop a subroutine that accepts the coefficients of a quadratic equation and returns two real numbers and an integer. If the roots are real, the subroutine returns an integer value of 0 and the two roots; if the roots are complex, the subroutine returns an integer value of 1 and the real and imaginary component of one of the roots.
6. Develop a function that returns the magnitude of the hyperbolic sine of a complex argument. That is, the function accepts the real part A and the imaginary part B of the argument and returns

$$shmag = sqrt((\sinh(A)\cos(B))^2 + (\cosh(A)\sin(B))^2)$$

   Test your function using the data in Review Question 3, Section 10.2 (p. 201).
7. Develop a subprogram that creates a file of sixteen-letter (character*16) names. (Suggestion: Use data from Appendix A as input.)
8. Develop a subprogram that reads a set of character*16 values from a file, sorts the names in alphabetical order, and writes the names into another file.
9. Develop a subprogram that searches an array of names for a specified name. If the name is located, the index identifying the name is returned; if not, a value of 0 is returned.
10. Develop a subprogram that searches an alphabetized array of names for a specified name. The search should start near the middle of the array. Each time a comparison is made to see if the name has been located, approximately half of the remaining names should be eliminated from the search space.
11. Refer to the INFO-type data defined in Example 10.3. Develop a subroutine that searches a file of INFO-type data and prints the names and ages of all individuals of a specified gender with salary greater than a specified number.
12. Develop and test a subroutine that searches a file of INFO-data and returns a value N, an array of N names, and an array of N phone numbers. The information returned

identifies individuals of a specified gender who are also between specified age limits. The salary, GPA, and quality rating of the individuals returned must equal or exceed specified minima. Test your routine for the following cases:

(a) All number-10 males.

(b) All females between ages 40 and 60 with a GPA greater than 1.9 and a salary greater than $14,599.

13. Develop FORTRAN subroutines to perform the following tasks on matrices whose elements are real numbers.

(a) Return an $n \times n$ identity matrix.

(b) Find and return the matrix product on an $m \times p$ matrix and a $p \times n$ matrix.

14. Develop FORTRAN subroutines that perform the same tasks as the Pascal procedures in Example 8.5.

15. Develop a FORTRAN function that accepts a matrix of coefficients and a vector of constants describing a set of independent linear equations. The function returns a value of one of the unknowns.

16. Develop a subprogram that accepts a matrix of coefficients and a vector of constants for a set of N independent simultaneous equations and returns a vector containing values of the unknowns.

17. Modify the subroutine developed in Exercise 16 so an error message will be printed if the set of equations is not independent.

18. Given that the elements of an $n \times n$ matrix are complex numbers, develop subroutines for each of the following tasks.

(a) Read an $m \times n$ matrix of complex numbers.

(b) Print an $m \times n$ matrix of complex numbers.

(c) Find and return the sum of two $m \times n$ matrices whose elements are complex.

19. Develop a subroutine that accepts a complex number and returns the magnitude and angle (in degrees) of the number.

20. Refer to Example 10.5. An expression for electrical current flowing through the transmission line is

$$I = IR * \cosh(\gamma * x) + \left(\frac{VR}{ZC}\right) * \sinh(\gamma * x)$$

Write a program that computes and prints the magnitude of the current flowing at twenty-five-mile intervals along the 400-mile line. Use the same data as in Example 10.5.

21. Develop a subroutine that finds the product of two conformable matrices of complex elements.

22. Refer to Example 8.11. Develop a FORTRAN program that performs the required task.

23. Refer to the program in Figure 10.22(a). What would the program output be if the three data statements were replaced with the following?

```
data mouse,bird,cat /6,4*5.,2*4,3*3,5*2/
data i,j /1,0/
data a,b,c /18*6.0/
```

24. Refer to the program in Figure 10.23(a). What would the program output be if the EQUIVALENCE statement were replaced with the following?

```
equivalence (k7,p(2),q(3)), (a((13:13),x(5:5)),(p(2),r(2,1))
```

Data Files for Exercises

The listings in this appendix consist of sample data related to certain example problems, review questions, and end-of-chapter exercises. The data files given are long enough so programs that access them will not produce trivial results. The file listings are intended to assist the student in checking and debugging programs.

GRADEFILE (for Example 2.3
and subsequent examples
and exercises)

1123	89	75	63	180
1134	100	100	95	200
1156	67	33	7	15
1172	45	74	91	175
1200	87	87	91	165
1203	91	42	98	200
1334	75	62	77	143
2222	100	68	100	193
2344	97	23	65	104
2553	73	71	70	141
2878	65	74	82	198
5444	61	31	3	15
6428	100	98	87	200
6888	100	100	100	200
7132	98	88	56	175
8200	87	89	81	160
8766	45	56	77	128
9000	91	73	66	156
9124	68	88	70	160
9299	30	56	40	170
9300	55	54	61	168
9855	77	77	77	177
9866	90	90	100	200
9900	32	98	100	200
9900	76	67	76	144
9987	80	90	80	188

SALFILE (for Example 3.4 and subsequent
exercises)

Dog, Dottie	12346	1008.98
Cat, Clem	2346	67.30
Mouse, Mickey . . .	2455	543.25
Mouse, Minnie . . .	2456	543.75
Duck, Donald	2465	53.98
Duck, Daisy	2466	2008.00
Duck, Huey	2467	1.49
Duck, Dewey	2469	1.49
Duck, Louie	2471	1.49
Jackson, Bo	11111	3245.00
Jackson, Kate	11200	2567.00
Taylor, Liz	11206	5698.75
Bull, Ferdinand . . .	13123	76.29
Cow, Clara	13888	246.66
Sajak, Pat	14445	777.77

SDATA (for creating file STUDENT_RECORDS, and for Example
4.5 and subsequent examples and exercises)

Doe,Jane	Bush,George	Evert,Chris
Female	Macho man	Female
38117	44110	44117
410–90–4320	273–32–1234	301–32–8705
JUnior	FReshman	SEnior
20	65	33
1000	100000	800000
2.93	2.09	3.82
82	25	132
Carver,George Washington	Jackson,Jesse	Kennedy,Jane
Man	Male	Female
38409	44109	44112
000–01–1234	273–32–8700	373–32–9102
GRaduate student	JUnior	SOphomore
97	44	30
11500	25000	150000
3.98	3.10	3.91
425	156	85
Jackson,Michael	White,Vanna	
Male	Female	
10002	38152	
555–55–5555	273–32–8710	
SOphomore	JUnior	
29	29	
999999	500000	
2.80	4.00	
42	100	

MYDATA (for creating a file of INFO
records, and for Example 6.6 and
subsequent examples and exercises)

Sajak,Pat	Glutz,Gloria
M	F
35	13
Wheel man	Weight lifter
200000.00	12.95
454–2234	555–4444
5	3
2.6	1.98
White,Vanna	Williams,J.Herman
F	M
29	53
Super star	Writer
5000000.00	53500.00
555–1212	682–0234
10	2
4.0	2.22
Jackson,Michael	Minh,Ho Chi
M	M
26	99
Singer	Top guy
3.2E18	200000.00
682–9999	000–0000
9	6
2.98	2.5
Thomas,Debbi	Redford,Robert
F	M
21	45
Olympic Skater	Actor
50.00	2230000.00
123–2222	876–5432
10	9
3.95	2.98
North,Ollie	Taylor,Elizabeth
M	F
42	54
Fawn's friend	Cover girl
98000.00	6.02E23
222–1234	999–9999
7	9
2.84	3.99

B

Answers to Review Questions

SECTION 1.1

1. The manufacturing technology at that time was not developed well enough to fabricate the components of his machines.
2. The principal components of a computer are the CPU, memory, and input/output devices. The CPU consists of an ALU, internal registers and a control segment.
3. A *microprocessor* is a computer CPU fabricated on either a single integrated circuit (chip) or a small number of chips.

SECTION 1.2

1. (a) 0100 1000 0100 1111 0101 0010 0101 0011 0100 0101
   (b) 0011 0101 0011 0010 0011 1000 0011 0000
   (c) 0101 0100 0100 1001 0100 0111 0100 0101 0101 0010
                    0011 1001 0011 1001
2. (a) 0001 0100 1010 0000   (b) 1111 1111 1101 0011
   (c) 0010 1001 0100 0000   (d) 1111 1111 1010 0110
3. (a) 0100 0101 1010 0101 0000 0000 0000 0000
   (b) 1100 0010 0011 0100 0000 0000 0000 0000
   (c) 0100 0010 0110 0101 0100 1100 1100 1101
   (d) 0011 1111 1111 0011 0011 0011 0011 0011
4. (a) −5.0 (b) 12.0

SECTION 2.1

1. *Declaration* statements and *executable* statements are found in Pascal programs.
2. Information may be passed to a subprogram *by value* or *by reference* to a variable.
3. program (output);
   begin
         writeln(' Isaac Newton, 13 years old');
         writeln(' Slippery Rock University');
   end.

SECTION 2.2

1. An *interpreter* translates and executes one command of source code. Sequentially numbered commands are translated and executed sequentially. A *compiler* translates one or more modules of source code into code that more closely resembles machine code (object code).
2. (a) *Source code* is computer code written in a format similar to that of natural language.
   (b) When source code is "translated" by a compiler or assembler, the lower-level code is called *object code*.
   (c) A *library* is a file of object programs. Each program performs some well-defined task.
   (d) A *linker* is a program that combines the various object modules needed in a program. The output of a linker is the absolute code or computer code for a program.
   (e) An operating system is a program or a set of programs that manages the operation of a computer.

SECTION 2.3

1. The COMMENT statement will not be terminated until line 160. Therefore, the program declaration statement in line 120 will be considered to be just part of the comment!
2. Character codes
3. Since "mouse" is a real number, the data assigned to "mouse" consist of a sign bit, a biased characteristic, and a significand. If 32-bit IEEE floating point representation is used, the binary number assigned to "mouse" is:

$$0100\ 0000\ 0100\ 1000\ 1111\ 0101\ 1100\ 0011$$

SECTION 2.4

1. (a) 19   (b) 61   (c) 13   (d) 15
2. (a) 3   (b) 12.6666 . . .
3. $Q1$: 5.0; $Q2$: -1; $Q3$: 24

SECTION 2.5

1. **(a)** 7   **(b)** 21   **(c)** 30 900 2700

2.
```
program review(input,output);
    (* Compute and print total in account for a fixed
       deposit of $1000 on Jan 1, 1990. Find total at
       end of each year from 1990 to 2050.  Rate is
       5.75%.  Interest is compound annually *)
    var tot: real; year: integer;
            begin
                tot := 1000.0;
                year := 1990;
                while (year <= 2050) do
                    begin
                        tot := tot*1.075;
                        writeln (year:10, tot:12:2);
                        year := year+1;
                    end;
            end.
```

3.
```
program review(input,output);
    (* Compute and print total in account for a fixed
       deposit of $1000 on Jan 1, 1990. Find total at
       end of each year from 1990 to 2050.  Rate is
       5.75%.  Interest is compound QUARTERLY *)
    var tot: real; year: integer;
            begin
                tot := 1000.0;
                year := 1990;
                while (year <= 2050) do
                    begin
                        tot := tot*(1.0 + 0.075/4);
                        tot := tot*(1.0 + 0.075/4);
                        tot := tot*(1.0 + 0.075/4);
                        tot := tot*(1.0 + 0.075/4);
                        writeln (year:10, tot:12:2);
                        year := year+1;
                    end;
            end.
```

SECTION 2.6

1. The average ID number will be computed.

2. Refer to Figure 2.8. Change line 200 to:

```
readln(GRADEFILE,id,test1,test1,test1,score);
```

Using the data in Appendix A, the average is 159.81.

3. In line 170, change;   count := 1;   to   count := 0;

SECTION 2.7

1. CONSTANT declarations make a program more readable and easier to maintain.
2. User-defined subprograms enable programming tasks to be developed in small, independent modules.
3. Line 35.

SECTION 3.1

```
1. program trig(output);
      const RAD =  0.01745329;
      var x: real;
          begin
               x := 30.0;
               while (x <= 60.0) do
                  begin
                      writeln(x:5:1,'    ', 1.0/cos(RAD*x),
                                    '    ', 1.0/sin(RAD*x));
                      x := x + 1.0;
                  end;
          end.
2. program hyper(output);(** hyperbolic functions **)
      var x,sinh,cosh: real;
          begin
               x := 0.0;
               while(x<=3.0) do
                  begin
                      sinh:= (exp(x) - exp(-x))/2.0;
                      cosh:= (exp(x) + exp(-x))/2.0;
                      writeln(x:6:1,sinh:12:3,cosh:12:3);
                      x := x + 0.1;
                  end;
          end.
```

SECTION 3.2

```
1. program functions(output);
  (*** SINH and TAHN functions ***)
     var x,y: real;
     function sinh(x:real):real;
        var y: real;
        begin
             y := (exp(x) -exp(-x))/2.0;
             sinh := y;
        end;
     function tanh(x:real):real;
         var y: real;
         begin
              y := sinh(x)/(exp(x) + exp(-x)) * 2.0;
              tanh := y;
         end;
  (** Start test program **)
        begin
             x := sinh(0.0); y := tanh(0.0);
             writeln(x:10:3,y:10:3);
             x := sinh(1.0); y := tanh(1.0);
             writeln(x:10:3,y:10:3);
        end.
```

2.
```
program degree_radian(output);
(** Solution to review question 3-2 **)
    function degrad(c:char; x:real):real;
        var y:real;
        begin
            y:= 0.0;
            if (c = 'R') then y := x * 3.14159265/180.0;
            if (c = 'D') then y := x * 180.0/3.14159265;
            if (c <> 'R') then if (c <> 'D') then
                    writeln('  Invalid argument in DEGRAD');
            degrad := y;
        end;
(** Start test program **)
    begin
        writeln(degrad('R', 180.0));
        writeln(degrad('D',3.14159265/4.0));
        writeln(degrad('r',0.0));
    end.
```

3. (a) 6   (b) 11

4. (a) 10   (b) 45

5.
```
program recur(output);
    function sum(n:integer):integer;
    (*** Returns sum of squares of even integers up to N ***)
    var y: integer;
        begin
            if (n <= 0) then y := 0
            else y := n*n + sum(n-2);
            sum := y;
        end;
(** Start test program **)
    begin
        writeln( sum(4));
        writeln( sum(10));
    end.
```

SECTION 3.3

1.
```
program  review(output);
    var s,c,t:real;
    procedure sct(x:real; var a,b,c:real);
(* Returns sin, cos and tan of angle expressed in degrees **)
        var r:real;
        begin
            r := 3.14159265/180.0;
            a := sin(r*x);
            b := cos(r*x);
            c := a/b;
        end;
(*** Start test program ***)
    begin
        sct(45.0,s,c,t);
        writeln(s:20:4,c:20:4,t:20:4);
    end.
```

```
2. program review(output);
      var big,small:real;
      procedure switch(var x,y:real);
          var temp: real;
          begin
              temp:=x; x:=y; y:=temp;
          end;
      procedure biglit(a,b,c:real; var small,large:real);
 (** Returns largest and smallest number **)
      begin
          if (a > b) then switch(a,b);
          if (b > c) then switch(b,c);
          if (a > b) then switch(a,b);
          small := a;   large := c;
      end;
 (*** Start test program ***)
  begin
      biglit(35.3,-32.0,15,small,big);
      writeln(small:10:2,big:10:2);
      biglit(4.0,3.0,2.0,small,big);
      writeln(small:10:2,big:10:2);
      biglit(1.0,2.0,3.0,small,big);
      writeln(small:10:2,big:10:2);
  end.
3. program review(output);
      var a,b:real;
      procedure hyp(x:real; var s,c:real);
      begin
          s := (exp(x) -exp(-x))/2.0;
          c := (exp(x) + exp(-x))/2.0;
      end;
  begin(*** program ***)
      hyp(1.0,a,b);
      writeln(a:10:3,b:10:3);
  end.
```

SECTION 3.4

1. Good programs should be readable, easy to modify or maintain, well documented, and developed in small, independent modules. Of course, they should work!

2. First, the task to be performed must be thoroughly understood. Then it should be subdivided into a set of simpler subtasks. Subdivision of subtasks should continue until the subtasks are simple. Then subprograms should be developed for the simple tasks. After this is successfully completed, these subprograms should be used to perform more difficult tasks. This general technique is called a *top-down bottom-up approach* to problem solving.

3.
```
program review(output,datafile);
(*** Find names of all males in salfile ***)
    type name = array[1..16] of char;
    var x:name; i,id:integer;
        datafile:text;
    begin
        assign(datafile,'salfile');   (** TURBO **)
        reset(datafile);
        while not eof(datafile) do
            begin
                for i := 1 to 16 do read(datafile,x[i]);
                readln(datafile,id);
                if odd(id) then writeln('      ',x);
            end;
    end.
```

4.
```
program review(output,datafile);
    type name = array[1..16] of char;
    var x:name; i,id:integer;  salary:real;
        datafile:text;
(** Find women who make at least $500.00 **)
    begin
        assign(datafile,'salfile');   (** TURBO **)
        reset(datafile);
        while not eof(datafile) do
            begin
                for i := 1 to 16 do read(datafile,x[i]);
                readln(datafile,id,salary);
                if not odd(id) then
                if (salary >= 500.0) then writeln('      ',x);
            end;
    end.
```

SECTION 4.1

1. **(a)** The file requires eighteen bytes of storage space, including space for two Newline codes and one EOF code.

(b) There are *no* integers. Only character codes are stored in a text file. Certain strings of character codes may be interpreted as integers.

2. *Buffers* are sets of contiguous memory bytes. Since CPU input is obtained from memory, data from files must first be transferred to memory buffers.

SECTION 4.2

1. Modify the algorithm given in Section 4.2 in the following way. Insert step 0 before step 1. Step 0 is:

0. Set sign to 1.

Change step 2 to the following:

2. If character is between 0 and 9, go to step 3. If character is a minus sign, then:
   (a) Set sign to -1.
   (b) Get the next character.
   (c) Go to step 3.
   Print error mesage and halt.

Add step 5(a) after step 5:

5(a). If sign = −1, replace the value assigned to the variable with the corresponding negative value.

2. The WRITELN procedure does the following:

   (a) Gets a binary value corresponding to the results of an expression or an assignment to a variable.

   (b) Converts these data to a coded character string representing the "value" of the data.

   (c) Writes this character string to the specified file. (Note: The default file is OUTPUT, which represents the user's console. Also, the WRITELN procedure performs this task with each argument in the argument list, then writes a Newline code in the specified file.)

3.
```
{100}  (* Program that counts the number of bytes in a textfile.
              The LOGICAL name of the file is dog_file *)
{120}  program count_bytes(output,dog_file);
{130}  var        n:integer;
{140}                 dog_file: text;
{150}                 c: char;
{160}  begin
{162}  (** In TURBO Pascal assignment of true file name to
              logical file name is made DURING program execution **)
{164}          assign(dog_file,'mydata'); (** TURBO Pascal **)
{170}          n := 1;   (** Tis is the EOF byte **)
{180}          reset(dog_file);
{190}          while not eof(dog_file) do
{200}            if eoln(dog_file) then begin
{210}                n:= n+1;  readln(dog_file)
{220}                                    end
{230}              else begin  n := n + 1;   read(dog_file,c); end;
{240}          writeln('  The number of bytes in the file is ',n);
{250}  end.
```

SECTION 4.3

1. READLN, WRITELN, and EOLN

2. Text files contain *lines*, that is, character codes followed by Newline marks. This file contains no Newline codes.

3.
```
program review (input,output,four_file);
      type four = array [1..4] of char;
      var four_file : file of four; x: four;
      begin
            assign(four_file,'four'); (** TURBO **)
            rewrite(four_file);
            writeln(' Enter four-letter words. Exit with EXIT');
            while x<> 'EXIT' do begin
                  readln(x[1],x[2],x[3],x[4]);
                  if x <> 'EXIT' then write(four_file,x);
                            end;
            close(four_file);   (** TURBO Pascal **)
            writeln; writeln;
            reset(four_file);
            while not eof(four_file) do
                  begin
                      read(four_file,x );
                      writeln(x);
                  end;
      end.
```

SECTION 4.4

1. ```
program search(STUDENT_RECORDS,output);
type student_record = array[1..50] of char;
var STUDENT_RECORDS: file of student_record; n:integer;
      function get_num:integer; (* Returns number of STU RECS *)
          var   i:integer; rec:student_record;
        begin
              reset(STUDENT_RECORDS);   i:= 0;
              while not eof(STUDENT_RECORDS) do
                  begin
                      i:= i+1;
                      read(STUDENT_RECORDS,rec);
                  end;
          get_num :=i;
          end;
 (*** Start test program ***)
 begin
      assign(STUDENT_RECORDS,'recs'); (** TURBO Pascal **)
      n := get_num; writeln;
      writeln(' There are ',n:2,' student records.');
 end.
```

2. ```
program search(STUDENT_RECORDS,output);
type name = array[1..16] of char;
     age = array[1..11] of char;
     student_record = array[1..50] of char;
var STUDENT_RECORDS: file of student_record;
      procedure look(x:char); (** Prints name and age for
          students of specified gender **)
          var n:name; i:integer; rec:student_record; a:age;
        begin
              reset(STUDENT_RECORDS);
              while not eof(STUDENT_RECORDS) do
                  begin
                      read(STUDENT_RECORDS,rec);
                      for i := 1 to 16 do n[i] := rec[i];
                      a[1] := rec[36]; a[2] := rec[37];
                      if rec[17] = x then
                          writeln(' ',n,'      ',a);
                  end;
          end;
 (*** Start test program ***)
 begin
      assign(STUDENT_RECORDS,'recs');    (*  TURBO PASCAL *)
      look('M');
 end.
```

3.
```pascal
program search(STUDENT_RECORDS,output);
type ssnum = array[1..11] of char;
     student_record = array[1..50] of char;
var STUDENT_RECORDS: file of student_record; i:integer;
    sr:student_record;
      procedure look(x:ssnum; var rec:student_record);
         var i:integer;  ss: ssnum; flag:boolean; y:student_record;
         begin
             reset(STUDENT_RECORDS);    flag := true;
             while not eof(STUDENT_RECORDS) do
                 begin
                     read(STUDENT_RECORDS,y);
                     for i := 1 to 11 do ss[i] := y[i+22];
                     if x = ss then begin
                                      flag:= false;
                                      rec := y;
                                      end;
                 end;
             if flag = true then for i := 1 to 50 do rec[i] := ' ';
         end;
(*** Start test program ***)
begin
     assign(STUDENT_RECORDS,'recs');    (*  TURBO PASCAL *)
     look('273-32-8710',sr);
     for i := 1 to 16 do write(sr[i]);  writeln;
     look('111-22-3333',sr);
     for i := 1 to 16 do write(sr[i]); writeln;
     look('373-32-9102',sr);
     for i := 1 to 16 do write(sr[i]); writeln;
end.
```

SECTION 5.1

1. True and True
2. CAT and MOUSE are printed.
3. CAT, DOG, and MOUSE are printed.

SECTION 5.2

1.
```pascal
program fahr_to_cels(output);
      procedure celsius(start,quit,inc:integer);
           var c: real;
           begin
               while (start <= quit) do
                   begin
                       c := start -32;
                       c := c * 5/9;
                       writeln(start:10,c:10:2);
                       start := start + inc;
                   end;
           end;
begin(** Start test program **)
     writeln; celsius(-300,500,20);
end.
```

```
2. program search(STUDENT_RECORDS,output);
   type student_record = array[1..50] of char;
        gpa = array[1..4] of char;
   var STUDENT_RECORDS: file of student_record;
        procedure look(x:gpa; sex:char );
           var  i:integer; z:gpa; flag:boolean; y:student_record;
           begin
              reset(STUDENT_RECORDS);    flag := true;
              while (not eof(STUDENT_RECORDS)) and flag do
                 begin
                    read(STUDENT_RECORDS,y);
                    for i := 1 to 4 do z[i] := y[i+43];
                    if (z >= x) and (y[17] = sex) then begin
                                           flag:= false;
                       for i := 1 to 16 do write(y[i]);
                       write('    ');
                       for i:= 23 to 33 do write(y[i]);
                       writeln;
                                                     end;
                 end;
              if flag = true then writeln('  None found!');
           end;
   (*** Start test program ***)
   begin
       assign(STUDENT_RECORDS,'recs');    (*  TURBO PASCAL *)
       writeln;
       look ('2.00','F');
       look ('3.00','M');
       look ('4.00','M');
       look ('4.00','F');
   end.
```

SECTION 5.3

(Note: Just the REPEAT-UNTIL structure is shown below. The remainder of each program is the same as in the previous examples.)

```
1. repeat
       read(STUDENT_RECORDS,rec);
       for i := 1 to 16 do n[i] := rec[i];
       if x = n then
              begin
                 found := true;
                 for i := 1 to 11 do ss[i] := rec[i+22];
                 writeln; writeln(n:20,ss:20);
              end;
   until  eof(STUDENT_RECORDS)  or  found;
```

2. repeat
```
    c := start -32;
    c := c * 5/9;
    writeln(start:10,c:10:2);
    start := start + inc;
until start > quit;
```

3. repeat
```
    read(STUDENT_RECORDS,y);
    for i := 1 to 4 do z[i] := y[i+43];
    if (z >= x) and (y[17] = sex) then begin
                        flag:= false;
        for i := 1 to 16 do write(y[i]);
        write('    ');
        for i:= 23 to 33 do write(y[i]);
        writeln;
                                    end;
until eof(STUDENT_RECORDS) or not flag;
```

SECTION 5.4

1.
```
var := exp1;
    while var >= exp2 do
        begin
            STATEMENT;
            var := pred(var);
        end;
```

2.
```
program for_loop(output);
    var s,c,t,x:real; i: integer;
    begin
        for I := 0 to 100   do
            begin
                x := i/100.0; s := sin(x); c := cos(x); t := s/c;
                writeln(x:10:4,s:10:4,c:10:4,t:10:4);
            end;
    end.
```

3. (a) 1
   (b) 1
   (c) ONE

SECTION 5.5

```
1. program search(STUDENT_RECORDS,output);
     type   gpa = array[1..4] of char;
            sal = array[1..6] of char;
            student_record = array[1..50] of char;
   var STUDENT_RECORDS: file of student_record;
          procedure look(sex:char;salmin,salmax:sal; gpamin:gpa);
             var i:integer; rec:student_record; x:sal; y:gpa;
             begin
                reset(STUDENT_RECORDS);
                while not eof(STUDENT_RECORDS) do
                   begin
                      read(STUDENT_RECORDS,rec);
                      for i := 44 to 47 do y[i-43] := rec[i];
                      for i := 1 to 6 do x[i] := rec[i+37];
                      if sex = rec[17] then
                         if (x > salmin) and (x < salmax) then
                            if y >= gpamin then
                               begin
                                  for i := 1 to 16 do write(rec[i]);
                                  write('   ');
                                  for i := 23 to 33 do write(rec[i]);
                                  writeln;
                               end;
                   end;
             end;
   (*** Start test program ***)
   begin
      assign(STUDENT_RECORDS,'recs');    (*   TURBO PASCAL *)
      look('M',' 20000','250000','2.50');
   end.
```

2. LORI, LISA, and LANA.

SECTION 5.6

1. **(a)** 10.0, 6.0, and 3.2
   (b) 15.0, 8.0, and 1.7
2.
12345	−8765
0	482
−26	0
−5	23456

3. Make the following changes to the function CONVERT shown in Figure 5.12(a):
   Change: (c <= '9')   to   (c <= '7')
   Change: num := 10 * num + n;   to   num := 8 * num + n;

SECTION 6.1

1. 180.62 and 170.00
2. 185, 365, and 0
3. Refer to Figure 5.12. Replace the CASE structure with the statement:

$$n := ord(c) - ord('0');$$

```
4. program hex(output);
       function hd(c:char):integer;
          var i:integer;
             begin
                i := -1;
                if (c >= 'A') and (c <= 'F') then
                    i := ord(c) - ord('A') +10;
                if (c >= '0') and (c <= '9') then
                    i := ord(c) -ord('0');
                if i<0 then writeln(' ERROR in HD arg.');
                hd := i;
             end;
     begin(** Test program **)
        writeln(hd('C'));  writeln(hd('4'));  writeln(hd('x'));
     end.
```

SECTION 6.2

1. User-defined variables may appear in argument lists of subprograms. Structured variables may not appear in argument lists.
2. 4

   > HELL

   5
   HELL

3. Washington,Georg
   Doe,Jane
   King,Martin Luth
   Chu,Ming

SECTION 6.3

1. To exchange the values assigned to two variables, the value of one of them must be "temporarily" assigned to a third variable.
2. This statement causes the sorting routine to execute more rapidly. Elements in the proper position in the array are no longer compared with unsorted elements.
3. Refer to Figure 6.11. Change the line

$$\text{if na[i]} > \text{na[i + 1] then begin}$$

to:

$$\text{if na[i]} < \text{na[i + 1] then begin}$$

SECTION 6.4

1. Smart,Becky   18
     Smart,Becky   18
   12
   3.25

2. and **3.**
```pascal
program review(input,output,herfile);
     type   str = array[1..16] of char;
            ph_num = array[1..8] of char;
            quality = 1..10;
                info = record
                           name:   str;
                           gen:    'F'..'M';
                           age:    0..110;
                           job:    str;
                           salary: real;
                           phone:  ph_num;
                           rating:  quality;
                           gpa:     real
                       end;
                black_book = array[1..100] of info;
     var   herfile: file of info;
           stu_recs: black_book; i,n:integer;
     procedure get_recs(var num:integer; var x:black_book);
     (** Reads file of INFO records into an array **)
         var rec:info;
         begin
             reset(herfile);   num := 0;
             while not eof(herfile) do
                 begin
                     num := num+1;
                     read(herfile,x[num]);
                 end;
         end;
     procedure sort_recs(n:integer; var x:black_book);
     (** Sorts an array of n INFO records alphabetically by name **)
         var sorted: boolean; i:integer; temp: info;
             begin
                 n := n-1;   sorted := false;
                 while not sorted do
                     begin
                         sorted := true;
                         for i := 1 to n do
                           if x[i].name > x[i+1].name then
                                                begin
                                                    sorted := false;
                                                    temp := x[i];
                                                    x[i] := x[i+1];
                                                    x[i+1] := temp;
                                                end;
                         if  n > 1 then  n := n -1;
                     end;
             end;
     (******  Start test program      *******)
     begin
             assign(herfile,'secretfile'); (** TURBO Pascal **)
             get_recs(n,stu_recs);
             sort_recs(n,stu_recs);
             for I := 1 to n do writeln('    ',stu_recs[i].name);
     end.
```

SECTION 6.5

1. The function may be written using a set of sixty-three characters and the IN command. The following method may be easier.

```
program check(input,output);
    var c:char;
    function check(x:char): char;
        var c:char;
            begin
                c:= '$';
                if (x>='a') and (x<='z') then c := x;
                if (x>='A') and (x<='Z') then c := x;
                if (x>='0') and (x<='9') then c := x;
                if (x = ' ') then c := x;
                if c = '$' then writeln(' INVALID CHAR');
                check := c;
            end;
  begin(** Test program **)
      repeat
            readln(c);
            c := check(c);
            writeln(c:20);
      until c = 'Z';
 end.
```

2. (a) dog   cat   mouse   bird   fish
         (* nothing *)
     dog   cat   mouse
     dog   cat   mouse
     cat
     dog   cat   mouse
     dog   cat   mouse   bird
         (* nothing *)
     bird

(b) Only the relationship $a = b$ returns a value True.

SECTION 7.1

1. (a) 3   **(b)** 2   **(c)** 5

2. Four lines are printed. The words printed are LISA, LANA, 3, and 4.

SECTION 7.2

1. A *dynamic* variable is one created while a program is running. For variables that are not dynamic, provisions for allocating memory space must be made prior to program execution.

2. (a) Get the pointer identifying the kth node.
(b) Create a new element and assign data to its fields.
(c) Write the pointer value stored in the kth element into the pointer field of the new element.
(d) Put the pointer value identifying the new element into the pointer field of the kth element.

3. Bill and Suzi

4.

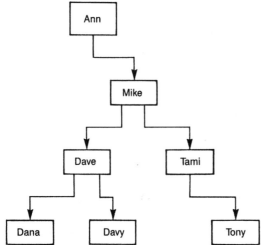

SECTION 7.3

1. The following function requires type definitions such as those shown in Figure 7.10.

```
function search(entry:pinfo; n:str): pinfo;
var flag: boolean;
begin
     flag:=false;
     while (entry<>nil) and not flag do
        if entry^.name = n then flag := true
             else entry := entry^.pl;
     search := entry;
end;
```

To test the function, the following commands may be used:

$$pt := search(entry, \text{'Bush,George} \qquad \text{'});$$
$$\text{if } pt<>nil \text{ then } writeln(pt\text{^.name)};$$

2. A binary tree created from a sorted set of data is a trivial tree structure since each node will have subsequent elements only on its right-hand side.

3. The names are printed in alphabetical order, then in reverse alphabetical order.

4. To remove the kth box, where $1 < k < n$:
   (a) Put the up-pointer in the kth box into the up-pointer field of the $(k - 1)$th box.
   (b) Put the back-pointer in the kth box into the back-pointer field of the $(k + 1)$th box.
   (c) Dispose of the kth box.

   To remove the first box:
   (a) Put nil into the back-pointer of the second box.
   (b) Replace the ENTRY pointer with the up-pointer in the first box.
   (c) Dispose of the first box.

To remove the *n*th box:
(a) Put nil into the up-pointer of the (*n* − 1)th box.
(b) Dispose of the *n*th box.

SECTION 8.1

1. 11.0   5.0   11.5
    30.8   24.85   20.9
    44.0   36.5   33.5

2.  ```
    rmat(3,4,a);   pmat(3,4,a);
    rmat(4,3,b);   pmat(4,3,b);
    rmat(3,3,c);   pmat(3,3,c);
    matmul(3,3,3,c,c,d);
    matmul(3,3,4,a,b,e);
    matadd(d,e,f);
    pmat(3,3,f);
    ```

3.  ```
    procedure add3(m,n:integer; a,b,c:matrix; var d:matrix);
        var i,j: integer;
        begin
            for i := 1 to m do
                for j := 1 to n do
                    d[i,j] := a[i,j] + b[i,j] + c[i,j];
        end;
    ```

SECTION 8.2

1. 2.0
2. (a) 1.0 and 4.0
    (b) not independent
    (c) not independent
    (d) 1.0, 2.0, 3.0, 4.0, and 5.0
3. EPSILON = 1.0
    (a) not independent
    (b) not independent
    (c) −5.8, 3.46, −1.45, 1.08

SECTION 8.3

1. −6.00   10.00
     3.00 + *j* 4.00
    −2.00 + *j* 1.00

2. 36.87
143.13
216.87
−36.87
0.00
180.00
Indeterminant form. 0.0 is returned.
0.00
90.00
−90,00

3.
```
procedure cpolar(mag,ang:real; var cc: complex);
   var x: real;
   begin
        x := 3.14159265/180.0;
        ccomplex(mag*cos(x*ang),mag*sin(x*ang),cc);
   end;
```

To invoke the above procedure:

cpolar(100.0,−120.0,c); cwrite(c);

SECTION 8.4

1. 0.0   6.50   0.00
10.00   0.19   −85.21
2. 0.40, −0.14, 0.57, 0.42, 0.02
3.   Matrix of coefficients   Vector of constants

15.0	−1.5	0.0	−4.0		4.5
−1.5	15.5	−3.0	−4.0		−4.5
0.0	−3.0	18.0	−8.0		10.5
−4.0	−4.0	−8.0	25.0		−1.5

The currents are: 0.34, −0.08, 0.65, 0.19

SECTION 9.1

1. 5 and 2 are printed on the first line, 5 and 8 on the second line.
2. **(a)** *a*, *c*, and *d* in FISH and *b* in DOG
      (b) CAT, FISH, HORSE, and PIG
3. Declare PIG before declaring HORSE.

SECTION 9.2

1. Eighteen

2.
```
procedure back_print(p:box_ptr);
    begin
        if p <> nil then
            begin
                    back_print(p^.p2);
                    writeln('    ',p^.name);
                    back_print(p^.p1);
            end;
    end;
```

3. 129

4. Forty

SECTION 9.3

1. 24, 7777, and 51541

2.
```
program base_B (input,output);
    procedure print_num(num,base:integer);
    (** Prints value of num using base-B **)
      var  rem,quot,i: integer;  c:char;
      begin
        quot := num div base;
        if quot <> 0 then print_num(quot,base);
        rem := num mod base;
        i := rem + ord('0'); (* Get ord of character *)
        c := chr(i);  write(c:1);
      end;
begin(** Start test program **)
    writeln; print_num(20,2);  writeln;
            print_num(4095,10); writeln;
end.
```

3.
```
function solve(j,n:integer; m:matrix; v:vector):real;

  (** Find jth unknown  in set of n equations **)
    var  x:real; top:matrix;
    begin
        x := det(n,m);
        if abs(x) < EPSILON then writeln(' NOT INDEPENDENT')
        else         begin
                        top:=m;
                        cnew(j,n,v,top);
                        x:=det(n,top)/x;
                    end;
            solve := x;
    end;
```

SECTION 9.4

1.
```
procedure deleteij(i,j,n:integer; var mm:matrix);
(** Deletes ith row and jth column from an nxn matrix **)
    var p,q:integer;
    begin
        for p := i to n-1 do
                for q:= 1 to n do mm[p,q]:=mm[p+1,q];
        for p := 1 to n-1 do
                for q:= j to n-1 do mm[p,q]:=mm[p,q+1];
    end;
```

2. (a) $\begin{bmatrix} -3 & 2 \\ 2 & -1 \end{bmatrix}$ (b) $\begin{bmatrix} .2 & .1 & -.05 \\ -.1 & .2 & .025 \\ .4 & -.8 & .4 \end{bmatrix}$

3. (a) Matrix is singular. There is no inverse.

   (b) $\begin{bmatrix} 4.00 & 0.00 & 0.50 \\ 2.00 & 4.00 & 0.00 \\ 0.00 & 8.00 & 2.00 \end{bmatrix}$

      $\begin{bmatrix} 1.00 & 0.00 & 0.00 \\ 0.00 & 1.00 & 0.00 \\ 0.00 & 0.00 & 1.00 \end{bmatrix}$

SECTION 10.1

1. 3.5, 3.0, 3

2. This part of the program prints n and 2 raised to the nth power for $n = 1$ to 8.

3.
```
        do 99 i = 1,99,2
        x = i
        a = x*x
        b = x**3.0
        c = x**0.5
        d = x**(1.0/3.0)
99      print*,x,a,b,c,d
        stop
        end
```

SECTION 10.2

1.
```
integer exp2
cube(x) = x*x*x
cubrt(x) = x**(1.0/3.0)
a = cube(2.0)
b = cubrt(27.0)
c = cubrti(8)
d = exp2(8)
print*,a,b,c,d
stop
end
function cubrti(i)
x = i
cubrti = x**(1.0/3.0)
return
end
integer function exp2(i)
exp2  = 2**i
return
end
```

2.
```
*     find real roots of a quadratic equation
          call root(1.0,5.0,6.0,x1,x2)
          print*,x1,x2
          stop
          end
          subroutine root(a,b,c,r1,r2)
          d = b*b -4.0*a*c
          if (d .lt. 0.0) then
              x1=0
              x2=0
              print*, ' No real root'
          else
              d = d**(1.0/2.0)
              r1 =(-b +d)/(2.0*a)
              r2 = (-b -d)/(2.0*a)
          endif
          return
          end
```

3.
```
a  = chmag(0.0,0.0)              function cosh(x)
b  = chmag(.048,.465)              cosh = (exp(x) + exp(-x))/2.0
print*,a,b                       return
stop                             end
end                              function sinh(x)
function  chmag(a,b)               sinh = (exp(x) -exp(-x))/2.0
x = cosh(a)*cos(b)               return
y = sinh(a)*sin(b)               end
chmag = sqrt(x*x + y*y)
return
end
```

SECTION 10.3

1. 4.0　　10.0　　18.0
　2.5 plus 5.5 plus 6.5 equals 14.5
2. Change the line

　　　　　　　　　　　if (c .eq. gen) then

　to:

　　　　　　　　　　if((c .eq. gen) .or. (gen .eq.'B')) then

3.

```
              open (unit=10, file='mydata',status='old')
              call look(21,59)
              stop
              end
              subroutine look(min,max)
              character*16 x,name
                  rewind(unit=10)
99            format(a)
97            read(10,99,end=13) name
              read(10,99)x
98            format(i3)
              read(10,98) iage
               do 96 i=1,5
96            read(10,99) x
              if ((iage .ge.min) .and. (iage .le. max)) then
                  write(6,95) name
              endif
95            format(20x,a)
              go to 97
13            continue
              return
              end
```

SECTION 10.4

1. (a) 168　　**(b)** 200
2. 190, 43.0, and 31.0

3.
```
            character*16 n(100)
            n(1) = 'dog            '
            n(2) = 'duck           '
            n(3) = 'danny          '
            n(4) = 'dannielle      '
            call sort(4,n)
            do 99 i = 1,4
  99        print*,n(i)
            stop
            end
  *      BUBBLE SORT
            subroutine sort(n,a)
            character*16 a(1),temp
            m = n-1
            do 99 i = 1,m
            do 99 j = 1,m
            if (a(j) .gt. a(j+1))then
                temp = a(j)
                a(j) = a(j+1)
                a(j+1)  = temp
            endif
  99        continue
            return
            end
```

4.
```
complex  a
a = cmplx(-0.5,sqrt(3.0)/2.0)
ang  = angle(a)
print*,ang
stop
end
  function angle(c)
  complex  c
  angle = atan2(aimag(c),real(c))*180./3.14159265
  return
  end
```

SECTION 10.5

1.
```
Illustration of ARITHMETIC IF statement
Illustration of COMPUTED GO TO statement
5   2.00000000    7.00000000   6  8
  4.00000000  7   5.00000000    5.00000000
6
  3.00000000    3.00000000   7   5.00000000
```

2.
```
    .333333343267440800   .33333333333333331E+00    12.0
  dog
             T                 F               T
  8  21 defghijklm 10
```

3.

```
      ***** Reads records  from file 'recs'. Prints each
      ****         name, age and gender.
            character*50 rec
            character*1 sex
            character*16 name
            character*2 age
            equivalence (age(1:1),rec(36:36)),(name(1:1),rec(1:1))
            equivalence (sex,rec(17:17))
            open(unit=13,file='recs'.status='old')
            rewind(unit=13)
    1       read(13,99,end=2)rec
   99       format(a50)
            write(6,98) name,age,sex
   98       format(10x,a,10x,a,10x,a)
            go to 1
    2       continue
            stop
            end
```

Index